Breaking Away from the Textbook

Creative Ways to Teach World History

Second Edition

Ron H. Pahl

Volume I: Prehistory to 1600

ROWMAN & LITTLEFIELD EDUCATION

A division of
ROWMAN & LITTLEFIELD PUBLISHERS, INC.
Lanham • New York • Toronto • Plymouth, UK

Published by Rowman & Littlefield Education
A division of Rowman & Littlefield Publishers, Inc.
A wholly owned subsidary of
The Rowman & Littlefield Publishing Group, Inc.
4501 Forbes Boulevard, Suite 200, Lanham, Maryland 20706
http://www.rowmaneducation.com

Estover Road, Plymouth PL6 7PY, United Kingdom

British Library Cataloguing in Publication Information Available

Library of Congress Cataloging-in-Publication Data

Pahl, Ron H., 1943-
  Breaking away from the textbook : creative ways to teach world history /
Ron H. Pahl. — 2nd ed.
    p. cm.
  Includes bibliographical references.
  ISBN 978-1-60709-190-5 (cloth : alk. paper) — ISBN 978-1-60709-191-2
(pbk. : alk. paper) — ISBN 978-1-60709-192-9 (ebook)
  1. History—Study and teaching. I. Title.
D16.2.P24 2010
907.1—dc22

                                                                2010017589

∞™ The paper used in this publication meets the minimum requirements of
American National Standard for Information Sciences—Permanence of
Paper for Printed Library Materials, ANSI/NISO Z39.48-1992.

Printed in the United States of America

Contents

List of Illustrations

Acknowledgments

This work could not have been accomplished without the unwavering support and commitment of my wife Jarvis and my grown children Mothusi and Leloba. The others whose suggestions greatly improved the quality of *Breaking Away from the Textbook: Creative Ways to Teach World History* are Dick and Judy Kraft, Nelson and JoAnne Woodard, Bill Lacey, John Bovberg, and Ron Evans. Also not to be forgotten are the many teachers and student teachers who tested, commented on, and corrected items in the Thematic Learning Pacs in these volumes.

Preface

The purpose of the series *Breaking Away from the Textbook: Creative Ways to Teach World History* is simple—to make the teaching and learning of world history a powerful and enjoyable experience in the classroom. All too often, our students tell us that world history is the most boring subject they have at school. This series of *thematic learning pacs* (TLPs) hopes to change this image of world history for both teachers and students. From the size of this volume, you can tell it is not a comprehensive world history guide, nor is it a text heavy into theory. Instead, this book focuses on the following:

- A wide variety of active teaching ideas for world history
- A large number of ideas on how to get students excited about world history
- How-to-do-it brainstorms for teachers who know they need help
- Neat ways to have students grapple with the major problems and issues humanity has faced throughout history
- Innovative ways to help students see the relevance of major people, events, and ideas of the past to our lives today

Simply put, the purpose of the book is to make world history fun. Teachers and students can select all or parts of the world history TLPs in this volume to enhance their study of a particular historical person, event, or idea. Personal choice from a wide variety of different activities is a key feature of the *Breaking Away from the Textbook* series.

These volumes, however, are not for everyone. Those who should not use these volumes are the following:

- Teachers who enjoy boring their students with endless lectures
- Teachers who believe that their students must memorize every name and date in their textbook
- Teachers who demand a quiet classroom with students reading their textbook, filling in the blanks of worksheets, and answering the questions at the end of the chapter

A word of caution, however, should also be made. Reading the textbook is important. The active learning strategies presented in this book are not meant to discourage reading. Rather, these strategies are designed to get students turned on to the ideas and problems that humans have faced throughout history. Students who are interested in the subject are going to want to read the text and other sources of history. These turned-on students are going to want to read more, write more, and think more about how to solve the major problems we have faced throughout history.

In these opening years of the 21st century, all of us are facing information overload. The amount of information in the world is doubling every year. The need now is *not* for more memorization of trivial facts from the past, but rather for the development of skills in the analysis of this information to decipher what is important in making present and future decisions. We know now from recent brain research that the neural networks of the brain can grow and change with stimulation. Turned on, stimulated kids increase their own brain power as they interact with each other to solve the problems of history. These are the kind of kids we want our students to be—the decision makers of the future.

You may ask, "Why should I buy *Breaking Away from the Textbook: Creative Ways to Teach World History, Volume I, Second Edition?* I already have volumes One, Two and Three—first editions, and I love them." The answer is simple: This new edition contains tons more TLPs to make the teaching and learning of world history an exciting and powerful experience for your students.

Some of the exciting new TLPs you can expect from Volume 1—Second Edition are:

1.2.4   *How Old Was Methuselah?* As in the first edition, the Second Edition does not stress the boring repetition of historical "facts," but rather asks critical questions that add to our understanding of history and human life. The new TLP

1.2.4 does this by looking critically at the Bible's statement that Methuselah lived 969 years, and creates a whole new understanding of history as we come to know that the ancient Middle East counted time in months, not years. Now how old was Methuselah?

1.3.2   *Our Dark Brown African "Eve"* Recent DNA research into early human history has revealed startling new findings. Now, what color was your and my grandmother's skin some 20,000 years ago?

1.13.3   *Can Climates Change Civilizations?* We humans on planet Earth are deeply worried about global warming in the 21st century. What does history tell us about how changes in climate have changed the way people live?

3.4.5   *Roger II's Kingdom of Sicily—Christian, Muslim, and Jew United Together* Will the tensions among Christian, Muslim, and Jew ever stop? There actually was a major kingdom during the Middle Ages—Roger II's Kingdom of Sicily—where Christian, Muslim, and Jew lived in full cooperation and harmony. How did they do it? Maybe we should begin to copy Roger II!

3.8.1   *Justinian's Plague of 541* CE One of the great conquests of all time was Justinian's reconquest of the Roman Empire, but why is it not given much coverage in our history books? And why did it fall so rapidly?

3.11.6   *The Alhambra—The Crown of Muslim Spain* So many art classes look to the Renaissance for examples of great art. Why do they not look at the Alhambra, constructed when the Muslims ruled Spain? Can there be a more beautiful building in the world?

4.3.4   *The Little Ice Age (1350–1850)* Ignored in most of our history books is the fact that humans experienced a recent mini-Ice Age. Let us go back in history to see some of the major ways this Little Ice Age of 1400–1850 impacted world history.

4.5.7   *Elizabeth of York—The Queen of Hearts* So many great women have been forgotten in our history books. Such a woman was Elizabeth of York, whose marriage ended the War of the Roses and who gave birth to one of the greatest kings in history, Henry VIII. And, oh, yes, she was also the original Queen of Hearts.

If you want your students to have fun in your world history class, but also have them deeply analyze some of the major issues that have confronted humankind from ancient times, through the present, and into the future, then *Breaking Away from the Textbook: Creative Ways to Teach World History, Volume 1, Second Edition* is for you and your students.

Introduction: History—What, Why, and How?

What is history? The original meaning of the word "history" in classic Greek was "inquiry" (Collingwood, 1956). More recently the word has taken the meaning "to inquire about the past."

Why history? Why do people "inquire about the past"? There are many reasons. Some people just want to know where they came from. Others want to look backward to find ancestors they can brag about to their neighbors. Some folks just do not like the present and want to complain that things just aren't like what they used to be in the good old days. Socrates (469–399 BCE) in ancient Greece was one of these. He made the following complaint:

> Children now love luxury. They have bad manners and contempt for authority. They show disrespect for their elders and love chatter in place of exercise. They no longer rise when their elders enter the room. They contradict their parents, chatter before company, gobble up dainties at the table, and tyrannize their teachers.

History today, however, has a much more important purpose. Humans, throughout history, have faced a variety of problems—some of which have never been solved. The result is that we still face many of these same problems—and many new ones as we move into the 21st century. As participating citizens of the world, we need to examine the records of the past to understand how humans in other times grappled with their problems: where they succeeded and where they failed. From this analysis, we can build on the experience of the past and better prepare ourselves for the future.

HOW SHOULD WE STUDY WORLD HISTORY?

Most world history books are structured chronologically, region by region (see Appendix A for a Full Thematic Table of Contents of *Breaking Away*). A result of this structure is that students often miss the truly global impact of many new ideas and changes in history and the different ways humans around the world reacted to these changes. The activities in this book are organized in chronological units around fourteen global themes in history to make it easier to grasp the monumental impact that different people, events, and ideas have had on the world as a whole. These fourteen global themes will form the fundamental structure for each unit in the book. The themes—plus a short description—are as follows:

1. HISTORICAL TIME LINE

In the physical universe, there may be no such thing as time, a beginning, or ending (Hawking, 1990). If we follow Hawking and the other quantum physics folks, the concept of time is a human invention. We humans seem to want beginnings and endings to our human story. Following this human convention of time, this book uses a simple BCE/CE (Before the Current Era/Current Era) dating pattern based on the birth of Jesus in developing a historical time line. As we pass into the 21st century, however, we must realize that this time scale is relative. Different cultures and religions have different time lines. Many of the dates used in this book are, by necessity, approximations.

Another interesting question is the shape of history. Is it circular and constantly repeating itself, as the Greeks saw it? Does history move in a straight line toward a distant goal, as in the Christian concept of salvation envisioned by St. Augustine, or the Marxist idea of Utopia? Does it move in wavy lines, tracing high and low periods? Or, does it parallel modern quantum physics and move chaotically, with repeating iterations, but also constantly changing at the same time?

2. SEPARATING FACT FROM MYTH AND PROPAGANDA

A major problem in history is the determination of what is fact and what is fiction. The cynic who said, "History is written by the winners" is often correct. We, as inquiring historians, must be aware of the point of view taken by an author and be able to distinguish blatant propaganda and deliberate misinformation from accurate information. A common problem also is when major people of history begin to take on super-human characteristics. This process of myth making has taken place throughout history, often innocently, as stories are repeated around the campfire. Often, however, this myth-making process becomes deliber-ate, as cultures invent their heroes and even their gods. This process of myth-making often takes on regular forms or archetypes, which we can see in all cultures throughout history (Pearson, 1989):

- The Warrior who can conquer any foe: Alexander the Great
- The Martyr who sacrifices his life for a cause: Socrates
- The Magician who has the power to defy nature: Moses
- The Wanderer who single-handedly discovers new worlds: Co-lumbus
- The Villain whose evil deeds darken even the sun: Attila the Hun

When people in history begin to take on the characteristics of these mythological archetypes, we, as inquiring historians, must be cautious about accepting this information as fact. Such mythological characters may be the central focus of our comic book heroes and antiheroes, but if we are not careful, they are treated as the factual characters of our his-tory books. Obviously, determining the facts of history from centuries of mythology is often a difficult task but one which we must undertake.

3. LOCATION AND MOVEMENT

Where an item or idea comes from is critical in its historical develop-ment, such as the spread of citrus fruit and grapes for wine from Persia. Equally important is how it spreads or does not spread across the world. If citrus fruit came originally from Australia, oranges would likely re-main a novel local food that would not have spread rapidly across the world until modern times. The Persian location, on the other hand, had trade routes both east to China and west to Europe at a very early date, and citrus seeds were easily carried along these routes to other corners of the world. The location and dissemination of historical items are therefore critical in understanding the successes and failures of indi-viduals and even whole empires.

4. POLITICS AND LEADERSHIP

Much of current textbook history focuses on the great deeds of heroic individuals and countries (see, "Separating Fact from Myth and Propaganda" above). To understand what happened in history, however, we must look behind the individual or country. What makes a leader or a country a success or a failure? What kind of political system was used to achieve success? What were its weaknesses, and what were its strengths? Is this a type of system we will want to use in the 21st century?

5. SOCIAL AND ECONOMIC LIFE

Was life better in the good old days? Or not? What social and economic features of past societies should we retain for the future, and which features should we leave in the history books? In eras of rapid change, such as our own, we need to carefully review our social and economic lifestyles, decide what we want and do not want, and then deliberately work toward creating a better life for all of us.

6. RELIGIOUS THOUGHT

Who is God? How have different people throughout history viewed God? Why is religious worship so different across the world? Why have some of the most powerful thinkers of humankind been devoted to religious thought? Why have some of the most savage acts in history been committed in the name of religion? Famed folklorist Joseph Campbell once said that "A myth is someone else's religion." Following Campbell, what is the difference between folklore and religion? The activities presented in this book are designed to further a wider understanding and respect of all our common human beliefs.

7. CONQUEST AND WARFARE

Conquests and warfare, at times, seem endemic to humanity. Traditional history books tend to spend a great deal of time fighting battles. The activities in this book are designed to go beyond these individual battles and examine the causes, repercussions, and possible diplomatic alternatives of war. The aim of these activities is to present students with options beyond war to draw from when they are faced with the critical decision of war or peace in the future.

8. TRAGEDY AND DISASTER

History is full of both man-made tragedies and natural disasters. Many of these disasters, such as the Black Death of 1331 CE–1369 CE, drastically changed the course of history. The activities in this book will bring the force of the massive impact these disasters had on contemporary people home to students. How can individuals, families, and nations cope with such disasters? Can students in class obtain the skills and the foresight to reduce the agony or avoid such tragedies and disasters in the future?

9. EXPLORATION AND DISCOVERY

Many of the high points of history are the culmination of human exploration and discovery. In some cultures, centuries can pass without much change in human knowledge or understanding. Then, suddenly, the conditions during a particular era are right, and humans begin to explore new lands and make discoveries that improve their lives. The seemingly simple discovery that seeds from grain could be stored and planted each year was one of the major discoveries of humankind—agriculture. Why do some societies explore widely and make new discoveries, and others do very little? What impact do new discoveries have on the human condition? What new discoveries can we expect in the future?

10. INVENTION AND REVOLUTION

The explorers in history get all the glory. Inventors, however, often make as many or more important changes, but we rarely ever know their names. New ideas also rarely happen in isolation. The activities in this book examine the conditions leading to several major historical inventions (such as the transistor in 1947), the impact of these inventions, and the social and economic revolutions that often follow their introduction.

11. ART AND CREATIVE THOUGHT

The joy and agony of human existence is often expressed in art, poetry, music, and other forms of creative thought. From the cave paintings of Lascaux (circa 15,000 BCE) to the singing of "Hard Day's Night" by the Beatles (1964), human creative expression is reflective of each historical era. The activities in this book examine such creative efforts of each era to better understand the joys and agony of what it means to be human.

12. SUCCESSES AND FAILURES OF AN ERA

At the conclusion of each era, it is important for inquiring historians to reflect back on the successes and failures of that era. What did humanity learn about itself during each period?

13. MAJOR HISTORICAL PROBLEMS

Kenneth Boulding (1964) proposed that history should be studied through major unresolved problems faced by humanity. Following Boulding, this book examines seven such problems throughout history:

- *The Problem of Justice.* Tyranny is universally recognized as being wrong, but it continues unabated in the 21st century. More difficult for a nation is the delicate balance between individual liberty and equality for all (see Mortimer Adler on this topic).
- *The Problem of War and Inhumanity.* War and Inhumanity toward other humans is universally recognized as evil. But, then, why do wars and inhumanity toward other humans continue, and even increase?
- *The Problem of Poverty.* Despite the tremendous wealth and resources available across the world, poverty not only remains a major global issue, but is growing rapidly.
- *The Problem of Ecology.* Human progress has often been made to the detriment of the quality of human life and the natural environment. How much of global warming is due to natural conditions, and how much is due to human lifestyles that depend on the continual burning of oil and coal?
- *The Problem of Ideology.* Good ideas often become ritualized into ideology, and important changes are rejected in the name of that

ideology. How can we ensure that our governments do not lock themselves into old corrupt ideas and reject new ideas that can improve all of our lives?

- *The Problem of Technology.* Technological advances often take precedence over thoughtful leadership as a society blindly follows new innovations that may force us down paths we do not want to go. How can humankind keep mentally ahead of the technology that keeps passing it by?
- *The Problem of Entropy.* Humans have limited amounts of resources. When these scarce resources are directed toward one goal, we only have a limited number of resources that can be utilized in other directions. Such a system—overcommitted to one direction—has a difficult time adapting to change. The result is an irreversible decline, followed by *entropy* (extinction), and replacement by another system. Should we accept entropy as our fate, or should we fight hard to prevent it?

14. ERA ANTECEDENTS FOR THE FUTURE

At the conclusion of each era, major antecedents of the future will be identified and analyzed. The activities in this second edition of *Breaking Away from the Textbook: Creative Ways to Teach World History* ask students to analyze the impact such inventions might have on the future. What do the antecedents of these inventions look like today? What will similar inventions look like in the future? At the conclusion of each era, students will role-play persons with five different viewpoints of that time period—from arch conservative to radical progressive—to decide whether or not humankind is ready to move on to the next era. At the completion of each Unit, students discover that the door to the future is never completely closed, and we humans are always drawn to peek around that door to see what the next era has in store. Einstein said it wisely: "To make new discoveries and improve the human condition, we must go beyond current thinking."

THEMATIC ORGANIZATION

The core of *Breaking Away from the Textbook: Creative Ways to Teach World History* is the *Thematic Learning Pacs* (TLPs) arranged according to each of the fourteen themes in each Unit. Each TLP has a short reading and a variety of creative ways to study each theme. Each TLP is numbered by both Unit and Theme to easily and quickly identify it. This thematic organization presents the teacher and the student with a great many interesting options for how to study history: Perhaps a study of myths and hero images across time following Theme 2 for each era of history. Or, perhaps a study of the major problems humankind has faced throughout history, following Theme 13 in each Unit. Better yet, just wander through *Breaking Away* and pick out those TLPs that look interesting and try them out in class. This book was designed as an enjoyable, challenging history cookbook for teachers.

A quick perusal of *Breaking Away* will also verify that each TLP follows a fairly regular pattern. This pattern is no accident, but rather a subtle form of instructional assistance that utilizes multiple intelligences that will be noticed when each TLP is used in class by the teacher:

- *Quick Writes* are often the first activity in each TLP, and these form easy-to-use Anticipatory Sets to settle a new class down on a specific writing assignment as the students come in through the door of the classroom. This also enables the teacher to take care of classroom administrative duties while students are writing. Each Quick Write focuses on relating the specific historical theme or problem presented by the TLP to each student's personal experience. Sharing these experiences with the class as a whole can be an excellent entry point for beginning the actual lesson.
- *Map Attacks, Art Marts,* and *Poster Powers* all focus on developing students' spatial intelligence.
- *Quick Calcs* focus on improving each student's mathematical-analytical intelligence.
- *Dramatizations* and *Quick Skits* add to students' bodily kinesthetic, verbal-linguistic, and interpersonal intelligences.
- *Diary Entries* improve each student's verbal-linguistic and intrapersonal skills.
- *Advanced (ADV) Historical Analyses* add to each student's verbal-linguistic and mathematical-analytical skills, and present challenges for more advanced students.

Some of the major active learning strategies presented in each TLP are as follows:

- Quick Writes
- Role Plays
- Viewpoints
- Photo Analysis
- Map Attacks
- Concept Webbing
- Venn Diagrams
- T Charts
- Time Lines
- Pair Shares
- Diary Entries
- Poet Corners
- Art Marts
- Songs and Rap Fests
- Front Page Newspapers
- Travel Brochures
- Dioramas and Models
- "You Were There"

- Slogans & Graffiti
- Bumper Stickers
- Quick Skits
- What If?
- Spin Doctors
- Counter Spins
- Time Travelers
- Talk Show Hosts
- Poster Power
- Quick Calcs
- History Chains
- Pro & Cons
- Research Projects
- Futurists
- Action Research
- Opinion Polls
- Interviews
- Decision Trees

For teachers who enjoy using the history lesson ideas from this volume in their classroom, it is recommended that they also check out Volume II, *The Enlightenment through the 20th Century, and Volume III, More Creative Ways . . . Ancient Times through the 20th Century and Beyond*, for more innovative ideas on teaching and learning about world history. Be sure to also use the Appendices in all three volumes for a traditional chronological table of contents, map resources, recommended background music, interesting CD-ROMs, and websites for world history teachers and students.

It is my sincere desire to get students excited about world history: From the results of recent brain research, we know that students learn better when they are excited and interested in their studies. This series is far from complete when considering all of the possible topics to cover in world history. It is my hope, however, that teachers will use this volume as a starting point for their own creativity. Apply the teaching ideas from this volume to other topics in history. History does not have to be an endless list of dead men entombed between the covers of a textbook. Use this volume (as well as Volumes II and III) as a starting point to turn students on to world history. Such excitement can have an amazing ripple effect. Teachers become more interested in teaching. Schools become more exciting places to be.

More learning takes place, and suddenly the world is becoming a better place. It can be done.

Ron H. Pahl California State University, Fullerton

Note: Do not forget my *Creative Ways to Teach the Mysteries of History, Volumes I and II,* for more great ideas to get your students excited about history.

Prehistory (4 Million BCE to 3000 BCE)

UNIT 1: TABLE OF CONTENTS

INTRODUCTION

The Prehistoric Era

Humans are certainly interesting animals. This chapter focuses on having students analyze the uniqueness of humans. In the four-billion-year history of planet Earth, we *Homo sapiens* have been here for only a blink of an eye—200,000 years. Through these activities, students will experience the painfully slow development of early human prehistory—the first discoveries of fire, tools, religion, art, and the rudimentary problems of living together. There are triumphs in the discoveries of early humans, but there is also a great deal of pain, hardship, and lack of advancement. We know that humans came close to becoming extinct many times in early history. The key question is, how and why were they able to survive? And why did it take so long for humans to develop simple things like knives, pots, and bread? These quintessentially human things were likely rediscovered and reinvented many times in early history. The students must grapple with these very basic and fundamental problems of being human. That is what we will study in Prehistory.

THEMATIC LESSON PACS

1.1.0 HISTORICAL TIME LINE

1.1.1 How Early Can We Date Real Human Beings?

How early can we date the first fully human beings? How can we tell human beings from other early pre-human beings and other members of the large ape family? We might never know exactly when the first humans emerged from prehistory. Archaeologists, however, have recovered many early creatures who were likely some sort of relatives of that first human being. This lesson has students pair up into teams to organize the *Early Pre-Human and Human Time Line* below:

- **Name Plates**: Photocopy enough sets of the following ten items in the *Early Pre-Human and Human Time Line* so that every two students has a set. Cut each name or item onto a strip of paper.

Illustration 1.1.1. *Four Prehistoric Skulls*

Place the strips of paper carefully into separate envelopes for each team and label the envelopes "1.1.1 The Prehistoric History Time Line" for later use in class.

- **Team Power:** Break the class into teams of two students each.
- **The Envelope:** Each team should be given an envelope containing the following random ten facts from the prehistoric era:
  1. The discovery of agriculture and farming across the world by modern humans (circa 10,000 BCE).
  2. Modern-looking pre-human *Homo antecessor* (circa 800,000 BCE) lived in Spain and England.
  3. The earliest direct human ancestor *Homo ergaste* (2–1.5 million years BCE) lived in Africa and used simple stone tools.
  4. Heavy-skulled pre-human *Homo sapiens neanderthalensis* (circa 300,000 BCE) lived in Europe.
  5. The first use of metal tools made out of bronze (3000 BCE) in the Middle East and Southeast Asia.
  6. The first small villages of modern human beings (8000 BCE) in many areas of the world.
  7. Magnetic pole reversal (740,000 BCE).
  8. Fire making and near-relative pre-human *Homo erectus* (3–1 million years BCE) lived in Africa and then Asia.
  9. Discovery of animal herding of reindeer in Europe by human beings (12,000 BCE).
  10. The first fully modern *Homo sapiens* (circa 200,000 BCE) appeared in southern Africa after living for thousands of years on protein-rich mussels along the seashore.

- **Quick Write:** Before beginning, each student should write a brief paragraph on what he or she thinks it might be like to be the first human in history. Several students can then share their quick write with the class. Later, at the end of the lesson, they can compare their quick writes with what they have learned.
- **Team Time Line:** The first job of each team of two is to correctly order the ten facts and artifacts according to time, with the oldest at the top and the most recent at the bottom. Each student should separately write the correct time line for the prehistoric names and artifacts on a personal sheet of paper for later reference.
- **Team Look Up:** Once every member of the team has the prehistoric time line written on a sheet of paper, the meaning and significance of each date in prehistory can be discussed by the team.

Especially important to note is when fully human individuals came into existence, and why they did so at that particular time. Once discussed by each team, the meanings of each prehistoric fact can be shared with the members of the class.

- **Poster Power:** On a large piece of paper, each team should construct its own time line for the prehistoric era using the ten facts, along with descriptions and illustrations to demonstrate the meaning of each name. When finished, these can be presented to the class and displayed on the classroom wall.
- **Music Mart:** Each team should pick what they think is the most important fact or event in the time line and then compose and present a short song or rap about the item or event. When finished, this can be presented to the class.
- **Journal Entry:** Each team member should then write a short journal entry speculating about what they now know about the development of humans during the prehistoric era—from the time line they developed—and possibly the most important things to happen during this era. When finished, students can first share their most important thoughts with their team and then with the class as a whole. Using student scribes to record information on the board, the teacher can then help summarize the findings of the whole class.

1.1.2   Create a Prehistoric History Chain

A fun way to conduct an end-of-unit review for assessment is to create a class history chain. The steps to conduct a history chain are as follows:

1. The teacher should place each of the ten major facts (without years attached) mentioned in the unit on an 8.5 × 11-inch sheet of paper, using a minimum of a 72-point typeface so that everyone can read the fact from across the room. These items should also be collected at the end of the lesson and stored in a folder for multiple use.
2. To begin the lesson, each of ten student should stand and come to the front of the room and randomly be given one of the facts. The students should then hold the item in front of them—facing outward—so that everybody in class can see the fact.
3. The students should now make themselves into a prehistoric history chain. Have the student holding the oldest name, event, or

thing stand at one far corner of the room, then have the students arrange themselves in chronological order across the front of the room, to the most recent name, event, or thing in another corner of the room. (Expect fun chaos, as students can talk to each other and determine—by themselves—their own chronological order.)

4. Once the prehistoric history chain has been established, the teacher can review the chain by having each student identify his or her name, event, or thing and its relative place in the time line. (The teacher can expect to have more than a few corrections to make as each student describes his or her item and its time in history—but remember, this is an excellent and fun way to review.)

5. As a second step in the history chain, the teacher should group the students into teams of about six students each, in order to have each team determine the most important item in chain for its impact on the world.

6. The teacher should then collect all the history chain name papers and save them to be used later. Students may then take their seats.

7. In a short journal entry, each student should then record what he or she thinks are the three most important things that happened in the Prehistoric era and then share them with the class to generate a full-class consensus on the meaning of the era.

1.2.0 SEPARATING FACT FROM MYTH AND PROPAGANDA

1.2.1   How Are Humans and Animals Different from Each Other?

In what ways are animals and humans similar? In what ways are humans and animals different from each other? The following very early pre-humans had many very human characteristics:

- "Lucy" (*Australopithecus afarensis*) lived 3.2 million years BCE. She stood and walked on two feet and was named "Lucy" by the archaeologists who found her in Ethiopia, Africa. She also had a small brain and long arms and lived near a forest.
- *Ardipithecus ramidus* was found in Ethiopia and dated at 4.4 million years BCE. He stood upright and walked on two feet. He also had long arms, a small brain, and lived in a forest.
- *Australopithecus anamensis* fossils from between 4.07 and 4.17 million years ago were recovered from Lake Turkana on the border

of Kenya and Ethiopia. These individuals stood and walked on two feet. They had small brains and long arms, and lived in the forest.

But do these very early pre-humans have the following human characteristics?

Early Human Criteria:

1. They had large brains.
2. They walked upright on two feet.
3. They had short arms: Apes lived in trees and swung from the branches with long arms. Humans with shorter arms lived in the grasslands.
4. They constructed, used, and carried sophisticated tools for hunting.
5. They used sophisticated language and social interactions with fellow humans.
6. Their DNA matches modern human beings.

- **Quick Write:** Each student should write a brief paragraph describing what it might be like to be an early pre-human, one million years ago. When finished, several students can share their thought with the class.
- **T Chart:** Using a T chart, make a list of at least five differences between animals and humans; for example, animals make noises to each other, but only humans can really talk to each other. Compare answers with everyone in class to make a large class T chart.
- **What's My Name?** Students can dress up to appear on the hot TV show *What's My Name?* Students in class then get to ask each of the guests questions to determine which pre-human or human each of the guests represents.
- **ADV Internet Search:** For an advanced project, students can search the Internet for recent pre-human discoveries and report their findings to the class.

1.2.2   Where Did Early Humans Live?

Contrary to most stories and cartoons, most early fully human individuals—circa 200,000 years ago—likely did not live in caves, nor did they live in trees. We know they lived near water in order to drink and to catch the animals that came to drink. Some early pre-humans knew how to make fire very early— about 1 million BCE—and make stone tools. They passed these skills down to humans. Early humans, but not likely pre-humans, knew how to make simple shelters out of branches and reeds. For the past several million years, early pre-humans have made many of their heavy tools out of stone and their lighter tools out of wood. Early humans used much smaller, easier-to-carry stone blades and arrowheads and wood tools as spears and arrow shafts. When it was cold, some early humans—and maybe some pre-humans—wore animal skins for protection.

- **Art Mart:** Make an illustration of what you think an early human homesite would have looked like. Include things early humans might have had, such as a fire, clothes, a small hut, and stone tools.
- **Bumper Sticker:** Create a bumper sticker that you think early humans might have worn on their animal skins—once they learned how to write.
- **Diorama:** Create a diorama or three-dimensional model of an early human site.
- **ADV Research Project:** Using your library or the Internet, pick one of the early humans or pre-humans and find out more about what is known about that early "person." When finished, report your findings to the class.

1.2.3   Were Neanderthals Human?

Homo sapiens neanderthalensis (Homo Neanderthal) were big, heavy-set people with large brow ridges who lived in Europe between 300,000 BCE and the end of the last Ice Age, approximately 12,500 BCE. Like modern *Homo sapiens*, Homo Neanderthal evidently descended from modern-looking *Homo antecessor* (circa 800,000 BCE) who lived in Spain and England. Although heavy and tough looking, Neanderthals were sensitive, loved flowers, and buried their dead with honor. As with other early human beings, they also practiced cannibalism in times of starvation. We also know that Homo Neanderthal was similar to modern human beings, but they had DNA sequences that differed from those of humans and therefore did not intermarry and were not ancestors of modern human *Homo sapiens* (Kunzig 1997).

- **Quick Skit:** Develop a short skit demonstrating what might have happened if a modern human met a Homo Neanderthal on the open plains near a stream of running water.

- **Tear Jerker:** Create a short, made-for-TV drama that depicts a heartbroken Neanderthal male who falls in love with a beautiful *Homo sapiens* female, but realizes that he will never be able to marry her because their DNA do not match.
- **Counter Spin:** Develop a late-developing news flash in which the brothers of a young human female rescue her from a kidnap attempt by a heavyset Neanderthal male.

1.2.4   How Old Was Methuselah?

Methuselah (Genesis 5:27) lived "nine hundred and sixty-nine years." How many times do we misunderstand ancient books? Quite often, we try to understand ancient books such as the Bible. The major problem is, however, that the language and concepts used several thousand years ago are easy to misunderstand, and easily lead to misinterpretation. A very good example is the age of Methuselah presented in the Bible as 969 years. Rather than an almost impossible biblical "miracle," we need to go back to the Middle East thousands of years ago to see how they first calculated time. We quickly find out that time in the Middle East was first calculated in "moons," rather than in the 365-day years as we know them. Ok, let's divide 969 "years" by 12 "moons" per year, and we arrive at 81 years in our own time. Methuselah really lived to be almost 81 years old—a respectable old man in our day. We have to realize, however, that the average age of a person in the ancient Middle East was likely under 30 years, so a man living to be 81 back then was a very old man in ancient times—but not almost a thousand years old. This is a good example of how, when reading about history, we must be careful to always look at how a word or a story is translated from one language to another, and how concepts such as time have changed over the centuries.

- **Quick Calc:** Every one in class can calculate their age in moons as they did in Methuselah's day by multiplying their age in years by twelve. Everyone should report their ages in moons to the whole class.
- **How Old?** Every student in class should think for a moment and decide how "old" is "old"? How many years old will they be when they become old? Every one in class should then share the age at which they will get "old." A student scribe should write these different ages on the board. How much difference is there between

what the students see as being old? Can the class as a whole come to some agreement as to what is old?

- **Eulogy:** Imagine you traveled back in a time machine, perhaps two thousand years, and were asked to give a eulogy at Methuselah's funeral. What would you say about the old man? Now be nice, because his family is surrounding you. But make sure that you correct the myth about how old he really was—in modern years. When finished, be prepared to present your eulogy to your class in a mock funeral for Methuselah.
- **ADV Research:** Students can search the Internet to find words in history that have been mistranslated and misunderstood. Can students identify tragic instances when mistranslations and misunderstandings have led to wars or the loss of life?

1.3.0 LOCATION AND MOVEMENT

1.3.1   Human Blood Types—Where Did They Come From?

The blood types among chimpanzees, gorillas, and humans are very similar, but with some very interesting differences. Chimps mostly have type A blood and never type B blood. Gorillas, on the other hand, have mostly B type blood, but never A type blood.

Among humans, type O blood has the widest distribution in the world—63% of all humans—with its highest concentrations in Central and South America (90%–100% of the whole population) and in Eastern and Southern Africa (80%–90% of the whole Bantu population). The lowest percentage of type O blood is found in Central Asia and Eastern Europe, without almost any type O blood found among the population. Although not conclusive yet, O'Neal (2007) and others believe that type O blood was the original blood type of humans when they first emerged 200,000 years ago in Southern and Eastern Africa.

About 21% of the world's population has type A blood, with highest concentrations in Northern Europe (25–40%), among the Australian Aborigine (30%–40%), and in North American Indian groups such as the Blackfoot (30%–40%). Almost 0% of the population of Central and South America has type A Blood. From its rather scattered distribution around the world, it is estimated that type A blood is a late human variation, likely associated with the development of herding animals and agriculture, perhaps as recently as 10,000 years ago.

Of the three major blood types, only 16% of the world's population have type B blood. We have to look to Central Asia from India and Pakistan to Siberia in the north to find the largest concentrations of type B blood (20%–30% of the population), with virtually no type B blood found in North and South America, parts of Southern Africa, and Australia. As with type A blood, type B blood evidently evolved very late in humans with the beginnings of animal herding and agriculture about 10,000 years ago (O'Neal 2007).

- **Quick Map:** With a partner in class, and using a blank map of the world, map the three major blood types of human beings and where they are found. Use colors to distinguish which areas have the largest concentrations of either type A, type B, or type O blood.
- **ADV Blood Research:** Every student, if possible, should find out his or her blood type, and the blood type, if possible of his or her mother and father. The class can then compare their blood types and that of their families.
- **ADV Family Map:** Each student, if possible, should find out what part of the world his or her ancestors came from. The teacher should then put up a large map of the world and have each student put his or her name on the map [with small pieces of sticky paper] to indicate where his or her family originated.
- **ADV Class Family Map:** The class as a whole should then merge these two maps together along with the information on each student's blood type. Student scribes should overlay the locations of the major human blood types on their family map. Students should now add their blood type to their names on the big map.
- **ADV Map Conclusions:** Using three-step analysis, students should now write a paragraph or two on what conclusions they draw from the map. In pairs, they should then share their findings with each other. The class as a whole should hear the conclusions of each student pair. The class as a whole should then draw their own conclusions as to the distribution of blood types across the world and their own family's place in this world.

1.3.2   Our Dark Brown African "Eve"

Almost 99.9% of our human genetic code, or genome, is identical for every human living on our planet called Earth. The one-tenth of 1% of the remaining DNA in all humans is responsible for little things such as differences in eye color, differences in skin color, how tall or fat we are, and how susceptible to disease we are. Scientists have studied human DNA samples from all over the world and have found that every one of us is descended from one dark brown African woman from east Africa who lived 150,000 years ago. Our earliest human ancestors were therefore very like the San hunter gatherer peoples of the Kalahari Desert of Botswana, Africa—with short, black curly hair, dark brown eyes, and dark brown skin—who hunted with spears and bows and arrows for their food. Biologists tell us that skin color only changes from black, to brown, and lighter shades of skin and not vice versa. Pale-skinned humans evidently evolved in northern Europe after migrating from Africa. Their skin began to change to lighter shades when they no longer lived in the intense sunlight of the tropics. This change of skin color evidently happened gradually over thousands of years. No matter their color now, we all have to realize that we—the people of planet Earth—all were originally dark brown and all came from Africa (Shreeve 2006).

- **Quick Write:** In a short paragraph describe your own skin color—exactly, if you can. Is it pink, brown, black, or some other shade of color? What happens when your skin is exposed to sunlight? How dark can it get in the sunshine?
- **Pair Share:** Now have a partner in you class describe your skin color—exactly, if they can. How are the two descriptions of your skin color different from each other? Report your findings to the class.
- **Three-Step Analysis:** Read the paragraph on "Our Dark Brown African Eve." Write a paragraph describing what you think about everyone's ancestor being one dark brown woman from Southern and Eastern Africa. Share your thoughts with a partner in class. Each pair of students should then share their thoughts with the class as a whole. Student scribes can briefly summarize the thoughts of the class on the board. The class can then summarize the class' thoughts regarding their dark brown grandmother.
- **Newspaper Reporter:** As a newspaper reporter for your town's *Daily Blat* go back in time 150,000 years ago to interview our first fully human female ancestor in Eastern Africa. Make sure to have a list of at least five questions you will ask her, and then with a partner in class, think about what her answers would be. Be sure

to mention to her that many of her great-great grandchildren will not only be black in skin color, but light brown and even pink. How would she treat her great-great grandchildren whose skin colors have changed over the centuries? Be prepared to give your interview, with your partner, in front of the class.

- **ADV Research:** Students interested in the topic can research the Internet for articles on skin color and our early ancestors from Africa.

1.3.3   Out of Africa

Our early human ancestors began to move out of Africa between 50,000 and 70,000 years ago, into the Middle East and across the world. Using very early archaeological data, let us use the following list (out of order) of major human archaeological sites to track how these early relatives of ours began to spread out around the world.

- **List of Early Human Archaeological Sites** [out of order]
    1. Omo Kibish in Ethiopia, Africa, 195,000 years old.
    2. Klasies River, South Africa, 120,000 years old.
    3. Qafzeh in Israel, Middle East, 92,000 years ago.
    4. Topper [pre-Clovis] in South Carolina, USA, 50,000 years ago.
    5. Monte Verde in Chile, South America, 14,800 years old.
    6. Lake Mungo in Australia, 45,000 years ago.
    7. Niah Cave, on the island of Borneo in south east Asia, 40,000 years old.
    8. Zhoukoudian (Shandingdong) in northern China, 11,000 years ago.
    9. Pestera cu Oase in Romania, eastern Europe, 35,000 years old.
    10. Yana River in Siberia, Russia (near Alaska), 30,000 years ago.
- **Teacher Directions:** Make sure every student or pair of students has a blank map of the world, or better, a world map with the major countries of the world, and a pencil or pen. Each student or pair of students will need the preceding list of early archaeological sites.
- **Student Directions:** The main purpose of this lesson is to find out how our early human ancestors spread out of Africa and across the world using the list of ten major archaeological sites:
    1. Make sure you have a blank map of the world from the teacher and a pen or pencil.

2. Make sure you have a list of the ten major archaeological sites concerning the early movement of humans around the world.
3. Using an atlas, locate the countries of each archaeological site on the list and mark it on the map with its site name and year.
4. When finished, draw arrows showing the direction of movement of our earliest ancestors across the world to these earliest archaeological sites. (Note that the largest number of years ago is the oldest and the smallest number is the most recent.)
5. When finished, you may present your findings to your class and compare your maps to determine which is the most correct.
6. As a final activity, each student should write an essay describing what he or she has learned about the early movement of humans out of Africa starting about 50,000 years ago.

1.3.4   Early Human Campfire

In a short dramatization, pretend that your class is a large family of early humans in Africa. Everyone is huddled around a large campfire (the middle of the classroom or outside in the grass).

A major debate is raging among the family members. Should the family leave Africa to live elsewhere in the world or not (circa 60,000 BCE)?

- **Pros or Cons?** Pick a side of the argument.
- **Defend It:** Write an argument supporting whether to leave or not, and then stand up in front of the fire and present your argument to the family.
- **Plenary Session:** After everyone has presented their arguments, have the family vote whether to leave Africa or not, and present the reasons for their choice.

1.4.0   POLITICS AND LEADERSHIP

1.4.1   Who Is in Your Early Human Family Tree?

The earliest humans most likely lived in small extended family units. In these very earliest of human days, there might not have been more than a few thousand humans on all of planet Earth. You are now one of these very earliest of human beings on our planet.

- **Family Tree:** Create a family tree of the family members and close friends who live with you.
- **What If?** Imagine that all of you are one of the only early human families living together on Earth over 60,000 years ago.
- **Task Master:** Make a list of tasks for each family member and friend to assist in the survival of everyone. Remember, early humans at that time had little more than simple stone and wooden tools for hunting and gathering plants to eat, a small simple shelter, and fires to keep warm and cook meat.
- **Art Mart:** Using large pieces of butcher paper (to simulate cave walls) paint a picture of some of the major things in your life as a very early human being.
- **Family Portrait:** Draw a picture of what you think your family might have looked like in 60,000 BCE.

1.4.2   How Should a Small Neolithic Village Be Ruled?

Sometime during the last stages of the last Ice Age, circa 12,500 BCE, a smart young woman, gathering seeds to eat, noticed that dropped seeds—with a little water—grew into full plants after a few months. She had made one of the major discoveries in the world—the discovery of agriculture. Soon, humans in many different parts of the world began to drop wheat, sorghum, and rice seeds in the ground. Archaeologists called this period the Neolithic, the New Stone Age. People who grew their own grain to eat had to live in one area to take care of their crops, instead of being a nomadic people wandering around looking for food. These New Stone Age farmers began to make fine, small stone knives to harvest their wheat. They also became the first people to live in small agricultural villages. Around 8000 BCE, the first real political leaders in the world were the men and women who developed the first small agricultural villages during the Neolithic around the world.

- **Quick Write:** In a short paragraph, give a description of what you think it would be like to live in one of the first small agricultural villages about 8000 BCE.
- **Name Maker:** In a team of four students from the same New Stone Age village, create a name for your village.
- **Rule Maker #1:** As the leaders of one of the first small villages in the world, what rules would your team of four create for the village?

- **Rule Maker #2:** How would your team create these rules?
- **Rule Maker #3:** Would your team involve others in making these rules? If so, how would you involve them?
- **Rule Maker #4:** How would you prevent one man from making all the rules and making a dictatorship out of your village?
- **Plenary Session:** Have each team share its ideas for ruling the village with the class, and have the class determine which team made the best rules.
- **ADV Historical Research:** As an advanced project, search your school library and the Internet for information on how early Neolithic villages and small states were ruled. When finished, report your findings to the class.

1.5.0   SOCIAL AND ECONOMIC LIFE

1.5.1   Making Early Human Tools

Animals, such as baboons, will occasionally use tools. The author of this work has personally seen a baboon in Africa grab a stick from a small boy and chase him with it (after the boy hit the baboon with the same stick!). Animals, however, do not know how to make tools for long-term use. This, anthropologists tell us, is a key difference between humans and animals. Humans purposely make tools for long-term and multiple uses.

- **Quick Write:** As fast as you can, make a list of thirty tools you use every day to make your life easier (for example, car, shoelaces, light switch, etc.). Share your list with the class.
- **What If?** For a moment, stop and think of what it would be like to be an early human with absolutely no tools to use. In a short paragraph, describe what it would feel like to be such an early human without any tools. In conclusion, describe the first tool you would make as an early human.
- **Pair Share:** Divide the class into pair shares (two students working together). Within three minutes, have each pair share make two lists, one of as many simple wood tools that early humans could make and one of simple stone tools early humans could make. The pair share with the most number of tools at the end of three minutes wins. The accuracy of the winning pair should be checked by having the winning pair share read their list to the class.

- **Plenary Session:** Conclude by having the class as a whole make a stone and a wooden tool list on the board by adding the suggestions from every group.
- **Design Team:** Teams of four students should design an "ultimate" stone or wooden tool. Each team's design should be put on a poster board and presented to the class. The best tool designs can be placed on display on the classroom wall.
- **ADV Museum Research:** Contact local museums to find out if any have displays of early stone and wooden tools used by early humans. If so, plan and conduct a field trip to see these tools.
- **ADV Action Research:** Check to see if anyone in your community knows how to make stone tools, and see if he or she will demonstrate this process to the class.

1.5.2   A Neolithic Ad Campaign

The year is 9000 BCE, at the end of the last Ice Age. The location is Iraq, in the Middle East, along the Tigris River, or in Chiapas, in southern Mexico. Your family is one of the first in the world to start planting wheat (in Iraq) or squash (in Mexico) to harvest and eat. Everybody is calling you Neolithic (New Stone Age) and laughing at you because your stone tools are not big and bulky, but are rather stone weights with center holes for digging sticks to plant the seeds, and small and sharp stones to cut the wheat in the fall. The trouble is, you need more people to help your family farm the lands, and the local nomads would rather just wander around the hills hunting and looking for wild berries and fruit. They are not very interested in working in the hot fields all day. You need an advertising agency to recruit some of the nomads to come and work in the fields with you.

- **Quick Write:** Close your eyes for a moment and imagine yourself as an early Neolithic human (9000 BCE) and one of the first human farmers on the planet. In a short paragraph, describe what it feels like to be one of the first farmers in the world.
- **Madison Avenue:** With a team of four advertising executives (students) from Madison Avenue, develop and present an advertising campaign promoting agriculture (the planting and harvesting of crops) to the hunting and gathering people who live near you (in your class).

- **Poster Power:** With your ad team, create a large poster promoting the advantages of agriculture over nomadic hunting and gathering.
- **Bumper Sticker:** Create a bumper sticker that criticizes nomadic hunters and promotes the good life on the farm.
- **Counter Sticker:** Create a counter sticker that opposes new inventions (such as farming) and wants to return to the good old days, when everybody was nomadic.
- **ADV Historical Research:** Using your school library and the Internet, research one "Neolithic" (key search word) site currently being excavated by archaeologists and report about their findings to the class.

1.5.3   Should Humans Swarm?

Why do bees swarm? And ants, and birds, and fish? But can humans swarm? Birds, fish, and large herd animals, such as wildebeests, often swarm when attacked by an enemy, such as a hawk, shark, or lion. A swarm can quickly surround an enemy, or distract the enemy with constantly changing movements until they tire out or flee. Bees and ants are sent out daily to find new sources of food or a new place to live. When they find a new source of food or a great new place to live, they quickly swarm to inform everyone where to find the food or the new hollow tree trunk. Trails are quickly set to the new source of food, and the bees or ants quickly swarm to consume it before it is found by some other insect. Swarming is efficient, rapid, and egalitarian for the whole nest of bees or ants. No individual decisions are made, everything is done quickly, efficiently, and equally. Everybody gets a share, and gets it as soon as possible.

So why do humans not use swarming more often to get what they want? Individual decisions are almost always very unequal; they are slow because a process has to be explained to everyone, and they are inefficient because not everyone is involved in the decision and not everyone gets to share in the rewards. Some new industries are starting to use swarming techniques and are making large profits for their companies due to swarming. Cemex, the large Mexican cement company, studies the patterns of cement use in the area every evening and determines the most likely areas to sell ready-mixed cement across the city. At daylight, all of the trucks are sent out to areas most likely to be using cement. When calls come in for cement, the trucks are usually already in the area, and the cement is delivered rapidly and efficiently. Another company, Southwest Airlines, uses swarming every night to determine which gate terminals are mostly likely to be open at the Phoenix airport when each of the hundreds of Southwest flights arrives at the airport. The swarming system has worked to save Southwest Airlines millions of dollars in wasted minutes of fuel and working hours waiting for gates to open up at the airport (Miller 2007). How else can humans start using swarming decision making efficiently?

- **Quick Write:** When was the last time you sat in a sports stadium or gym and cheered for your home team? Or, when was the last time you did the wave with thousands of people in a baseball or football stadium? What did these swarming actions feel like to you? What purpose did these swarming actions serve? How powerful were they? Write a paragraph on your personal experiences with swarming, and share these with the class.
- **Class Swarm:** On three, the whole class yells all together: "Go Team!" Now, that was not loud enough. On three, 1, 2, 3, yell "Go Team!" Now, that's better! Discuss then why swarming actions such as these are so powerful.
- **Action Jackson:** In student pairs, think of ways that humans could use swarming types of decisions to improve their lives. When finished, report their ideas to the class as a whole for general discussion.
- **ADV Research:** Using the Internet, look-up "Swarming" and how it has been used in history by the military and protestors. In what future ways can swarming be used effectively by humans? Be sure to report your findings to the class.

1.5.4   Domesticated Cats—Where Did They Come From?

Meow! When was the last time you thought about the history of kitty cats? When did they get so attached to human beings? DNA testing of domestic cats has placed their origin approximately 10,000 years ago in the Middle East. This is almost the same time as the Neolithic Revolution and the beginning of farming. People started living in villages and saving the grain they harvested. Guess what happens when you leave some bags of seed on the ground? Mice and rats started eating the grain. Of course, when you have rats, you have cats. And the cats started chasing and eating the rats and mice. Humans started to like having the cats around to chase the rats. Domestic cats were the results.

- **Art Mart:** On a piece of paper, draw a cat chasing a mouse, 10,000 years ago in the Middle East. Share your drawing with the class.
- **Egyptian Cat Mummy:** The ancient Egyptians liked their cats so much that they mummified them just like the pharaohs. Create an illustrated story of an ancient cat mummy from Egypt. Be sure to share your story with the class.
- **Time Machine:** Use your desk as a time machine to carry you back to ancient Egypt to interview the great Pharaoh Ramses II. Focus your discussion on how the ancient Egyptians used their cats and why they mummified them.
- **ADV Research:** Look up "History of cats" on the Internet and report what you find to your class.

1.5.5   American Corn 10,000 Years Ago?

"Agriculture started in Mesopotamia, in the Middle East, 10,000 years ago." That has been the simple answer for history tests for over a century. But is it correct? When the Spanish first conquered Mexico and Peru almost 600 years ago, corn was without question the major crop across the Americas—and only in the Americas. But no one knew how long corn had been grown in the Americas. Archaeologists in the Americas have long been looking for ancient microscopic pollen grains from corn to give us some idea of the age of this major food of the Americas. Recently, archaeologists found such ancient corn pollen, dated 7,000 years ago, in the Mexican state of Tabasco. Also recently, in Belize, archaeologists found ancient corn pollen from 5,000 years old. Put together, it is now estimated that early American Indians were already planting corn 10,000 years ago. If this is correct, then agriculture started not only in the Middle East, but also in the Americas at about the same time—10,000 years ago (Bryant 2007).

- **Quick Write:** Imagine you are an archaeologist who has just made the major discovery that corn in the Americas is at least 10,000 years old. Briefly describe in a paragraph how you feel about making such a major discovery.

- **News Flash:** Write and deliver in front of your class a 30-second news flash about the famous discovery of 10,000-year-old corn in the Americas.
- **Time Line:** With a partner, create a time line that compares the beginnings of agriculture 10,000 years ago with other major events in history, such as the first human beings 200,000 years ago, the Norman conquest of England in 1066, and the first airplane flight 1906.
- **Art Mart:** Draw a poster for your classroom that illustrates both the beginnings of agriculture in the Middle East and the beginnings of agriculture in the Americas, 10,000 years ago.
- **ADV Research:** Using the Internet, search on the words "Corn history" and the "Beginnings of agriculture" to see what additional information you can gather on the beginnings of food crops in the Middle East and in the Americas.

1.5.6   Licorice Power

Licorice is not only a favorite candy of many people—it is 50 times sweeter than sugar! It is also one of the world's oldest medicines. The ancient Roman historian Pliny the Elder described how the Romans used licorice to cure colds, treat asthma, and heal wounds. Ancient herbalists in China and India also used licorice for similar healing properties, including sore throats. Modern medical researchers have also found that it is good for killing cells infected with cancer, hepatitis, and even human immunodeficiency virus (HIV) (Williams 2006).

- **Quick Taste:** In a short paragraph, describe what licorice looks like and tastes like to you when someone gives you a piece. When you are finished with your paragraph, share your impressions of licorice with your class.
- **Ancient Poster Power:** As an ancient herbalist of 500 BCE, from either Italy, China, or India, create an advertising poster for the wall of your "drug store" that describes the medical benefits and great taste of licorice.
- **TV Commercial:** As the fast-talking and loud announcer of a TV commercial, create and present to the class a quick 30-second spot advertisement for licorice.
- **ADV Research:** Do an Internet search on "Licorice" to find out what else you can learn about this ancient medicine, which is also a very sweet candy. Be sure to report your findings to your class.

1.6.0   RELIGIOUS THOUGHT

1.6.1   A Poem of Nature

Stand quietly some evening, away from the city lights, and look at the stars and the crescent moon on the horizon. Sit alone on the beach and listen to the roar of the ocean's waves pounding on the shore. Lie down in a forest some day by yourself and look up at the wind bending the branches and the clouds moving across the sky. Even in our day of jet travel, traffic jams, gigabyte hard drives, and exploring the planet Mars, we can still stand in wonder at the power of Nature. From the largest telescope probing our endless universe to the smallest photon in an electron microscope, we still wonder at the power of Nature that we do not understand. We humans are so small when we try to understand this beautiful chaotic symmetry around us. It is this attempt to understand such a magnificently complex, ever-changing, and yet symmetrical universe that led to the first religious thoughts of early humans. This is a key distinguishing feature that separates human beings from animals—an initial sense of wonder that becomes a scientific curiosity about how things work, and then a religious question of whether a supreme being might be out there someplace guiding everything.

- **Quick Write:** Think for a moment about Nature. In a short paragraph, describe three things that absolutely amaze you about Nature.
- **Pair Share:** When finished with your thoughts about Nature, share your thoughts with a partner in the classroom.
- **Poet's Corner:** As an early human being looking at the universe, write a short poem describing your wonder at what you see.
- **Song Fest:** Create a song or a rap that describes your wonder at the universe around you.
- **Mythology:** The famed folklorist Joseph Campbell once said, "A religion is someone else's myth." Take a moment and think back to a day in early human history. From your imagination, create a myth that becomes popular and eventually becomes a major religion in the world. When finished, share your thoughts with the class.
- **ADV Historical Research:** Use your library and the Internet to research what anthropologists think are the earliest forms of mythology and religion, and share your findings with the class.

1.6.2   Mother Earth

From archaeological evidence and our own language, we have evidence of early human religious beliefs. This evidence focuses on the concept of Mother Earth (Gaia) who controls the human cycle of birth and death, the cycles of the moon, and the yearly cycle of the seasons—dying in the fall and rising again in the spring with new life. She went by several different names: Dictynna in ancient Minos on Crete, Artemis in ancient Greece, Diana in classical Rome.

Note from the Future: Most scientists today follow the practice of studying many small parts to try to understand the whole, but some scientists are reversing this and finding evidence that the idea of Mother Earth as a living whole might indeed be true. They call this theory the *Gaia hypothesis* (Capra 1996, 22–23).

- **Quick Write:** Think for a moment about the name "Mother Earth" and then write a short paragraph describing what you have heard about the "Mother" of Nature.
- **Pair Share:** Share with a partner in class what you have heard about "Mother Earth." Be sure to allow each partner in the pair to talk for at least one minute.
- **Concept Web:** When the pair share is finished, each pair should share what they said with the class. Two students can act as recorders on the board to develop a class concept web of what we understand about "Mother Nature."
- **Front Page:** As a team of four student reporters for the *Stone Age Daily News* (an oral campfire news-reporting service), ask several early humans around the campfire (the classroom) what amazes them the most about the wonders of "Mother Earth," and then report your findings in a front-page edition of the newspaper at the next evening campfire.
- **Poster Power:** Create a poster of your view of how "Mother Earth" might look and of all of the powers she possessed.
- **Action Research:** Interview parents, neighbors, and friends to gather what impression they have of the "Mother Nature" myth.
- **ADV Way Back in Time:** The idea of "Mother Earth" dates well before most modern religions. Compare the ancient concept of "Mother Earth" with modern religions. How are they similar, and how are they different?

- **ADV Gender Bender:** Why are the earliest religions we know female-oriented and the newer religions male-oriented? Some historians think that men were the first people to write, and they used this skill to dominate women. What do you think? Discuss this in class.
- **ADV Futurist:** Read current research on the Gaia hypothesis, which sees the Earth as a living entity, and report back to the class on your findings.

1.6.3   Stonehenge

As early as 10,000 BCE, early humans began to formalize their religions by conducting religious services around major stones or forests, and they began to erect stone monuments as centers of worship. A magnificent example of such a center is Stonehenge (circa 3000 BCE) in southern England. Imagine these early prehistoric peoples dragging these huge stones—each over 13 feet high and 6 feet wide—over 15 miles to Stonehenge. A prehistoric observatory and cemetery, the stone monument lines up perfectly with the rising and setting sun at each yearly summer solstice (June 21st, the longest day of the year). From Stonehenge, we can understand that prehistoric humans were quite sophisticated in their knowledge of the universe. They carefully plotted the yearly cycle of the seasons and the points at which the sun set and rose every day. The builders of Stonehenge must have wondered in awe at the magnificent cycle of life and death in Nature that they saw around them, and they based a major part of their religion on what they saw.

- **Quick Write:** Think of a time when you stood in a quiet spot and watched the sun slowly go down to the horizon. In a short paragraph, describe your feelings as you watched the sun slowly sink and then disappear. What do you think prehistoric humans thought when they witnessed the same daily event of nature?
- **Poster Power:** Using the illustration or another one you find, create a poster that illustrates what ancient humans must have thought when they witnessed a sunrise at Stonehenge on the summer solstice.
- **Model It:** Create a diorama or model of a prehistoric monument, such as Stonehenge, out of paper, cardboard, clay, or stone, and then label the different parts of your model. If you wish, you can

use a flashlight to simulate the sun at summer solstice to illustrate how the real Stonehenge lines up with the rising sun on June 21 each year.

- **ADV Prehistoric Research:** Research your library and the Internet for "Stonehenge" (key search word) to find out what else you can learn about this magnificent ancient religious observatory. Be sure to report your findings to your class.

1.7.0   CONQUEST AND WARFARE

1.7.1   Are Humans Violent or Peaceful?

Anthropologists debate whether humans—especially men—are basically violent or peaceful. As far back as the human record exists, it is clear that humans were often violent toward each other. As recent as the daily news from yesterday, it is clear that humans—again especially men—have a strong tendency toward violence. James Watson and Francis Crick, the famed scientists who discovered DNA, think that, for us to survive, men actually have a violent gene in them that has to be repressed by social rules. The question remains, however, whether this violence is natural to human beings toward each other, or whether it is learned and passed from one family to the next. It is also clear from the archaeological record that humans can be peaceful, living in small villages and extended families together, and sharing all work and the food they produce. Humans also enjoy peaceful things, such as art, music, and storytelling. The question whether humans are basically violent or not still remains to be answered (Dubos 1974; Sussman 1997).

- **Quick Write:** In a short paragraph, describe whether you think humans—especially men—are basically violent toward one another or basically peaceful toward each other.
- **Pair Share:** With a partner in class, share (for one minute each) your ideas on whether humans are basically violent or peaceful.
- **Bumper Sticker:** Are humans basically violent or peaceful? Pick a side, and then create a bumper sticker that supports your position.
- **Poster Power:** Create a poster that illustrates this disagreement over the basic nature of humans.

- **Quick Skit:** With a team of four student actors, create a short dramatization of a struggle between two families of early humans over a water hole. Present your dramatization at your next campfire (your next classroom plenary session).
- **You Were There:** As the ace reporter for the *Stone Age Daily News*, give a play-by-play description of a fight between two early human families over the only water hole within ten miles.
- **Stone Age Mediator:** Many wars are fought over simple things, such as food and water. Make a list of alternatives the two families might have to fighting over a water hole, and then propose a mediated settlement.
- **ADV Historical Research:** Using your library and the Internet, research a minimum of two wars and try to identify the root cause of the war. Could it have been avoided? When finished, present your findings to the class at their next campfire.
- **ADV The Futurist:** Conduct surveys in your school, neighborhood, and on the Internet to inquire as to the possibilities or impossibilities of a future world lived without warfare.

1.7.2 Otzi the Ice Man

In 1991, some hikers found a frozen human body at the top of an Alpine pass, 10,530 feet high, on the border between Austria and Italy. To the amazement of everyone, the human body was found to be 5,300 years old. It had been frozen at the top of the pass since the Late Stone Age. Archaeologists named him Otzi, and worked hard to keep his body frozen so they could study it for as long as possible. Otzi was by far the oldest human body to survive intact, with his clothing, his bow and arrows, and a copper axe. Otzi also amazingly had tattoos across his body—interestingly, in the very places where acupuncture is performed today. But what killed poor Otzi at the top of the pass? Archaeologists using X-rays discovered that he had an arrowhead imbedded underneath his shoulder blade. Someone had attacked him with a bow and arrow at the top of the pass and killed him there. The arrow pierced an artery leading from the heart, and Otzi quickly bled to death. He froze solid and remained where he died for over 5,000 years (Hall 2007).

- **Quick Write:** What if you discovered a frozen body while hiking in the mountains? What would you do? What would you think?

What would you do when you found out that the body was over 5,000 years old? Share your thoughts with the class.

- **Front Page:** As a red hot newspaper reporter, write the first newspaper front page account of the discovery of the Ice Man. Be sure to have a short and sharp two-inch-high headline for your news piece.
- **Ice Age Drama:** With a team of four from your class, create a short drama that gives an idea of how the Ice Man might have died on the mountain. Be sure to present your drama to your class.
- **Time Line:** Place the Ice Man on an early historical time line with the first humans (200,000 years ago), the last Ice Age (12,000 years ago), the discovery of how to make pottery (9,000 years ago), and the discovery of metal tool-making using copper (6,500 years ago).
- **ADV Research:** Using the Internet, search on the words "Ice Man" and see what you can learn about Otzi, the Ice Man, and report your findings to the class.

1.8.0 TRAGEDY AND DISASTER

1.8.1 How Did Humans Survive During the Ice Age?

We can only imagine the great tragedies of early humans because we have no written record of these events. The last Ice Age (35,000 to 12,500 BCE) was certainly one of these tragedies. How advanced were human beings before the last Ice Age covered the planet? How many humans, plants, and animal species died because they could not survive the radical drop in the temperature of the planet we call Earth? How many human innovations and ideas were lost because of the vast sheets of ice that covered much of the earth? We actually know very little about how humans survived during the last Ice Age. As the temperature of the Earth plunged, vast amounts of the planet's water became frozen in massive glaciers, and the average sea level dropped as much as ninety feet around the world. Because many Ice Age people lived along the oceans, many of the archaeological human sites from the Ice Age are currently under water, making them very difficult for archaeologists to excavate.

- **Quick Write:** Describe in a short paragraph the coldest you have ever been. What did you do to become warm again?
- **Banner Power:** Create a banner to hang on trees around the campfire to encourage early humans to think of better ways to keep warm and improve their lives. (In reality, early humans could not read or write, nor did they have pen and paper.)
- **Epic Teller of Tales:** Oral stories told around the campfire on cold nights were the great literary works of the Ice Age. Imagine yourself as a great Ice Age Epic Teller of Tales and create a grand oral epic of how humans survived during the last Ice Age. You may accompany the epic with a musical instrument or with appropriate music from a CD player.
- **The Futurist:** As a team of four famed underwater archaeologists from the future, present to your class a report on a major human Ice Age site you have just excavated. Be sure to describe the hazards of excavating underwater, a map of your imaginary excavations, and illustrations of some of your major finds.
- **ADV Prehistorical Research:** Using your library and the Internet, research what archaeological evidence has been found of human life during the last Ice Age and report back to the class on your findings.

1.8.2   Why Early Human Cannibalism?

Starvation was a constant threat for early humans. Food was scarce—especially in the winter. From archaeological evidence, we know that cannibalism was widely practiced by early humans, due to near starvation. Early humans would even crack open the bones of their dead to suck out the marrow. It also has taken place in more recent history, in such tragic events as the Donner Party during the California Gold Rush of 1849.

- **Quick Write:** The word "cannibalism" is a frightening word in the English language—or in any language. In a short paragraph, describe your feelings and any questions you have when you hear this word.
- **Letter to a Friend:** As an early human being, write a letter to a friend describing the horror of seeing someone you know being eaten due to starvation.

- **Pros and Cons:** Do you think cannibalism is justified in times of extreme starvation? Take a position on this question and be prepared to defend it when your class meets again around the campfire.
- **Decision Tree:** In teams of four students in the class, discuss starvation and cannibalism among early humans in terms of a decision tree to decide what alternative early humans had. The problem "cannibalism" is the trunk of the tree. Each student team thinks of a minimum of three alternatives (branches) early humans had considering starvation and cannibalism. Each team then considers the positive and negative aspects of each alternative (branch). Based on their decision-tree analysis, the team then makes a decision as to the best alternative when faced with starvation and cannibalism.
- **ADV Historical Research:** Using your library and the Internet, look for modern instances when people have resorted to cannibalism. When finished, report your findings to the class.

1.9.0   EXPLORATION AND DISCOVERY

1.9.1   What Did Fire Do for Humans?

Two major concerns of early humans were getting enough to eat and keeping warm at night, and these two concerns were closely related to each other. The human body gets its energy from eating food, and over 90% of the body's energy is used in keeping the body warm. If early humans could get more food and keep warmer, they would live a much better life.

Crucial to this equation between food and warmth was the discovery of fire. A few early humans learned about the existence of the phenomena of fire from lightning starting a grass fire. It must have been a frightening experience as the searing heat, smoke, and flames roared through the grass, forcing animals and early humans to flee for their lives. Early humans also found, however, that this terrible thing called "fire" also had its advantages. Returning a few days later, early humans—always hungry—found that roasted animals trapped and killed by the fire were much easier to eat and tasted rather good. They also found that sleeping by the still-burning embers of an old tree kept them warm at night. Wow! Something so dangerous was also so very useful! We can imagine the arguments of early humans: "Stay away from it, it's dangerous!"

(conservative position); "No, I like cooked meat and keeping warm at night—let's find out how to use it" (progressive position).

Just imagine what it must have been like to have been an early human to wait around for lightning to start a grass fire before you could have your next cooked meal or heater to keep you warm at night. Some bright young pre-human *Homo erectus* innovator about 1 million years BCE had a brilliant idea: What if humans keep adding dry wood to a fire to keep it going and take pieces of this fire and build fires elsewhere? Life suddenly became much better due to this major discovery. Early humans with fire as a tool now had more food to eat, because cooked meat was much easier to digest than raw meat. With more food to eat and a nice fire at night to keep them warm, suddenly life was much better for early humans.

- **Quick Write:** In a short paragraph, describe what it is like to try to eat a piece of raw chicken. From your own experience, tell why you think that cooked chicken is better than raw chicken. (Never actually eat raw meat; raw meat can harbor dangerous bacteria that can make you sick.)
- **Cave Painting:** Create a cave painting with a large piece of poster paper that illustrates both the dangers and the advantages of fire for early humans. When finished, show it to the rest of the early humans in your classroom.
- **Madison Avenue:** With a team of four student advertisers, develop a worldwide ad campaign to sell early humans on the idea of using fire to cook meat and keep warm at night.
- **Quick Skit:** With a team of four student actors, create a short skit that illustrates how early humans lived before and after the discovery of fire.
- **ADV Action Research:** From the library and the Internet, find out how early humans made fire with a bow, a stick, and dried leaves. Make a fire bow and demonstrate it to your class (outside the classroom). With your demonstration, make a chart that carefully illustrates how to make fire with a fire bow.

1.9.2   Why Tin and Copper?

The early history of humankind is very slow. New human discoveries did not happen very fast. Fire was certainly a major discovery, but that happened about 1 million years BCE. The tools early humans made tell us this very slow story. For several million years, the only tools humans and pre-humans made were out of stone and wood. A real change in tool making came when someone at the end of the last Ice Age, in Serbia, circa 12,500 BCE, was trying to make a stone tool from a hot rock, but found that the stone bent instead of chipping or shattering, as had other stones. The toolmaker must have been mad at first, but then began to be curious about this strange hot stone he could bend by hitting it. The toolmaker suddenly realized that this strange stone lasted longer and could be sharpened more easily than stone tools. Something else strange about this bending rock: The hotter this toolmaker made the rock, the softer and easier to bend it became. This early toolmaker had discovered copper, and thus began the age of metal making.

The problem with copper and tin, however, is that they are very soft and keep bending all sorts of directions when hit too hard. Copper and tin occur together naturally in only two areas of the world: Turkey in the Middle East and Thailand in Southeast Asia. In both Turkey and Thailand, about 4500 BCE, an accidental discovery led to a major human advance in toolmaking. In both cases, someone accidentally dropped copper and tin into the same fire at the same time. Imagine their surprise when the two soft metals—copper and tin—melted together and formed a much harder metal called bronze. Suddenly, humans had a very strong metal that would not break when dropped, as stone tools did, and would not bend when hit, as copper and tin had. After a million or more years, the Stone Age was now over. Humans had a new source for their tools and weapons—spearheads, plows, knives, kettles, and hundreds of other items could now be made out of bronze. This was the beginning of the Metal Age, with many other metals (such as iron and steel) to be discovered a few thousand years later.

- **Quick Write:** Think of a moment in your life when you made a major discovery that really surprised you. Write a short paragraph describing your discovery and why it surprised you.
- **T Chart:** On the left side of your T chart, make a list of tools that could be made with either stone or wood. On the right side of the chart, make a list of tools that could be made with metal.
- **Time Traveler:** Traveling back in time to the very end of the Stone Age and the beginning of the Metal Age, describe in your diary the momentous change in human history that you are witnessing.

- **Song Fest:** Make up a song, a rap, or a poem (for nonsingers) about this great discovery of metal making.
- **Art Mart:** Create a drawing or painting for your classroom wall that illustrates the amazing discovery of bronze.
- **ADV Historical Comparison:** Using your library and the Internet as sources, compare the discovery of metal making to the other great discoveries of human history, such as agriculture, fire, and human flight. From your research, how does the discovery of metals compare to the other great discoveries of human history and prehistory?

1.10.0   INVENTION AND REVOLUTION

1.10.1   How Did Simple Pots Change the World?

The simple invention of pottery in the Middle East (circa 9000 BCE) had an immense impact on humans. For the first time in history, humans could carry water with them when they traveled any distance. For the first time, humans could cook food by soaking it and boiling it in water.

- **Quick Write:** Make a list of foods that could not be prepared and cooked unless you had a pot, bowl, or pan.
- **Concept Web:** Develop a concept web with the word pottery and list all of the things that early humans and humans today can do with pottery—include the nose cones of space shuttles.
- **T Chart:** Make a T chart focused on the concept of water. On one side of the chart, list items early humans could do with water before they had pottery. On the other side, list all of the things early humans could do with water once they had invented pottery. For example: Without pottery, early humans had to live near water (they could not carry it). With pottery, humans could live in villages safely on hills because water could be carried there in pots.
- **Collage:** Make a collage of photographs of a minimum of twenty different shapes and uses of pottery: pots, jars, pans, bowls, plates, and sculpture, for example.
- **ADV Action Research:** Watch someone make a pot on a potter's wheel and then make a simple coiled pot out of clay. As you are making the pot, imagine that you are the first person in history to make a clay pot. In your diary, then write a short entry describing what it must have felt like to be the first person making a pot.

1.10.2   Why Wear Clothes?

Why do we wear clothes, especially when it is hot? Many people, even in the tropics, wear few if any clothes. Some people do the opposite and jump into ice water without any clothes! Burrrrrr! Interestingly enough, the first clothes we can find in the archaeological record have nothing to do with either being warm or cold. The earliest "dress" for a woman was a belt made out of beads with dangling strings of beads flowing from the belt. Not very practical, except that it obviously enhanced the way the young girl looked as she walked with a sway across the campground. Today we call it Sex Appeal. These first clothes were made to attract the attention of the opposite sex. A second type of early clothing was "the crown"—something a leader could wear on his or her head to symbolize leadership. We all wear clothes today to cover our bodies for modesty. Obviously, the earliest people on Earth had no such desire—they used their early "clothing" as beads and crowns to show themselves as someone special.

- **Quick Write:** Write a short paragraph on why you wear clothes and what you would do if you did not have any clothes. Be ready to share your thoughts with your class when finished.
- **Designer:** As the world's very first clothes designer—according to archaeologists—design the world's first beaded skirt for girls and a fancy crown for your local monarch. Share these masterpieces with your class when you are finished.
- **Shirts and Pants:** As the world's first clothes designer, when nobody else wears clothes, present an argument to the world for people to start wearing clothes. Share you ideas with a partner, and then to the class as a whole.
- **ADV Research:** Research your library and the Internet for information on early clothing and then present your findings to the class.

1.11.0   ART AND CREATIVE THOUGHT

1.11.1   Who Made the Early Cave Paintings?

One of the true indications that humans are different from animals is art. Animals do not make art; humans make art. There is a stereotype that ancient humans lived like primitive animals, concerned only with food, shelter, and an occasional battle with a neighbor. Prehistoric cave and rock paintings from around the world tell us a different story. Many of these early rock and cave paintings are some of the true wonders of the world. They often depict a very trained and sophisticated talent at observing Nature and great skill at producing something very beautiful.

- **Quick Write:** Think for a moment about the most beautiful painting you have ever seen. In a short paragraph, describe this painting and share your description with your class.
- **Prehistoric Art Mart:** On large pieces of paper, have the early humans in your cave (class) become cave painters. Each student should create a simple drawing of a person, animal, or thing.
- **Prehistoric Story Line:** When each student is finished with the simple drawing, all of the class should stand up in a long line around the room, holding their drawing in front of them. The first student should create a story about the character or animal in his or her drawing. The imaginary story should then be carried on by the next student—adding on to the story—until every student has had a chance to add to the story.
- **Prehistoric Art Gallery:** Prehistoric artists with the best drawings can display their work on the cave (classroom) wall; visiting students from other classes may be given a gallery walk of artwork in the class once they are finished.
- **ADV Prehistoric Art Walk:** Go to the library or the Internet and find pictures of the magnificent cave paintings from Lascaux, France (circa 10,000 BCE). Just wander through the book or website to look at these magnificent prehistoric works of art. Imagine that you have just discovered the Lascaux caves; keep a log of your impressions of what you see, and share it with the other early humans in your cave (class).
- **ADV Prehistoric Art Research:** Find other books or websites on prehistoric cave and rock paintings from other areas of the world, such as the Tassili Highlands in southern Algeria, Altamira in northern Spain, and the Tsodillo Hills in northwest Botswana. Make a list of the major subjects in each of the paintings at these sites. What similarities and differences are there between these prehistoric paintings from across the world? What kind of materials did each artist mix in his paints? Which do you think are the

most beautiful? When finished, describe what you have learned about early prehistoric artwork to the other members of your class.

- **ADV Rock Art Field Trip:** Many areas of the United States and the world are full of ancient rock art. Pay a visit to see these ancient treasures, and then report to the class on what you saw.

1.12.0 SUCCESSES AND FAILURES OF THE PREHISTORIC ERA

1.12.1 Your Race to Prehistoric Success

- **Quad Race:** OK, quads (groups of four students), this is your chance to show your abilities to identify the most important successes of humanity during the prehistoric era.
  1. Pick the name of one of the following inventions or discoveries out of a hat for your quad.
  2. Then make a long list of reasons why this invention or discovery is the most important during the prehistoric era.
  3. When each quad is finished, the teacher will read each quad's list to the class.
  4. Each quad should listen carefully to each other quad's answer to ensure that it is acceptable.
  5. A scorekeeper will keep count of each quad's point total of acceptable answers on the board.
  6. The quad with the most number of acceptable reasons wins the game.
  7. The prehistoric inventions and discoveries are as follows:
     - fire
     - stone tools
     - pottery
     - metals
     - towns
  8. On your mark, get set, go! (And may the best quad win.)

1.12.2 A Failure to Communicate

Humans created new inventions throughout the prehistoric era. The greatest failure of the prehistoric era was the failure to communicate these new inventions and ideas to others. The great Paul Newman flick,

Cool Hand Luke, had a famous line: "What we have here is a failure to communicate." This line is certainly true about the early history of humans on planet Earth. New discoveries were certainly made, but they were not passed on to others and so died with the inventor. All around the world, small families made important discoveries or created inventions, but the news of them did not spread, and they were forgotten. As a result, humankind did not make much progress in improving the way we lived for thousands of years.

- **Quick Write:** How often have you forgotten to tell someone something very important? In a short paragraph, describe such an instance and then share it with the class.
- **The Power of Music:** With a partner in class, write a ballad about the importance of sharing ideas around the prehistoric campfire (classroom) to encourage early humans to develop better ways of communication.
- **Drama Power:** Create a short drama with a partner around the campfire (your class) to encourage early human beings to share their new ideas with each other. When finished present it to your class.
- **Quick Skit:** With a team of four early humans (students), create a quick skit that illustrates the need for humans to communicate with each other.
- **ADV Historical Research:** Look through your library and the Internet for other historical examples of major errors that took place because people failed to let everybody know what they needed to do.

1.13.0   MAJOR WORLD PROBLEMS FOR THE PREHISTORIC ERA

1.13.1   The Utter Poverty of Early Human Beings

The major continuing historical problem of the prehistoric era was the utter poverty of early humans. Every bone discovered by archaeologists from prehistoric humans shows signs of malnutrition. A large number—if not most—of early humans died from starvation during this era. The widespread practice of cannibalism (see TLP 1.8.2) was also an indication of the utter poverty of early humans.

- **Quick Write:** When you see a homeless person who is unable to take care of himself or herself, what reaction do you have? In a short paragraph, describe how you feel about such a person, what you can do to help them, and what they can do to help themselves.
- **Graffiti Power:** With a partner in class, create graffiti on poster paper to hang in their cave for early humans giving them ideas on new ways to do things so they can escape the terrible poverty of their existence in prehistoric times.
- **Front Page:** With a team of four student reporters for the *Stone Age Daily Times*, interview early humans (fellow students) from around the campfire (the classroom) to hear different views on how the utter poverty of early human beings can be reduced in the future. When finished, create a front-page edition of your newspaper focusing on this major problem for early humans.
- **ADV Action Research:** Conduct a campfire (class) project of asking parents, friends, and neighbors about ways early humans could escape the constant starvation they all faced. When completed, discuss the findings of all the students around the campfire. What are the implications of these findings for history and for our own day?

1.13.2   Mosquitoes! Ugh!

This little bug the size of a grape seed has killed great leaders, decimated armies, and decided the fate of nations. No animal or human has had such a profound effect on the history of humans on this planet. Even today, in the 21st century, millions of people die each year from diseases carried by this little bug—malaria, yellow fever, dengue, encephalitis, and West Nile Virus. But no one realized it was the mosquito that caused all of these deaths until 1894, when Ross and Manson discovered that a mosquito bite transmitted the malaria parasite into the blood of humans.

Some of the first humans—200,000 years ago—certainly died from mosquito bites. Even ancient Rome was a center for mosquito-borne fevers. While the Romans themselves became immune, malaria attacks stopped many invaders such as the Visigoths, Vandals, Ostrogoths, and Huns. But Rome was not alone. Ancient Egypt, ancient China, and ancient Mesopotamia all had millions of people killed by this little bug. Even Alexander the Great was likely killed by malaria in 323 BCE.

Even the early founding of the United States was impacted by this little bug. Philadelphia, the capital of the newly formed United States, was attacked by the yellow-fever–bearing mosquito in the summer of 1793, and everybody—including Washington, Jefferson, and Adams—fled Philadelphia until the fever subsided in the fall of that year.

But surely, in the 21st century, we know how to control the mosquito? Everybody across the world sprays many types of insecticide. Insecticides may work for a little while, but the sneaky mosquito continually adapts to be immune to new sprays. Even now, new insecticide-resistant mosquitoes are beginning to spread across the world (Spielman & D'Antonio 2001). What new diseases will these little bugs bring to human beings? How many more millions will die? And will humans across the world learn how to fight these little monsters—over and over again?

- **Quick Write:** Write a brief paragraph about your last experience with a mosquito. What happened? Did it get you? Were you able to kill it?
- **Quick Skit:** With two other people in class, create a short skit from your favorite period of history. In the skit, demonstrate how the ancient ones might have combated mosquitoes. Did their methods work? Be ready to present your skit to the whole class.
- **ADV Research:** To date, no effective means have been invented to control mosquitoes for any length of time. Window screens, invented in the 1880s, were certainly a help. DDT was a help for a number of years. But mosquitoes seem to know how to develop immunity to every bug spray invented. Research the Internet to find of any recent discoveries that may be of help in controlling mosquitoes. Report your findings to the class.

1.13.3   Can Climates Change Civilizations?

Six thousand years ago, planet Earth had a lot more rainfall. Great deserts such as the Sahara were lush, large plains full of lakes and water-loving animals such as hippos, crocodiles, and water buffalo. The same is true in the Middle East, India, and western China. In all of these areas, archaeologists have found rich sites of early Acheulian stone tools dating back perhaps one-half million years and other modern sites with Middle and Late Stone Age tools. The evidence is very clear—humans lived in these areas for many thousands of years. These early humans obviously were satisfied with their lives and their surroundings, full of wild animals that they hunted for food and with plentiful supplies of water to drink.

But suddenly, around 5,500 years ago, things began to radically change. Major areas of the world, such as the Sahara in northern Africa, dried up. The rainfall ceased. The lakes began to dry up. All the animals began to migrate or die off. And the humans followed the animals and water to areas where they could survive, such as along the Nile River in Egypt, the Tigris and Euphrates Rivers in Iraq, and the Yangtze River in China. These human migrations to the great rivers of the world, some 5,000 years ago, seems to have sparked human brain cells around the world for innovation and change. Suddenly, almost at the same time, people began to live together in cities, cultivate crops, and raise domesticated animals. Someone had the idea to form cities and governments. Someone else started to write things down. And someone else had the terrible idea to create an army to conquer neighbors. Now they call this "The Beginnings of Civilization." The question remains, however, whether all of these "civilized" human actions are the result of the radical weather change and desertification, or the result of human ingenuity (Chandler, 2007)?

- **What If?** What if all the sources of water around your home and town suddenly dried up? What would you do? Write a short paragraph describing your reaction to the sudden change of weather around you. When finished, be prepared to present your ideas to the class.
- **Song Lyrics:** As a great songwriter and singer from 4,000 years ago, write and sing a song describing the beautiful life of the Sahara Desert—before it was a desert—and how sad it is now without any people, plants, animals, or water.
- **Political Speech Writer:** Two people 5,000 years ago in the Middle East want to be mayor of their newly formed town. Write a speech for the guy/gal who insists that climate change and desertification is what caused people to settle down and form towns, governments, and writing. Or, write a speech for the guy/gal who insists that humans changed on their own to form governments and writing without the influence of desertification. Present your speech to the class in a debate over which of these views is correct.
- **ADV Research:** Go on the Internet and study the early history of the Sahara Desert and the development of ancient Egypt to see how the history of the two are interconnected.

1.14.0   PREHISTORIC ERA ANTECEDENTS FOR THE FUTURE

1.14.1   Is Humankind Ready to Advance?

It is now time to judge whether or not humankind is ready to advance into the next era.

- **Viewpoints:** Five members from around our campfire will state their basic viewpoints of whether or not enough advancement has been made during the prehistoric era. Should humankind move forward? The five illustrious members are as follows:
  1. **Lodak Betrink,** the arch-conservative of the campfire, believes that humankind has gone far enough with enough progress. Betrink believes strongly that the good old days were the best and that humankind needs to hold strongly to past values and beliefs.
  2. **Movar Derudzuk,** one of the rising young voices at the campfire, is a more moderate conservative who believes that we need to be very cautious with any change and be very sure that no harm will come to the campfire if change takes place. Movar is willing to accept some change, but only in very small amounts and only when the time is right—and he wants to decide when that time will come.
  3. **Pokaldar Wookbot,** the wishy-washy middle-of-the-roader around the campfire, is willing to accept change for a few minutes after one speaker, but might have a change of mind in an instant to oppose change after another speaker has finished.
  4. **Yeemul Vatsmeer,** the moderate progressive of the group, is willing to support change for the good of the people around the campfire. Vatsmeer is especially in favor of change when Vatsmeer's own family will directly benefit.
  5. **Quikdok Varull,** the radical progressive around the campfire of early humans, is very willing to support any change that will move humanity away from the drafty old prehistoric campfire into something more modern and comfortable for humanity.
- **Pick a Position:** Each member of early humans (students) around the campfire (classroom) now must choose one of the five positions for humanity to take and support that position with evidence of what they have learned about prehistoric human beings.

- **Vote for Humanity:** A vote will then be taken of all early humans around the campfire to determine whether or not humanity should move on to the next era. The consensus decision of the imaginary early humans around the imaginary campfire will determine their own future and the rest of humanity. (In reality, just such decisions by early human families were key in deciding whether humans stayed the way they were or progressed to new levels of development.)

Ancient History (4000 BCE to 500 CE)

UNIT 2: TABLE OF CONTENTS

INTRODUCTION

The Ancient Era

Humans around 4000 BCE suddenly got their act together. They discovered and invented more things—such as iron and steel tools—and they told more people about these inventions. Small city-states grew into large empires. Small, local religious beliefs and myths were transformed into major religions, such as Hinduism, Judaism, and Christianity. The activities in this chapter share the excitement of the era and have students sense the impact of major inventions, such as writing and the wheel. They will also analyze the significance of some of the major people of these ancient times, the reasons behind the rise and fall of some of the classical civilizations of the world, and the development of the major religions of the world. Through the activities in this chapter, students will discover that the world changed dramatically from prehistoric times, when things had remained the same for centuries. Human beings suddenly improved their existence with new ideas and inventions—such as reading and writing—along with the ability to pass these new ideas and inventions to future generations. But students will also learn that change is not always in a positive direction. Large and powerful empires—the Roman Empire, for example—reached their peaks and then eventually fell. Many great ideas, inventions, and writings from across the ancient world were lost through carelessness, war, and just plain apathy.

This is an important chapter of activities because it enables students to realize what humans can do with new ideas, the need to fully communicate these ideas, and the knowledge that even good ideas and empires can fail if not constantly challenged to improve.

THEMATIC LESSON PACS

2.1.0   HISTORICAL TIME LINE

2.1.1   Ancient History Time Line

- **Name Plates:** Photocopy six sets of the thirteen names and items below. Cut the list of names or item into strips of paper. Place the strips carefully into separate envelopes for each team and label the envelopes "2.1.1 Ancient History Time Line," for later use in class.
- **Team Power:** Break the class into six teams.
- **The Envelope:** Each team should be given an envelope containing the following random thirteen names from the ancient era:
    1. Siddhartha Gautama started Buddhism (circa 560 BCE)
    2. Fall of Rome (410 CE)
    3. Shih Huang Ti built the Great Wall of China (221 BCE)
    4. Julius Caesar shifted Rome to an Empire (44 BCE)
    5. Hammurabi law code written (circa 2200 BCE)
    6. Hindu Upanishads written (circa 400 BCE)
    7. Moses established formal Judaism (circa 1300 BCE)
    8. Lao Tse started Taoism (circa 604–531 BCE)
    9. Invention of writing and wheels (circa 4000 BCE)
    10. Jesus started Christianity (circa 30 CE)
    11. Confucius started social reforms (circa 551–479 BCE)
    12. Step Pyramid at Saqqara, Egypt, built (circa 2686 BCE)
    13. Pericles established democracy (circa 460–429 BCE)
- **Team Time Line:** The first job of each team is to correctly order the thirteen names and facts according to time, with the oldest at the top and the most recent at the bottom. Each student should separately write the correct time line for the thirteen names and facts on a personal sheet of paper for later reference.
- **Team Look Up:** Once every member of the team has his or her own ancient time line on a sheet of paper, each of the thirteen items should be divided between members of the team to find

out the meaning of each item from their textbook. Once found, the meanings of each ancient name or fact can be shared with the members of their team to write on their own time lines.

- **Poster Power:** On a large piece of paper, each team should construct its own time line using the thirteen names, with descriptions and illustrations to demonstrate the meaning of each name. When finished, these can be presented to the class and displayed on the classroom wall.

- **Music Mart:** Each team should pick what they think is the most important name or event in the time line and then compose and present to the team a short song or rap about the name or event. When finished, this can be presented to the class.

- **Journal Entry:** Have team members write a short journal entry speculating about what they now know about the development of humans during the period from 4000 BCE to 500 CE—from the time line they developed—and possibly the most important things to happen during this era. When finished, students can first share their thoughts with their team and then with the class as a whole for a general discussion about what they think are the most important things that happened during the era.

2.2.0   SEPARATING FACT FROM MYTH AND PROPAGANDA

2.2.1   How to Make a Myth

- **Quick Write:** Instruct the class to think for a moment of a favorite mythological character and then write a short paragraph about this character.

- **Poster Power:** Make a poster illustrating the five major archetypes found in human mythology (Pearson 1989). Note that the characters in many comic books and cartoons on TV are archetypes. These five archetypes are as follows:
  1. The Warrior who can conquer any foe
  2. The Martyr who sacrifices his life for a cause
  3. The Magician who has the power to defy nature
  4. The Wanderer who single-handedly discovers new worlds
  5. The Villain whose evil deeds darken any day

- **Quick Skit:** With a team of four student actors, create a short skit that illustrates one of the five major archetypes of mythology.

- **ADV Mythological Analysis:** Pick one historical person from ancient history, such as Alexander the Great, Attila the Hun, Moses, Jesus, or Cleopatra. Conduct a mythological analysis on that person by reading about that person and determining whether or not he or she fits one of the five mythological archetypes above. If so, decide whether the person is now more of a myth or still a real historical figure, according to the evidence gathered.

2.2.2   Sophia—Myth, Religion, or Philosophy?

Who is Sophia? Translated from the ancient Greek, she is Wisdom—our knowledge of what is true, right, and just. Clearly "Wisdom" is an important concept for our decision-making abilities as human beings. But that is where it begins to get confusing. In many old religions, she becomes the Goddess of Wisdom. For example she was Wisdom or Athena for the ancient Greeks.

For the early Israelites, at many early archaeological sites, she sits next to the Jewish God in temples as his wife and the Cannanite Goddess Asherah. In the Old Testament of the Bible, various verses of Proverbs 8 picture Sophia as a female source of wisdom: "Does not wisdom (Sophia) call? Does not understanding, raise her voice? . . . Take my instruction instead of silver, and knowledge rather than choice gold, for wisdom (Sophia) is better than jewels . . . I, wisdom (Sophia), dwell in prudence, and I find knowledge and discretion."

In the Eastern Greek Orthodox Church, Sophia, "Wisdom," is revered as the Hagia Sophia—The Holy Wisdom. The best example of this can be seen in one of the world's most magnificent churches—the Hagia Sophia—built by the Byzantine emperor Justinian, in Istanbul, Turkey (537 CE). The Western churches, both Catholic and Protestant, however, try to ignore the presence of a female named Sophia in their male dominated "Holy Trinity"-focused religion. One group of early Christians, the Cathars, in southern France, also called the Gnostics, actually saw Sophia as the "Holy Ghost" in the Christian trinity, but they were killed for this belief by the Pope in Rome.

How then should we view Sophia, "Wisdom"? Is it important personal thinking that we should all have and improve on? Is it philosophy? Is it religious? Or is it myth?

- **Quick Write:** Sit back and consider for a minute what you think the difference is between myth and religion. Write a short paragraph about your ideas, and share these with your class when you are finished.

- **Pair Share:** With a partner in class, write down three or four of myths you know and three or four religions you know and share these with the class. Again, what is the difference between them?
- **Art Mart:** As an ancient artist, draw a picture of Sophia as either the Greek Goddess Athena, the Jewish/Cannanite Goddess Asherah, or the Hagia Sophia (the Holy Sophia) of the Byzantine Empire and Eastern Orthodox Church. Be sure to share your artwork with your class, and put the best images on your classroom wall.
- **ADV Myth, Fact, or Religion?** As an advanced class discussion and final essay, look at Sophia in terms of what she has been throughout history—a myth, a fact, or a major part of several different religions. Or, has she been parts of all three in history?
- **ADV Research:** Look up Sophia to find out what you can learn in your library or the Internet. Report your findings to the class.

2.3.0 LOCATION AND MOVEMENT

2.3.1 Who, What, and Where Did It Happen First?

Where did the major ancient era inventors and their new ideas come from?

- **Pair Share:** Divide the class into student pairs (pair shares). Have each pair share pick one person, idea, or invention from the history time line (see 2.1.1) and then speculate on the origins of the idea or invention, or on what caused the person to do what he did.
- **Look Up:** Each pair share should then use their textbook or other source book to locate where the person, idea, or invention started in the world.
- **Map Attack:** On a blank map of the world, each pair share should indicate this starting point on their map with an illustration of the person, idea, or invention. Each pair share should then share their findings with the rest of the class.
- **ADV Historical Research:** Using the school library or the Internet, find out how the news of this person, idea, or invention spread around the world and then report your findings to the class.

2.3.2   Great Ideas and Inventions That Did Not Make It

Many of the great ideas and inventions in the world never became well known until a much later date. Why did such great ideas and inventions rapidly spread across the world?

- **Pair Share:** Using a map of the world, each pair share should brainstorm a minimum of five ways why a great idea or invention from ancient history might fail to spread around the world. (Suggested ideas and inventions include: pyramids, the wheel, iron making, and writing—see 2.1.1.) Each pair share should be sure to think of such geographic barriers as mountains, deserts, and oceans and the lack of any reliable long-distance transportation during ancient history in their discussions.
- **Plenary Session:** Each pair share should then share their five ways with the class and a recorder should list all of the different ways on the board. The teacher can lead a discussion with the class to decide which five ways are the most likely reasons why an idea or invention failed to spread for such a long time.

2.4.0   POLITICS AND LEADERSHIP

2.4.1   Why Pyramids in Ancient Egypt? (2600 BCE)

Organized central states can do things that small groups of people in villages cannot do. After 3000 BCE, humans were suddenly doing very large organized projects that early humans did not even dream of—such as building pyramids. They were the world's first symbols of the power of a centralized state. The pharaohs were buried in the pyramids as symbols of the state, not for their own glory. The great pyramids of Egypt, contrary to myth, were not built with slave labor but by free Egyptians working three months each year while the Nile was flooded (Boorstin 1992, 88).

- **Quick Write:** In your mind, imagine standing next to the great pyramids at Giza in Egypt. In a short paragraph, describe what you think about these gigantic stone monuments.
- **Pair Share:** In student pairs, brainstorm for two minutes and make a list of five things people can do with a pyramid. (This is really a trick question. Pyramids are more symbolic and really not very useful.)

- **Strategy Session:** Student quads (teams of four students each) should brainstorm and plan strategies on what it would take to have people from all over Egypt work together on a large project (such as a pyramid) three months at a time for ten years.
- **Poster Power:** Create a large poster encouraging the people of Egypt to cooperate and build one of the great pyramids of Egypt more than 4,000 years ago.
- **Bumper Sticker:** Create a funny bumper sticker to encourage the Egyptians building the pyramids to enjoy their work.
- **Speech Writer:** As a bright and upcoming pharaoh-to-be of Egypt, write a speech to your countrymen urging them to keep building pyramids as a means of keeping the country together.
- **Political Rally:** Stage a pro-pyramid political rally in your class-room—with banners, posters, and speeches—promoting the building of more pyramids.
- **Survey Team:** Divided into survey teams with four surveyors (students) each, the class as a whole can measure the school's sport fields to see if the Great Pyramid of Giza could fit there. The Great Pyramid is 481 feet high and 733 feet long on each of its four sides. Can it fit?
- **The Futurist #1:** Times have changed. What do you think it would take to get anybody to volunteer the time to build a pyramid today? Conduct a poll in your school and neighborhood to see how many people would volunteer to help build a pyramid in the sports field next to your school. When completed, report your findings to the class.
- **ADV The Futurist #2:** During the early fourth dynasty of Egypt, the pyramids were the symbol of the power of the state. Research your library and the Internet to identify the symbols of power of the state today.

2.4.2 Why Did Hammurabi Make Laws? (circa 2200 BCE)

Hammurabi, the first king of Babylon, also wrote the first known law code. Two of Hammurabi's laws were as follows (Harper 2000):

> #3: "If any one brings an accusation of any crime before the elders, and does not prove what he has charged, he shall, if it be a capital offense, be put to death."
>
> #22: "If any one is committing a robbery and is caught, then he shall be put to death."

- **Quick Write:** In a short paragraph, describe what you think it might have been like to live in a time that did not have any laws.
- **Quick Skit #1:** With a team of four students, write a short skit depicting what it would be like without any written laws and present it to the class.
- **T Chart:** Create a T chart that compares things that happen when people do not have laws (for example, stealing somebody's food) and then how this would be different if laws existed.
- **Poster Power:** Create a poster that encourages people to create laws and to live and work together peacefully.
- **Quick Skit #2:** In a team of four students, create a short skit that illustrates what it might have been like to live under Hammurabi's laws (2200 BCE). When finished, speculate how these laws are different from our laws today.
- **The Futurist:** With a partner, rewrite Hammurabi's laws so they could possibly be used today and present them to your class.
- **ADV Historical Research:** Using your library and the Internet, research other examples of Hammurabi's laws in early Babylon and share them with the class.

2.4.3   The Great Female Pharaoh—Hatshepsut

Hatshepsut was one of the first great women in our historical record. Foreigners, called the Hyksos (shepherd kings), had ruled northern Egypt for a hundred years after 1700 BCE. As the pharaoh after the death of her husband, Thutmose II, Hatshepsut drove the Hyksos out of Egypt and reestablished a strong, centralized Egyptian government based in Thebes. She was not only an able ruler, she also had artistic taste and had the most beautiful temple in Egypt constructed on the west side of the Nile from Thebes. All, however, were not pleased with her rule. Her stepson, Thutmose III, resented her rule; when she died, he quickly covered up her name with plaster on every monument he could find, and replaced her name with his own. Thanks to the plaster protection from Thutmose III, we know a great deal about Hatshepsut due to her many well-preserved monuments (see Canby 1961).

- **Quick Write:** In a short paragraph, present your opinion of women being strong leaders of countries.
- **Bumper Sticker:** Create a bumper sticker either for or against one of the great female rulers in history, Hatshepsut.

- **Quick Skit:** With a team of four students, present a short skit that illustrates the rule of Egypt's first female pharaoh.
- **Front Page:** With a team of four, develop a front-page edition of the *Classical Times* newspaper that focuses on the rule of the Pharaoh Hatshepsut.
- **You Were There:** As the host of this popular TV program, have the studio audience each write down one question for them to interview this week's guest, Hatshepsut (a student in costume), visiting us from over 3,500 years ago.
- **What If?** What if Hatshepsut visited our country today? What would she say about the role women have in our country's politics? Write a short speech you think she might give on this topic.
- **ADV Historical Research:** Using the library and the Internet, find other major women rulers who made important contributions to their nation's well-being. When finished, report your findings to the class.

2.4.4   Volcanoes, Hyksos, and Hebrews?

There is no historical record of a Hebrew people in Egypt except for the Bible. Many historians, however, believe that the biblical Hebrews were one of the shepherd tribes of the Hyksos, who were the foreign rulers of northern Egypt for 100 years at the end of the Middle Kingdom (circa 1700–1600 BCE). Also a major, early Hyksos archaeological site exists in southern Israel, not far from northern Egypt. Circumstantial evidence from the Greek island of Thera (Santorini) also ties the Hebrews to the Hyksos. Egyptian artifacts from the era of Pharaohs Hatshepsut and Thutmose III (circa 1630 BCE) date from the remains found on Thera at the time of the gigantic volcanic explosion (1628 BCE)—one of the largest in history—that destroyed most of the island. If matched to the biblical stories in Exodus—dark skies, a pillar of fire, and a tidal wave—the volcanic eruption 500 miles to the north might provide some confirmation to the stories of Moses. Exodus says that Moses parted the waters of the Red Sea. Could this have been a tidal wave? Although the Red Sea is not part of the Mediterranean, the written word "Reed" is very close to "Red" in Hebrew. A "Sea of Reeds" is a major location in northern Egypt along the Mediterranean and would have been directly affected by a tidal wave from Thera. A simple copying mistake by a scribe thousands of years ago could explain this possible change of location.

Also according to Egyptian records, the former Hyksos rulers (Moses and the Hebrews?) were chased out of Egypt by Hatshepsut and her stepson, Thutmose III. The Hebrew version of the story says they were escaping from Egyptian slavery. Exodus also mentions that Moses was raised as a royal prince in Egypt. His name, Moses, has a great deal of similarity to the other royal prince of the same time, named Thut-mose. Were they related? We do not know, but with other circumstantial evidence tying together the Hebrewswith the Hyksos, it might be possible (Pellegrino 1993; Assmann 1997).

- **Quick Write:** Imagine for a moment a gigantic volcanic explosion near your town. In a short paragraph, describe what reactions you would have in such an instance and what you would do.
- **Map Attack:** Using an atlas and a blank map of the Mediterranean area, locate the Greek island of Thera (Santorini) just north of Crete. Then, simulating the volcanic eruption on Thera, draw a circle 400 miles in circumference around the island to indicate the area where volcanic ash from the volcano likely fell. How much of Egypt would have been affected by this explosion? Looking at your map, could a tidal wave from the volcano have hit Egypt?
- **Bumper Sticker:** Create two bumper stickers: one for the Egyptian version of the chasing of the Hyksos rulers (Hebrews?) out of Egypt and the other for the Hebrew version of escaping from Egyptian slavery.
- **Quick Skit:** With four student actors from the classroom, create a short drama that illustrates the difference in interpretations between the Egyptians and the Hebrews about the Hyksos (if they were indeed Hebrew).
- **ADV Interpretive Research:** Through classroom discussion and research in the library, try to explain why peoples such as the Egyptians and the Hebrews would have different interpretations of the same events in which both people took part.

2.4.5 Was There Democracy in Ancient Greece?

Our concept of democracy comes from the ancient Greeks in the time of Pericles (circa 460–429 BCE). In theory, the idea of democracy is to give everyone an equal say in how the government of a city or country is run. But we also know that this has not been true in many instances of history. Thomas Jefferson and the Declaration of Independence of

1776 really did not mean that "all men are created equal" when he wrote those famous words. In reality, he was really thinking of only European males who owned property in 1776. The signers of the Declaration of Independence did not plan to include in their "democracy" any poor men who did not own land, any American Indians, any African Americans—free or slave—or any females of any ethnicity. The democracy of Pericles in ancient Greece was much the same. Only respected Athenian men of some wealth were included in this ancient "democracy." No females were also allowed to voice their opinions or vote. Also, no slaves were allowed to speak or to vote.

Now, let us recreate that period of history. Your classroom is now the classical city-state of Athens and your classmates are the citizens of Athens: How are you going to run your "democracy" of ancient Athens? How should we run our "democracy" today?

- **Quick Write:** In a short paragraph, describe what you think is meant by the word "democracy" and who should be included in your definition. When finished, share your thoughts with your class.
- **Amphitheater:** Rearrange the desks in the class into concentric circles facing the front to represent an ancient Greek amphitheater. Two thousand of the leading citizens of Athens have gathered here in our amphitheater to debate the major issues of the day. Listen to the excitement of the crowd. With the person next to you, make a list of topics you think might be discussed by these citizens of Athens and who should be allowed to vote on these issues.
- **Dictatorship or Democracy:** Make believe that you are a citizen of ancient Athens. The people of the city have gathered to decide whether they want to live under a dictatorship or under a democracy. You have been asked to be one of the major speakers to speak either in favor of democracy or dictatorship. Pick the form of government you will support. Write a strong, short speech calling for the people of Athens to support your choice and deliver it in front of the gathered citizens of Athens (students in the class).
- **The Rowdy Crowd of Athens:** The Athenian crowd (students) may cheer, boo, or hiss their favorite (or not so favorite) speakers as they speak.
- **Take a Vote:** When all the speeches are finished, the citizens of Athens may then vote on whether they want to live under a dictatorship or a democracy.

- **ADV Historical Research #1:** Analyze the following quote. Shah Cyrus of Persia commented on the political organization of the Greeks after he had conquered them: "I have never yet been afraid of any men, who have set a place in the middle of their city, where they could come together to cheat each other and tell one another lies under oath" (Boorstin 1992, 96). The great American humorist Will Rogers also once said: "We have the best Congress money can buy!" What did these two men mean in criticizing democratic government? How can we correct their criticisms of democracy?
- **ADV Historical Research #2:** Using your library and the Internet, compare dictatorships and democracies as political systems. What are the advantages and disadvantages of each? When finished, describe which one you think is a superior political system and share your thoughts with your class.
- **ADV Historical Research #3:** Ben Franklin and the state of Pennsylvania during the building of the Congress wanted a single house legislature—without a Senate for rich landowners. Franklin's idea was defeated by Washington, Jefferson, and Madison who wanted an upper house in Congress where the wealthy would have a vote. Who was more "democratic": Franklin, or those who opposed him? And, today, how much real democracy do we have in the United States and the world, where everyone can speak from all ethnicities, rich and poor, male and female? How can we improve on "democracy" for the future?

2.4.6   Did the Great Wall of China Work?

Great walls have been used throughout history in an attempt to keep people from crossing borders into other countries. Shih Huang Ti, the first emperor of China during the Ch'in Dynasty (221 BCE) constructed the first Great Wall we know of in order to keep the Mongols out of China. It is the longest and most massive human structure in the world and the only one that can be seen from space. Other large historical walls include the following:

1. Hadrian's Roman Wall (circa 122 CE) to keep the Scots out of England
2. The Great Wall of the Caucus (circa 570 CE) to keep the Huns out of Persia (See TPAC 2.4.7 below)

3. The Maginot Line (1914) to keep German troops out of France before World War I
4. The Berlin Wall (1949–1989) to keep East Germans from fleeing to West Berlin, Germany
5. The Israeli-Palestinian Wall (1948-Present) to keep the Palestinians from entering Israel
6. The Tijuana Wall (1996 to the present) to stop Mexican illegal immigrants from entering the United States

- **Quick Write:** In a short paragraph, describe what you would think of a neighbor of yours who put up a tall cement wall between his house and yours. Why do you think the neighbor put up the wall?
- **Map Attack:** Using your textbook or a historical atlas and a blank map of Asia, draw the Great Wall of China and measure its length.
- **Poster Power:** Create a poster to attach to the Great Wall (of your classroom) that illustrates why the Great Wall of China was first built.
- **Graffiti:** On a large piece of butcher paper, create a saying that might have been placed on the Great Wall as graffiti.
- **Wall Simulation:** Walls are very intimidating structures and can change the way people interact with each other:
    1. Divide your class in half with a wall of chairs, with only one entryway where students can pass through the wall.
    2. Half of the class (the Groks) will stand on one side. The other half of the class (the Zulls) will stand on the other side.
    3. Each Grok and Zull should keep a journal to record his or her feelings at each stage of this activity. They can record their initial feelings now that a wall separates them.
    4. The Groks and the Zulls should each design a badge or paper hat indicating who they are.
    5. The Groks and Zulls should write slogans and tape them on the wall describing why their side of the wall is better than the other.
    6. The Groks and the Zulls can write and sing a rap or a song about what they think of each other.
    7. Groks and Zulls can e-mail messages to any remaining friends they might have on the other side of the wall describing what they feel about the wall.
    8. The Groks and the Zulls should each make special rules for when one of the others want to pass through their territory, and

any other rules they think necessary to keep their territory free from the other group.

9. Time-out should now be called to have each Grok and Zull write a journal entry about what is happening.
10. After the journal writing has been completed, the wall should be taken down and students take their regular seats.
11. The activity now needs to be debriefed. How were the Groks and the Zulls beginning to feel about each other? What would start to happen if the wall was left up for several days?
12. Each student (Groks and Zulls) should write concluding essays examining what the wall did to the class. Students should also speculate as to what happens when such a wall is constructed in history.

- **ADV Historical Research:** Use the library and the Internet to find pictures and stories of the walls that were constructed by one country to keep a certain group of people from crossing a border. In your research, find evidence as to whether each wall was successful or not. When finished, report to the class on whether or not this strategy of constructing walls was successful or not.

2.4.7 Did the Great Wall of the Caucus Work?

Persia (modern day Iran) was one of the earliest of the great empires of the world. A series of great Persian empires survived for thousands of years at perhaps the major crossroads of the ancient world. To the east were ancient China and India. To the west were the great ancient powers of Egypt, Greece, Rome, and ancient Babylon. How was ancient Persia able to be so strong for so long? This is not just a question of leadership. It is also a question of security. The major threat against Persia throughout most of ancient history was the nomadic tribes sweeping down from modern Russia through the narrow pass between the Caucus Mountains and the Caspian Sea into Persia. As early as 400 BCE—over 2,700 years ago—the Greek historian Herodotus noted the importance of this 30-mile-wide pass at modern Derbent along the Caspian Sea in keeping the Scythian invaders out of Persia. Almost 400 years later, in 65 BCE, the Roman General Pompey made the same comments about this important pass and how the early Persians had created a fortress there to protect their northern border. But 600 years later, in 570 CE, the great Persian Shahanshah (King of Kings) Khosrow I needed to build a major wall at Derbent, spanning the whole pass, to keep out the dreaded Huns whose horsemen destroyed much of the Roman Empire. The wall ran 20 feet high and 30 miles long and was secured by a mighty 60-foot-high fortress—Narin Kala—above today's Derbent along the Caspian Sea in Russia. The wall was successful in keeping the Huns out of Persia. But, almost 700 years later, in 1258 CE, the Mongol invasion swept over the walls to destroy Persia as well as most of the Middle East (Powell 2008).

- **Quick Write:** In a few sentences, describe the most impressive wall you have ever seen. What was the purpose of the wall? Do you think it is right that walls be constructed between countries and peoples?
- **Map Attack:** On a blank map of the Middle East, indicate the location of the Great Wall of the Caucus at Derbent, between the Caspian Sea and the Caucus Mountains. Also indicate the great Persian Empire below it in current Iraq and arrows to indicate the route of the nomadic invaders as the Scythians, Huns, and Mongols who used the pass to attempt to invade Persia.
- **Art Mart:** On a large piece of paper, teams of two student artists each should create a picture of what they think the Great Wall of the Caucus might look like with the Huns to the north of the wall and the Persian forces of Khosrow to the south.
- **War Council:** With four members of your class, create a war council of 570 CE to advise the Persian Shahanshah (King of Kings) Khosrow how he should handle the Huns invading from the north. Should he attack them directly? Should he build the Caucus Wall to protect Persia? Or, should he negotiate a treaty with the Huns? Each war council should then report its findings to the class.
- **Editorial Spin:** As a newspaper editor of the Huns, write a short editorial complaining that the wall is preventing the Huns from invading Persia. Then, in an opposite spin, write a second short editorial supporting the construction of the Caucus Wall by the Persian Emperor Khosrow in 570 CE.

2.5.0   SOCIAL AND ECONOMIC LIFE

2.5.1   Ancient Civilization Travel Promotion

It must have been fascinating to be alive during one of the great classical civilizations of ancient times.

- **Middle East Travel Brochure:** In groups of four students each, pick one of the great civilizations of ancient times (such as classical Egypt, Mesopotamia, Persia, Greece, or Rome) and develop a promotional travel campaign to that civilization. Be sure to use your textbook, library, and the Internet for information on your civilization. Your promotional campaign should include the following:
  1. A large map of the civilization
  2. A poster advertising travel to that civilization
  3. A presentation of what to go and see in the civilization
  4. A Strong/Weak T Chart analysis of the civilization
  5. A list of ideas and inventions we acquired from that civilization
- **Plenary Session:** When you are finished with your travel promotion, your team may present it to the class.

2.5.2   Aspacia—Ancient Greece Did Not Know What to Do with Her!

Aspacia lived in ancient Greece while Pericles ruled Athens (460–429 BCE). Unfortunately, she was from lowly Miletus and not Athens— where all the snobs lived. She had only recently come to "The Big Apple"—Athens and all the big city folks wanted nothing to do with lowly Aspacia. But the snobs in Athens really hated something else about Aspacia—she had brains. Athens was then clearly the intellectual capital of the world, with no room for a smarty-pants young lady like Aspacia. But something very interesting began to happen. With her beauty and brains, she slowly began to climb the social and intellectual ladder of Athens. Soon, she was having deep discussions with top thinkers of the day, men such as Socrates, and even major politicians, such as Pericles began to seek her political insights. But Pericles also saw something else in Aspacia—as a divorcee, he found a companion who could also be his political advisor. With still much grumbling from the Athenian snobs, Aspacia and Pericles lived together for the rest of the Pericles' life and eventually had a son, also named Pericles. Unfortunately for Aspacia and Athens, Pericles died during a plague attack in 429 BCE, which also wiped out over one-third of the city's population. Aspacia continued to live in Athens, with all the city's grumbling, but some Athenians obviously thought very highly of her. In the major archaeological museum in Athens a statue of Aspacia still remains—

looking carefully at the statue's face, we can certainly see her beauty and almost sense the intellectual rigor that lay inside (Leon 1995).

- **Quick Write:** Who is the smartest woman whom you have ever met or seen on TV? In a short paragraph, describe why you think she is so smart. When finished, share your thoughts with the class.
- **Time Traveler:** As a TV news correspondent, travel back in time to interview Aspacia in 540 BCE for your TV *Ancient News Hour*. With a partner in class, write a set of interview questions and the answers that Aspacia might give to you. You and your partner can then present the interview to class, with one taking the correspondent's role and the other Aspacia's role.
- **Brain List:** With a partner in class, make a list of all the major women you can find in your history book, with a brief note about what each did. Compare your list with the rest of the class, to see if you missed any.
- **No-Brainer:** Why does your textbook have the histories of so many males and so few females? Discuss this in teams of four, and develop reasons how this might be made more equitable in the future. This topic can then be discussed in an open forum in class.

2.6.0 RELIGIOUS THOUGHT (4000 BCE–500 CE)

With the exception of Islam, most of the major religions of the world appear during this classical period of history. The following activities focus on understanding the major ideas of each religion or religious leader as they appear chronologically in history—Hinduism, Moses and Judaism, Buddha, Lao Tse, Confucius, and Jesus and Christianity. (The rise of Christianity and Muhammad and Islam will be considered later, during the Middle Ages in Unit 3.)

2.6.1 Hinduism: The More Gods the Better

There is no one belief or dogma in Hinduism. Everyone can create a new god—this is acceptable in Hinduism. Even Jesus is acceptable in Hinduism as a god. Hindus believe that the splendor of the world is so vast that no one god could have made it all. In such a complex world, the more gods, the better. In this complex of many gods, a trinity of three major gods exists—a supreme, but distant father figure named Brahma, who is above everything; Vishnu, a god of life and vitality; and Shiva, a god of death and rebirth. Life and death, however, are not permanent for a Hindu—they are a cycle of birth and rebirth, of being born into a next life, with each life hopefully better than the last one. The idea of worship is also quite different between Hindus and Christians. Hindus do not go to a temple (church) to worship. In Christianity, worshipers enter their church (temple) to hear and read the word of God. Hindus, instead, stand outside the temple and look in to see the image (or dar'san) of god in the temple and present fruit as offerings. In the beginning (what Christians call "Creation"), Hindus believe that everything was together as one in Nature. While Christians have the goal to go to a place called "Heaven," it is the aim of every Hindu eventually to return to a state of oneness with Nature.

- **Quick Write:** Imagine that you are a Hindu. As a Hindu, you must choose the most important things in life to you. Once you have made that decision, you may pick the gods you wish to worship to assist you with these important things—but you may worship only one god at a time. In a short paragraph, describe the most important things in life to you and what things you would like to see in the god or goddess you choose.
- **Poster Power:** Create a poster that illustrates your impression of the Hindu idea of the cycle of death and rebirth, and the eventual hope of going back to being at one with Nature.
- **T Chart:** With a T chart, compare the Hindu form of worship to the Christian concept of worship, based on the information in the previous paragraph.
- **Venn Diagram:** Use a Venn diagram to compare the differences and similarities of this Hindu idea of creation with that of the Christian concept of creation, using the information in the above paragraph.
- **Field Trip:** If a Hindu temple exists near your home, take a field trip there and then write a report to the class on what you saw.
- **Art Mart:** Find a picture and a description of a Hindu god in your library or on the Internet, and draw a picture of this god in a temple so that others can see his dar'san.
- **ADV Religious Comparison #1:** Using sources in your library and on the Internet, compare the three major gods in Hinduism (Brahma, Vishnu, and Shiva) to the three parts of the Christian

god (Father, Son, and Holy Ghost). Develop a Venn diagram to illustrate the similarities and differences between them.

- **ADV Religious Comparison #2:** Develop a poster illustrating your understanding of the differences between Hinduism and Christianity.

2.6.2   Lao Tse—The Ultimate Simplicity (circa 604–531 BCE)

Lao Tse, in his *Tao Te Ching*, set the direction of Chinese religious thought for more than 1,200 years. His teachings and philosophy were the ultimate in simplicity.

- **Reader's Corner:** To set the mood to read from the *Tao Te Ching*, be sure everyone is quiet. Have soft music playing in the background. Have an excellent reader recite the following passage to the class, softly with feeling (Tsu 1972):
  Better stop short than fill to the rim.
  Oversharpen the blade, and the edge will soon blunt.
  Amass a store of gold and jade, and no one can protect it.
  Claim wealth and titles, and disaster will follow.
  Retire when the work is done.
  This is the way of heaven.
  (If you wish to read more of the *Tao Te Ching* to your class, pick up a copy at your library or on the Internet.)
- **Contemplation:** Be sure the students have a moment of quiet after the passage is read to contemplate what was said. Read each line separately and ask the students to record on paper what the line means to them.
- **T Chart:** With a T chart, compare the American ideal of a successful man or woman with the teaching of Lao Tse.
- **Time Traveler:** Imagine a Chinese time machine bringing Lao Tse to the United States today. What would he say about life in America?
- **Finding Ch'i:** Go outside and draw a tree on a piece of paper to see if you can feel the ch'i of the tree and nature. European painters found the beauty of landscape painting (ch'i) during the 1700s (1,200 years after Lao Tse).
- **ADV Comparing Art:** Using sources in your library, look at the great early paintings of Europe's best painters—Michelangelo, Velasquez, and Rubens. They painted great people of importance.

Look at the works of the great painters of China; they painted landscapes. Chinese painters sought the simple Taoist ideal of balancing the opposites of life (yin and yang) to obtain oneness with Nature (ch'i).

- **ADV Religious Comparison:** Using a T chart, compare the ideals of Lao Tse and the "Taoist religion" with what you know of Christianity.
- **ADV Reader's Corner:** Check out a copy of Lao Tse's *Tao Te Ching* from your school library, find a favorite quiet corner, and read it to experience a sense of ch'i (oneness with Nature).

2.6.3   The Buddha—Follow the Inward Voice (circa 560 BCE)

Prince Siddhartha Gautama (the Buddha), from India, was born into great wealth, but was shocked when he witnessed the poverty and suffering of most of his fellow human beings. Siddhartha's answer was not to try and improve the world but to escape from suffering through enlightenment (*nirvana*). This enlightenment or nirvana for the Buddha was to end suffering by not craving earthly things. Asoka, the king of the Mauryan Empire in India, was the first major ruler to convert to Buddhism (321 BCE), after being horrified by the massive deaths caused by warfare. Asoka and Buddhists throughout history have remained nonviolent. The famous short novel *Siddhartha* (about the Buddha) by Herman Hesse gives a good description of the self-imposed sufferings that humans put on themselves during this life, and the enlightenment or nirvana needed to end this suffering:

Siddhartha also realized why he had struggled in vain with his Self. Too much knowledge had hindered him; too many holy verses; too much doing and striving. He had been full of arrogance; he had always been the cleverest, the most eager—always a step ahead of the others, always the learned and intellectual one. Now he understood it, and realized that the inward voice had been right, that no teacher could have brought him salvation. That was why he had to go into the world, to lose himself. That is why he had to be a merchant, a dice player, a drinker, and a man of property. That is why he had to undergo those horrible years, suffer nausea, learn the lesson of the madness of an empty, futile life till the end, until he reached bitter despair, so that Siddhartha the pleaser-monger and Siddhartha the man of property could die. He had died and a new Siddhartha had awakened from his sleep. He also would grow old and die, but today he was young, he was a child—the new Siddhartha—and he was very happy. (Hesse 1951)

- **Quick Write #1:** Make a list of ten favorite people you love and ten favorite things you own.
- **Pair Share #1:** In a pair share, talk about these favorite people and things with a fellow student and then share them with the class.
- **Quick Write #2:** In a short paragraph, describe how you would feel if all of these people and things were no longer available to you.
- **Pair Share #2:** In a pair share, discuss your suffering due to the loss of your favorite people and things. (Note: This is the suffering for material things spoken of by the Buddha. The aim of nirvana is to do without these feelings of want for earthly things.)
- **Meeting of the Minds:** For a classroom presentation, stage a meeting between a typical TV couch potato/junk-food fanatic of today (a student from class) and the Buddha (another student from class) from 2,500 years ago. Have each member of the class write down a question to ask each guest, and then let the interviews begin.
- **Time Traveler:** As a time traveler, bring the Buddha to your hometown today and have him describe what he sees in your material world through Buddhist eyes.
- **Front Page:** As the ace reporter for the *Ancient Times* newspaper, write a newspaper article from 321 BCE describing Asoka's conversion to Buddhism and present it to your class.
- **ADV Religious Comparison:** Using your library and the Internet as resources, research the similarities and differences between Buddhism and Christianity, and make a Venn diagram comparing the two.
- **ADV Poet's Corner:** Read *Siddhartha* by Herman Hesse for a short, simple story of the life of the Buddha. After finishing this little book, write a poem describing your feelings about life through the eyes of Siddhartha.

2.6.4   Confucius—Serve Our Fellow Humans (circa 551–479 BCE)

Many Westerners are confused about Confucius. He did not found a religion. He was not concerned with creation, worship, or the idea of god.

He had no commandments or rules to follow. He was never a crusader or a leader in battle. The teaching of Lao Tse had become the major religion in China. The teachings of Confucius, however, were more of a social movement than a religion. His sayings were—and still are—a means of improving how we can serve our fellow humans. The following readings are from his *Great Learning* (Confucius 1971):

1. When the mind is not present, we look and do not see; we hear and do not understand; we eat and do not know the tastes of what we eat.
2. Riches adorn a house, and virtue adorns the person. The mind is expanded, and the body is at ease. Therefore, the superior man must make his thoughts sincere.
3. From the loving example of one family, a whole state becomes loving, and from its courtesies the whole state becomes courteous, while from the ambition and perverseness of one man, the whole state may led to rebellious disorder—such is the nature of the influence. This verifies the saying: "Affairs may be ruined by a single sentence; a kingdom may be brought down by one man."

- **Quick Write:** In a short paragraph, write down and describe the meaning of a favorite saying of yours.
- **Bumper Sticker:** Create a bumper sticker honoring the wisdom of Confucius.
- **Poster Power:** Create a poster illustrating the meaning of each of the sayings of Confucius.
- **TV Talk Show Host:** Imagine you were a famous talk show host and Confucius (a member of your class) has agreed to appear on your show. Have each member of your studio audience be prepared to ask him a question.
- **Role Play:** Imagine you are Confucius visiting the United States today. What would you say about how people lived? What recommendations would you have for Americans? In a class plenary session, tell the class what you would say to Americans today.
- **ADV Research:** Many Christian churches teach that "faith is more important than good works." Confucius taught just the opposite—that what is important is the good work we do helping others, and not necessarily what we believe. Interview your family and friends to see what they think about this issue, and also

see what you can find in the library and Internet on this important question. Be prepared to report your findings to your class.

2.6.5   Judaism—The Unnamed God of Moses (1600 BCE to the Present)

In the book of Exodus 2:1–10, we can see the beginnings of Judaism and the major monotheistic religions of today, embodied in a leader from Egypt named Moses (circa 1600 BCE). The God of Moses had no name, and he appeared to Moses at the top of a mountain to give the Jewish people the ten rules by which they must live. Several of the rules that God gave Moses on the mountain were as follows:

1. Thou shalt worship no other gods before me.
2. Thou shalt not kill.
3. Thou shalt make no statues of any living thing, for I am a jealous God.

The Jewish God also had no hesitation about going to war. Moses sang to his God (Exodus 15:6–7):

Thy right hand, O Lord, glorious in power.
Thy right hand, O Lord, shatters the enemy.
In the greatness of thy majesty thou overthrowest thy adversaries.
Thou sendest forth thy fury, it consumes them like stubble.

Many of the early religions of the world practiced human sacrifice. The god of the Jewish people, however, was different and outlawed the practice of sacrificing humans (Genesis 22:1–19). Many other people, such as the Greeks and Romans, believed that men could become gods. This, however, was not so with the Jewish religion. Jewish holy men, such as Moses, could perform magic and miracles, and rise to heaven without dying, but men could not become God, not even Moses, the holiest man of Judaism. Greek and Roman rulers, on the other hand, regularly proclaimed themselves to be gods. For many years, Rome ruled the central part of the Jewish homeland—Judea—and insisted on placing statues of their Roman emperor/gods inside the main Jewish temple in Jerusalem. We can only imagine the anger of the traditional Jewish religious leaders—opposed to having more than one god, opposed to statues, and opposed to men becoming gods—at having statues of a Roman emperor/god in their temple. (Historical note: It was this same Jewish/Roman struggle that Jesus was involved in during his lifetime.)

- **Quick Write:** In a short paragraph, give your view of a monotheistic God.
- **Poster Power:** Create an illustration of Moses meeting his God on Mount Sinai.
- **Map Attack:** Using an atlas and a blank map of the Middle East, locate Egypt (the birthplace of Moses), Mount Sinai in the Sinai Peninsula in eastern modern Egypt, and Judea/Israel (the traditional home of the Jewish people).
- **Ace Reporter:** Imagine yourself as a reporter for the local *Sinai Papyrus* newspaper. With another student, develop a spirited interview between the news-papyrus reporter and Moses after he comes down from the mountain. When finished, present this interview of the millennium to the class.
- **Role Play:** Imagine that your class is now a courtroom in Roman Judea where a panel of neutral judges (students) has been called in to arbitrate the ongoing battle between the Jewish people and the Roman rulers.
  1. Two teams of lawyers (students)—one team representing the Jewish leaders, the other team representing the Romans—will prepare arguments for arbitration judges in order to settle the fighting between the Jewish radicals and the Romans. (Both the Jewish leaders and the Romans [in our fictional recreation] have agreed to abide by the rulings of the court.)
  2. The lawyers and the judges should focus on the facts that the Jewish leaders believe in only one God, that no man can become God, and that no statue of God can be erected. The lawyers and the judges, on the other hand, should focus on the fact that the Roman emperor has declared himself to be god and wants his statue to sit in the Jewish temple.

(Historical note: In reality, the Romans finally got tired of Jewish opposition to their rule and destroyed Jerusalem, the capital of the Jews, in 69–70 CE.)

- **ADV Religious Comparison #1:** In a quick write, compare the Jewish concepts of worshiping only one God within a temple and of making no statues, with the Hindu beliefs of having many gods with statues within a temple (dar'san) that they do not enter to worship.

- **ADV Religious Comparison #2:** Compare the teachings of the God of Moses with the teachings of Buddha and Lao Tse with a T chart. Why do you think these religions are so different?
- **ADV Religious Comparison #3:** Compare the Jewish teachings of a monotheistic God (no human sacrifice, and no humans becoming God) with the Christian teachings of a three-in-one God, the sacrifice of Jesus on the cross to save sinners, and Jesus being God and man at the same time.

2.6.6   Alexandria—The Ancient Intellectual Capital of the World (265 BCE–59 CE)

Poor Alexandria (Egypt) gets mistakenly overlooked in many world history textbooks. Alexandria was the intellectual capital (not Athens or Rome) of the classical Mediterranean world for more than 300 years. An exciting mixture of Greek, Jewish, and Egyptian thinkers in Alexandria made several major contributions to world history and especially world religion.

1. The lighthouse of Alexandria—one of the first in the world—was one of the wonders of the ancient world.
2. The Great Library of Alexandria—another wonder of the ancient world—had more than 500,000 scrolls containing the major writings of the classical world.
   (Historical note: Only a few hundred of the scientific, poetic, religious, and historical works stored in this great library are still with us today, 2,000 years later.)
3. The Jews, even in the ancient world, were known for their old religion. The Greeks were known especially for their philosophy. The Jewish religion and the philosophy of the Greeks met in Alexandria, with some very large repercussions for both Jewish and Greek ideologies. One result of this Jewish/Greek meeting in Alexandria was that over 100 Jewish/Greek scholars translated the Jewish Bible (Old Testament) into Greek during the reign of Ptolemy II (circa 265–246 BCE). It became known as the Septuagint. The Greek writers of the Christian New Testament (60–150 CE), including Paul, used this Greek Septuagint (not the Hebrew Bible) in their work.

4. A Jew by the name of Philo of Alexandria (circa 25 BCE–50 CE) created the concept of *theology* by explaining Judaism through Greek philosophy and the use of *allegory*. (Note: Allegory is explaining something not by the obvious meaning of words, but through hidden meanings and references.) Philo's use of allegory enabled Christians to use both the Old Testament and Greek philosophy to explain their religion. Simple biblical stories could now be analyzed allegorically for deeper hidden meanings. Philo also developed the concept of *Logos*—the idea that the "word of God" is God (Boorstin 1992, 52).

- **Quick Write:** Think of a time in your life when you saw two different ideas merge together to become a powerful new idea. Describe this in a short paragraph, and share it with the class when finished.
- **Poet's Corner #1:** Imagine you are an ancient Greek sailor on the Mediterranean Sea late at night, and you see this magical light on the horizon. You know that this is the light from the Great Lighthouse at Alexandria. In free verse poetry, describe what this light during the night means to you.
- **Art Mart:** Create a drawing or painting of what the Great Library at Alexandria might have looked like when it contained most of the great writings of the classical world.
- **Letter Home:** Imagine you are the first time traveler to visit the Great Library of Alexandria in 200 BCE. In a letter back home to your class, describe what it means to be in the biggest library in the classical world.
- **Poet's Corner #2:** In a poetic "Ode to Alexandria," describe what it has meant to the world to have lost forever most of the world's knowledge during the classical times.
- **ADV Biblical Scholar:** Imagine yourself as a Biblical scholar following the ideas of Philo of Alexandria. Look through the Christian New Testament and find a minimum of three stories that can be told simply at the surface level and then allegorically at a deeper level to explain a religious principle. (Example: Matthew 13:3–9 "Some [seed] fell on rocky soil." Allegorically, Matthew [through Jesus] explained that, in this parable, "seed" referred to people who refused to believe in God.)
- **ADV Religious Comparison:** Christians, with a complex three-in-one God, needed allegorical explanation in their developed theology based on the concepts of Philo of Alexandria. Using sources

in your library, trace the development of the concept of theology with the rise of Christianity.

(Historical note: Hindus and Buddhists did not need theology and allegory to explain their religions.)

2.6.7   Jesus—The Poor Jewish Rebel

Jesus, from the stories in the Bible and from archaeological evidence (Crossan 1991; Silberman 1994), was obviously a poor Jewish rabbi with the radical idea of purifying the Jewish faith by taking back the temple in Jerusalem from the corrupt high priests and Roman sympathizers. He taught that "The poor shall inherit the Earth." He tried to "purify" the main temple in Jerusalem from Roman influence by force, but failed (Matthew 21:12). As with many others who rebelled against Roman rule during the period, Jesus was promptly executed by crucifixion.

- **You Were There:** Led by top-flight anchor person Bop Top (a top student in class) the popular panel show "You Were There" travels back in time to 33 CE, to cover the recent crucifixion of a Jewish radical rabbi called Jesus. For your panel show, you will need five prominent local participants (from the class) as panel members (possibly in costume) who witnessed the execution:
  1. Simon Cleophus, an assistant to the chief priest
  2. Maximus Vainius, an officer in the Roman army
  3. Drusilla Felixus, an upper-class Greek lady (pro-Roman)
  4. Zaddik the Nazarene, a radical follower of Jesus
  5. Aeneas Nailemhigh, a local cross maker

  Bop Top, the anchor of the show, can introduce each of the panel members and have them describe what they saw. The rest of the students in class should each develop at least one probing question for each panel member.
- **Debrief:** When finished, each student in class should write a brief essay describing the event that they just "witnessed" and discuss its importance to history.

2.6.8   Jesus—God or Man?

Some of the followers of Jesus claimed to have seen Jesus after his death by crucifixion (circa 33 CE), and claimed that he rose into heaven shortly afterward. Paul (died circa 66 CE), an early Christian convert, began to teach that Jesus was the "Son of God," and was sent down from heaven to become man and save everybody by sacrificing or martyring himself on the cross.

About 100 CE, Christian writers, such as John, began to develop a full theology for Christianity following Philo of Alexandria. They used Philo's concept of allegory to see hidden meanings in the Jewish Bible (Old Testament). They also used Philo's concept of Logos or "the Word" as God. Christians applied this concept of Logos to Jesus and saw that he was the "Word of God" (Logos) and therefore God himself (John 1:1–14). The early debate between Christians asked whether Jesus was a human political savior (messiah), like Moses who saved the Jewish people, or was Jesus a religious savior (messiah) or God. The debate was a major one and led to early divisions among Christians. Eventually, Emperor Constantine called for the leaders of Christianity to come to Nicaea (325 CE) and decide this issue. After much debate, the bishops voted and a majority of mostly Eastern bishops agreed to the concept of a three-in-one (trinity) God—Father, Son, and Holy Ghost. All other early Christian beliefs were declared to be false.

- **Poster Power:** Create a poster that illustrates the struggle within the early church to decide whether Jesus was God, man, or both.
- **Venn Diagram:** Make a Venn diagram to compare the similarities and differences between the major teachings of Judaism (see 2.6.5) and Christianity. Be sure to compare the concepts of human sacrifice and humans becoming God.
- **ADV Five-Way Comparison:** Make a chart comparing the major features of the following religions: Hinduism, Buddhism, Taoism, Judaism, and Christianity (see 2.6.1–2.6.8).
- **ADV Poster Power:** Note the key difference between Hindus, who wish to see a vision (or dar'san) of God, and Christians, who want to hear the word of God because they believe that the word or Jesus is God. Create a poster illustrating these very fundamental differences between Hinduism and Christianity. What are some possible implications of this great difference between religions in the future?
- **ADV Essay:** Using your chart and poster, write an essay describing the major similarities and differences between these classical religions of the world.

(Note: The rise of Christianity and Islam will be covered in Unit 3.)

2.6.9   Was Helena the Discoverer of the "True Cross"?

The Roman Emperor Constantine I (280–337 CE) loved his mother and made her his Empress. Not satisfied with worldly possessions, he also had a vision in the clouds of the "True Cross," and later in 316 CE, made Christianity the official religion of the Roman Empire. He also moved the capital of the Empire from Rome to Byzantium in 324 CE—of course, he then renamed his new capital Constantinople after himself.

But let's talk about his mother, Helena. She also became a devout Christian and literally became the first tourist to visit the Holy Land, what we call Palestine and Israel today. Guided by her belief in Christianity, eighty-five-year-old Helena proclaimed a piece of wood that she found in Jerusalem to be part of the "Holy Cross," and she built the Church of the Holy Sepulcher where she found it. But the Empress did not stop there. She found a robe that she proclaimed was a holy relic which Jesus wore. In Bethlehem, she used her faith to find the manger where Jesus was born, and she built on the spot the Church of the Nativity, one of the holiest spots in Christianity today. Nobody in the 4th century CE knew where the town of Nazareth was—Helena took everyone with her to an empty field in modern central Israel and proclaimed that this was the location of the town of Nazareth where Jesus was reared 300 years before. She even went down to the Sinai Desert and proclaimed a mountain there to be Mount Sinai—where Moses was first given the ten commandments. Without the visions of Helena, Palestine and Israel would not have become one of the world's major tourist spots for Christian holy religious relics for the last 1,700 years (Leon 1995).

- **Quick Relic:** Rapidly look around the room you are in to see if you can find any possible Special Relics. If you do, quickly write a short paragraph on the Special Relic you think you have found. When finished, be sure to share your thoughts with your class. And make sure you tell your class, in reality, whether you think your Special Relic is real or not.
- **Belief, Myth, or Fact?** Look up in the dictionary the difference between the words *belief, myth,* and *fact.* Compare these definitions to that of the major folklorist Joseph Campbell (1968), who said: "Myth is just someone else's religion" (Campbell 1968). What is your personal opinion about the difference between these

three words? How do holy relics, as found by Helena, fit into the differences between these three words?

- **Time Traveler:** As a time travelers, with a partner in class, go back in time to 330 CE to interview Helena about her discovery of the major holy relics of modern day Israel and Palestine. What questions will you ask Helena? And what answers do you expect to hear from her? Present your time traveler interview to the class in the form of a play in which one student is the interviewer and one student is Helena.
- **Daily Rag Editorial:** As the major editor of your local *Daily Rag Newspaper*, write an editorial describing your opinions of the discovery of holy relics by Helena, and how these relics affect us today.
- **ADV Research:** Using the Internet, research the background on Helena's major discovery of the holy relics of Christianity, and report your findings to the class.

2.7.0 CONQUEST AND WARFARE

2.7.1 The Ancient Greek Warrior

From as early as the great epic tales of Homer, the Greeks took pride in their soldiers and their great battles, such as Troy, where Greek soldiers hid themselves inside a wooden horse and secretly opened the gates of the city for the waiting invaders outside. Most early Greek battles were fought only between the strongest individual soldiers on both sides of a battle. Their helmets, armor, weapons, and shields were made out of heavy bronze, and they would often fight until one of the combatants died. Death for such brave warriors was considered to be full of valor and honor for their family, in order to lessen the sorrow and grief of loved ones.

- **Quick Write:** In a short paragraph, create a description of a mythical warrior who can vanquish any foe and conquer any land.
- **Diary Entry:** As a Bronze Age warrior from ancient Greece, imagine what it feels like to go into battle dressed as described. If you wish, read your diary entry to the class when finished.
- **Armor Sticker:** Create a bumper sticker for ancient-era warriors of Greece to put on their heavy bronze armor.
- **Poster Power:** Create an advertising poster to recruit more Bronze Age warriors into one of the armies of the Greek city-states.

- **Quick Skit:** In a team of four student actors, create a short skit that illustrates what it might have been like marching off to war with several hundred other Bronze Age warriors from one of the classical Greek city-states.
- **ADV Action Research:** Conduct a series of interviews in your class, in your school, and in your neighborhood to see if people view "war" as something to be glorified or something to be resisted at all possible costs.

2.7.2 How Great Was Alexander?

At the age of twenty-two, the amazing Alexander the Great (356–323 BCE) of Macedonia led his army on a ten-year march in which he traveled over 2,800 miles and conquered most of the Middle East. He never had more than 100,000 people under his command, and yet he was able to conquer Egypt, the mighty Persian Empire under Darius, and numerous smaller kingdoms along the way. Considered to be one of the great military geniuses of history, the young general was always more interested in fighting and conquering than in actually ruling his people. He died of a fever, likely from a mosquito bite, at the age of thirty-two while he was building a new army for more conquests. Alexander left no organization or appointed leaders for his gigantic empire; on his death, his empire collapsed (Grant 1964, 61).

- **History Chain:** Place the following fifteen battle names and dates associated with Alexander the Great on regular 8.5 × 11-inch paper and give them to fifteen students. These students should hold their name and date cards in front of them and place themselves in correct chronological order. Place the following battles of Alexander the Great in their correct chronological order. (Remember that BCE—Before the Current Era—dates go in descending order, not ascending order):
    1. Persepolis (early 330 BCE), in southern Iran—the capital city of the Persian Empire.
    2. Ancyra (early 333 BCE), in central Turkey, near modern Ankara.
    3. Taxila (326 BCE), on the northernmost Indus River in modern Pakistan, where Alexander's troops mutinied against him and insisted on returning home.

4. Damascus and Tyre (early 332 CE), in modern Syria and Lebanon.
5. Damghan (late 330 BCE), in northern Iran to the south of the Caspian Sea.
6. Alexandria (late 332 BCE), in Egypt, where he named the major seaport after himself.
7. Patala (325 BCE), at the mouth of the Indus River in modern Pakistan where the Greek fleet of ships met Alexander and his army on their return home.
8. Gaulamela (early 331 BCE), in northern Iraq on the upper Tigris River, where Alexander defeated the Persians for a second time.
9. Babylon (323 BCE), in southern Iraq, where Alexander died of a fever.
10. Granicus (early 334 BCE), near the current town of Istanbul, Turkey, was Alexander's first major victory.
11. Ephesus (late 334 BCE), on the western shore of modern Turkey.
12. Babylon (late 331 BCE), in modern southern Iraq, the ancient capital of the Mesopotamian Empire.
13. Kabul (329 BCE), in modern Afghanistan.
14. Samarkan (328 BCE), in modern Uzbekistan, the commercial center of the ancient Silk Road to China.
15. Issus (late 333 BCE), in southern Turkey on the modern border with Syria, where Alexander defeated Shah Darius of Persia.

- **Map Attack:** With a partner in the classroom, a blank world map, and a world atlas, trace the approximate 2,800-mile conquest of Alexander the Great in correct chronological order. Each set of partners should share their map with the other partners in the class to compare their routes. The class in plenary session can then come to a general consensus of the route taken by Alexander the Great and his army between 334 and 323 BCE. (Note that the exact locations of many of his battles more than 2,000 years ago are not known, but indicate the approximate locations of these battles from the clues given.)
- **You Were There:** As the talk show host of the popular TV program "You Were There," interview Alexander the Great (student in costume) to get his spin on why he was such a great military general. Each member of your studio audience should also have at least one question to ask this great general.

- **Counter Spin:** As the ace reporter of the *Classical Times* newspaper, write up an (imaginary) interview with one or more peoples conquered by Alexander the Great and his army. Be sure to ask them about the devastation, looting, and destruction caused by his army. Do they consider Alexander to be "Great"?
- **Obituary:** As a major political commentator for Classical Radio—323 BCE on your radio dial—comment on the recent death of Alexander the Great and whether such great generals should be considered heroes—or tyrants, who bring only death and sorrow to the world.
- **ADV Military Research:** Using the library and the Internet for resources, find out about other ancient-era military leaders, such as Thutmose III (circa 1504–1450 BCE) of Egypt, Darius (circa 558–486 BCE) of Persia, Julius Caesar (circa 45 BCE) of Rome, and Trajan (98–117 CE), emperor of Rome. From your research, discover if they took pride in their military achievements, or did they eventually regret all the bloodshed they caused? When finished, report your findings to the class.

2.7.3   Tomyris—The Female Warrior of Ancient Scythia

History is full of macho male military leaders and conquerors, but very few females. One of the few was Tomyris, who was from an ancient group of Scythian nomads called the Massagetaes. They lived along the western side of the Caspian Sea on the border between modern Azerbaijan and Iran (ancient Persia). In 550 BCE, Shah Cyrus of Persia had hacked his way through the Middle East to build a gigantic empire that stretched from the Mediterranean Sea to India. Only one people remained for Cyrus to conquer: the Massagetae, Tomyris' Scythians to the west of the Caspian Sea. Cyrus first attempted to trap Tomyris into becoming one of his many wives. She refused. He attempted to trap her again, but ended up only with her son, who died in his hands. The result was a gigantic battle, and one of the most bloody in ancient history, ending with over 200,000 dead Persian warriors—including Cyrus. Tomyris, the female warrior of the Scythians, was victorious and although the battle took place over 2,500 years ago, the battle still marks the northern boundary of ancient Persia and modern Iran along the Araxes River (Leon 1995).

- **Quick Write:** Write a short paragraph describing who you think was the most famous woman in history (e.g., Cleopatra, Queen

Elizabeth I, Nefertiti). Why do you think this woman was so famous? Compare this woman to Tamyris. Be ready to share your opinions with your whole class.

- **Rumper Sticker:** Create a rumper sticker that Tomyris could have put on the back end of her horse as she rode into battle.
- **You Were There:** As a firsthand observer of the battle between Cyrus of Persia and the Scythians of Tomyris, describe for your TV viewers how the battle took place.
- **Map It:** Using an atlas, find the location of the battle between Cyrus and Tomyris, and on a blank map, label the location of the battle and the major surrounding landmarks. Be sure to include the reason why the battle was so important.

2.8.0   TRAGEDY AND DISASTER

2.8.1   The Loss of the Library at Alexandria

Some 500,000 of the known manuscripts from the classical world were stored at the Great Library at Alexandria. Some of the manuscripts in this great library were destroyed by one of several fires, some were destroyed by neglect, and fanatical Christians destroyed others in their religious fury to eliminate anything not Christian. As a result, we know of only a handful of the 150 or so great Greek writers, and have lost countless thousands of scrolls of classical science, art, and literature. Imagine if we only had a few thousand or even a few hundred more of these great writings of the ancient world that were stored at the Library at Alexandria in Egypt! Just think how much more we would know about the world around us (Boorstin 1992, 27).

- **Quick Write:** Imagine what it must have been like to see the only great library in the world burning. In a short paragraph, describe your feelings for everything that was lost in the library. When finished, share your feelings with the class.
- **You Were There:** As the popular ancient-era TV show host for "You Were There," ask five guests (students in costume) who knew the library in its greatness to comment on its loss. Each member of the studio audience (students in class) should also have a minimum of three questions each to ask the guests:
  1. Zeno Liberius, the former head librarian of the Great Library
  2. Lothus Maximus, a Christian iconoclast

3. Philonius the Elder, a renowned Greek thinker
4. Caesar Augustus, who sent his scribes to study at the great library
5. Cleopatra, who liked to go to the library to read in peace away from her many followers

- **ADV What If?** Research the library and the Internet on the contents of the library at Alexandria and then speculate as to how far and how fast world civilization might have progressed had the works of the Great Library at Alexandria remained intact for the scholars of the world to study. Write a short report detailing what you think would have happened to the history of the world as a result. When finished, report your thoughts to the class.

2.8.2   What Caused the Collapse of the Akkadian Empire (circa 2170 BCE)?

The Akkadian Empire in Mesopotamia may have been one of the earliest large states to fall due to a severe drought. Following the Sumerians in present day Iraq, the Akkadian Empire was established around 2300 BCE. The empire stretched from the present-day Persian Gulf across Syria and into Turkey. It was very likely the world's first very large empire, coving most of the Middle East. But it abruptly collapsed less than 200 years later. Why?

By 2170 BCE, archaeological records present evidence of a mass exodus from the north, with settlements abandoned and refugees escaping into southern Mesopotamia. Excavations at one of the Akkadian settlements—Tell Leilan—show evidence of a thick layer of windblown dust. Three hundred years later, nomadic groups again ventured into the region, but the empire was not reestablished.

Geologists recently found strong evidence of a great drought in a deep-sea sediment core drilled from the Gulf of Oman. The core sample shows a dramatic 300-year period of windblown dust that could be dated to roughly the same period as the Akkadian collapse. Chemical traces in the dust allowed the scientists to pinpoint its origins in central Mesopotamia—home of the early Akkadians.

- **Quick Write:** In a short paragraph, describe what you would do if your town and state suddenly ran out of water. Be ready to share your thoughts with your class.

- **Map Attack:** On a blank map of the Middle East, label and shade in the early large Akkadian Empire that covered all of modern Iraq, Syria, Lebanon, and eastern Turkey.
- **Semitic Arrows:** The Akkadians were the earliest known Semitic language speakers in the Middle East. Draw arrows from the central Akkadian Empire to illustrate how the Semitic language spread to areas like Israel to become Hebrew and to Saudi Arabia, where it became Arabic.
- **6 O'Clock News:** With classroom anchor teams of four (student) news reporters, go back in time to report on the growing disaster of 2170 BCE and the collapse of the large Akkadian Empire to an ever-expanding drought that lasted several hundred years.
- **ADV Research #1:** Use the library and the Internet to find other such examples of droughts and other extreme weather conditions causing the decline and fall of other cities and countries. When finished, report your findings to your class.
- **ADV Research #2:** Using the library and the Internet, identify other countries and areas of the world that are in danger of being destroyed by drought. What means are available to stop or slow down droughts in large areas around the world? Be sure to report your findings to the class.

2.9.0 EXPLORATION AND DISCOVERY

2.9.1 How Were Iron and Steel Forgotten?

Iron smelting first took place (circa 2000 BCE) in an area around Greece, Turkey, and Romania, but iron smelting spread slowly due to the high temperatures required to melt iron—1,535 degrees Centigrade (2,795 degrees Fahrenheit). The earliest bronze—constructed from melting soft tin and copper together—was forged in Iran in circa 4,000 BCE at the beginning of the Bronze Age. Iron, however, was stronger than bronze and easier to find. Steel is the much stronger form of iron and requires much higher smelting temperatures. The earliest steel furnaces in the world have been found by archaeologists on the island of Sri Lanka (circa 2,200 BCE). Ancient China, India, and Rome followed, with more blast furnaces (400 BCE) for cast iron and, later, for steel. Along with many important ideas, the early process for making steel was lost to Europe after the fall of ancient Rome in 410 CE. The steel-making process was not rediscovered until the 16th century in Italy and only reintroduced to England in 1610.

- **Quick Write:** Open an oven when it is 450 degrees Fahrenheit—it's hot! In a short paragraph, describe what it must feel like when opening a blast furnace at 2,795 degrees (more than five times hotter). In your description, be sure to note what kind of protection you would want to withstand this kind of high temperature needed for iron smelting.
- **An Iron-Maker Sticker:** Create a sticker boasting about the early Greeks and Turks who were able to smelt iron in 2000 BCE, far before the rest of the world.
- **Role Play:** Role-play two steelmakers in ancient Sri Lanka in the Indian Ocean describing to a visitor what it is like to be the first real steelmakers in the world.
- **Action Research:** Next time you have a fire in the fireplace or around a campfire, place a piece of iron on the fire and leave it for a time. When you come back, is it glowing red yet? If not, puff a bellows at it to make it hotter. Can you make it hot enough to melt it (2,795 degrees Fahrenheit) with a bellows? Be safe if you try to do this and do not be disappointed if you fail. (Sri Lankans could melt steel in a blast furnace in 2000 BCE; Europe could not do this for another 1,600 years because they did not know how to get their fires hot enough.)
- **ADV Historical Research #1:** Using your library and the Internet for resources, make a list of all the Middle Eastern and Asian discoveries made long before they were made in Europe and America. Speculate why these discoveries did not take place in Europe and the Americas.
- **ADV Historical Research #2:** Why did Europeans forget how to make steel after the fall of the Roman Empire circa 410 CE? How could this major mistake of history have been avoided? Research your library and the Internet to try to find answers to this major historical problem, and report your findings to your class.

2.10.0 INVENTION AND REVOLUTION

2.10.1 Read and Write Egyptian Hieroglyphics

Egyptian hieroglyphics evolved at an early date (3100 BCE) from pictographs. The ancient Egyptians, like the ancient Mesopotamians with their early cuneiform writing (also 3100 BCE), thought that writing came down as a gift from the gods. Illustrated here is simple phonetic

A		B		CH	
D		E		F	
G		H		K	
KH		L		M	
N		O		P	
Q		R		S	
T		W		Y	
Unpronounced sign at the end of a female's name.					

Illustration 2.10.1a.   *Phonetical Egyptian Hieroglyphics*

translation of several Egyptian hieroglyphic symbols. You might notice that, as with most Middle Eastern languages, hieroglyphics did
not contain vowel sounds. The circle or cartouche around the group of
characters means the word is a name. A half circle at the bottom of the
cartouche means the person is a female. (For examples of Mesopotamian cuneiform see PAC 8.10.1 in Volume III.)

- **Who Was That Egyptian?** Can you identify the cartouche of the
  famous ancient Egyptian found in this section? (A cartouche is a
  round circle with a stand at the end that symbolizes the existence
  of a name in Egyptian hieroglyphics.) Using the translation of the
  hieroglyphics here, see who can be the first to correctly translate
  the name of this famous ancient Egyptian in the cartouche. Remember, the name is written in consonants only.
- **Write Your Own Name:** Now write your own name in hieroglyphics. Remember to encircle it with a cartouche. When fin-

Illustration 2.10.1b. *Ancient Egyptian Cartouche*

ished, exchange name papers with two classmates—one after the other, to mix them up. Have each student then go to the board, eight at a time, to write the hieroglyphic name they have. Who can identify which cartouche belongs to which student in class?

2.10.2   Read and Write Chinese

Chinese writing also developed at an early date (circa 1400 BCE), eventually encompassing almost 40,000 characters. As with the ancient Egyptians, the ancient Chinese believed that writing was given to them by a

Illustration 2.10.2. *Five Classical Chinese Words*

divine being. With so many characters, Chinese writing is obviously very hard to learn. Because Chinese characters are independent of pronunciation, these same characters have been adopted by other Chinese dialects (such as Cantonese) and other languages (such as Korean, Japanese, and Vietnamese) to mean very different things in each language.

- **Write It:** Practice writing five classical Chinese words. They are translated into English as the words (a) water, (b) word, (c) to be able, (d) river, (e) to criticize.
- **Language Analysis:** Looking carefully at the five classical Chinese words in illustration 2.10.2, note which words are repeated and appear within other words. They are called "keys" and help us to understand how the classical Chinese characters were created (Jean 1992, 45).
  1. The word "river" in classical Chinese is composed of which two Chinese words?
  2. The word "criticize" is composed of which two Chinese words?
- **ADV Pronounce It:** Learn to pronounce the formal greetings and count from one to five in the following languages. Can any similarity in the languages be noted from how they sound? (Note: The following activities can be done using Microsoft's Encarta on CD-ROM, which also has most other major languages in the world.)
  1. Mandarin (spoken in the north of China)
  2. Cantonese (spoken in the south of China)
  3. Korean

4. Japanese
5. Vietnamese

2.10.3   The Phoenician Shift—Why Did It Happen?

About 1100 BCE, something interesting began to happen to languages in the Middle East. Highly trained male scribes had been writing and reading complicated Egyptian hieroglyphics and Mesopotamian cuneiform for almost 2,000 years. The problem was that normal people could not read or write these complex languages. What if a daughter wanted to write a letter to her mother? It did not happen before 1100 BCE. Suddenly, some brilliant person in ancient Phoenicia (modern Lebanon and Israel) set up a simple alphabet of simple letters that anybody and everybody could write on simple parchment or paper. Suddenly, almost overnight (say one thousand years), people all over the Middle East began to use the Phoenician alphabet and make it their own. Aramaic (derived from Phoenician circa 1000 BCE) became an early alphabetic rage across the Middle East and widely replaced the clunky ancient Mesopotamian cuneiform. From the Aramaic alphabet, other peoples began their own alphabets: The Hebrews (circa 1000 BCE) and the Arabs (circa 400 CE) are two major examples. Another major group of Phoenician alphabet users were the Greeks (700 BCE), who took the Phoenician phonetic consonants and added vowels to produce an "alphabet" of vowels and consonants together. For some odd reason, the Greeks also began to write their letters from left to right—something very familiar to most of us. About 400 BCE, the early Romans began to use their own Phoenician/Greek-based alphabet—the basic one we still use today.

- **Write It:** Using the Greek alphabet, write your name in Greek. What changes must take place for you to fully recognize your own name as it is written today in Latin letters?

Illustration 2.10.3.   *Classical Greek Writing*

- **ADV Research:** Using the Internet, search for the different alphabets described in this lesson: Phoenician, Aramaic, Hebrew, Arabic, and Latin. In how many of these languages can you write your name? Now try to write your name in complicated cuneiform and hieroglyphics. It is clear why the people of the world dropped these clunky ancient languages for modern alphabetic languages based on the Phoenician alphabet. Be sure to share your findings with your class.
- **ADV Language Shifts:** A great many language shifts are taking place today. Some languages are disappearing, while others are becoming larger and dominating the world. Research your library and the Internet to find out what major language shifts are taking place today and how these changes may affect you and the world in the future. Be sure to report your findings to the class.

2.10.4   Will Our Written Languages Disappear?

Why have some written languages failed while others have continued down to our own day? How is our own written language changing? What changes has our language undergone during the past century? What changes will our written language undergo in the future? What specific technological changes in the future will change how we write and how much we write? (For example, consider that as more people use computers rather than handwriting on paper, the skill of handwriting may disappear within the next 100 years. Also consider voice-recognition word processors that write down automatically what you say into the microphone.) What would happen if we completely lost the ability to write our language and robots do all the writing in the future?

- **Quick Write:** Imagine for a moment what it would be like to not have a written language. In a short paragraph, describe what you could and could not do if you did not have a written language. When finished, share your ideas with the class.
- **T-Shirt Logo:** Create a T-shirt logo that promotes the use of written language for those who do not know how to write.
- **Poster Power:** Create a poster that describes the advantages of written language.
- **Quick Skit:** With four other student actors from your class, develop and present a short skit demonstrating what it might be like for humankind to lose written language. What would they use in its place?

- **The Futurist:** Do you think that humankind—with all its rapid technological advances in voice recognition software—could lose its written language in the future? With a classroom partner, develop a presentation that illustrates how this might happen. If so, what would replace written language?
- **ADV Linguistic Research #1:** Use your library and the Internet to research possible answers to why cuneiform in ancient Mesopotamia and hieroglyphics in ancient Egypt did not survive. Share your findings with the class.
- **ADV Linguistic Research #2:** Using the same sources, try to find out why the Chinese- and the Phoenician-based written languages (such as English, Spanish, Greek, and Arabic) survived.
- **ADV Linguistic Research #3:** Two thousand years ago, most of the great thinking and writing of the world was located in Alexandria, Egypt, and used the Greek language. One thousand years ago, most of the great thinking and writing was in Baghdad (in modern Iraq) using the Arabic language. Five hundred years ago, most of the world's great thinking and writing shifted to Europe, with the invention of the printing press using German and other European languages. Using the library and the Internet, study the reasons for these great language changes and their impact on the world. Be sure to report your findings to the class.

  (Note: To answer these questions, focus your readings on the advantages and disadvantages of each language. Focus also on who was using the language in each culture. Did everybody use the language, or was each language used only for the elite scribes?)
- **ADV Linguistic Research #3:** Using library and Internet resources, look back at the development of written language. What advantages did written language give to individuals over those who could not read? What advantages did written language give to the whole development of humanity?

2.10.5   What Would We Do Without the Wheel?

Wheels for carts and wagons were invented almost at the same time as a potter's wheel (3500 BCE) in Mesopotamia.

- **Quick Write:** For a moment, imagine life on our planet Earth without the wheel. Write a short paragraph describing what life might be like without this most important of inventions. When finished, share your ideas with the class.

- **Letter to the Editor:** Imagine that you are the inventor of the first potter's wheel in the world. Write a letter to the editor of the *Classical Times* newspaper describing your new invention.
- **Make a List:** Have a competition in class to see who can list the most uses for wheels in one minute.
- **Art Mart:** Draw a picture of what you think the first wheeled cart might have looked like.
- **Working Model:** Make a cardboard model of a two-wheeled cart with a wooden or metal axle and moving wheels. Write out a description of the difficulty of making the wheels and axle turn. How did you solve this very basic problem (which was not understood by humans until 3500 BCE)?
- **Make a List:** Make a list of all the things that would be needed to make wooden wheels and carts run better (for example: better roads, ball bearings, and rubber tires).
- **Action Research:** Watch a potter make pottery in coils without a wheel, and then make pottery with a potter's wheel.
- **ADV Impact Research:** Using your library and the Internet for resources, describe the impact of the invention of the wheel on the world and report your findings to the class.

2.10.6   The Pythagorean Theorem: $A^2 = B^2 + C^2$

The Classical Greeks, such as Socrates and Pythagoras (circa 569 BCE–500 BCE), did not have modern Arabic numbers (See PAC 3.10.1 The Power of Zero, in Volume I) that we use today. Instead, they study mathematics using geometric shapes such as squares and triangles. Perhaps the most famous of these early mathematical discoveries was the Pythagorean Theorem $A^2 = B^2 + C^2$. Let us do the Pythagorean Theorem the way the Classical Greeks did, using squares and triangles.

Teacher Directions to Test the Pythagorean Theorem:

1. For each student, the teacher should cut a piece of thick paper into a right triangle, with the vertical line (A) being two inches long, a horizontal line (B) being three inches long, and the slanted line or hypotenuse (C) to connect the other two lines.
2. Each student should then be given one of the right triangles along with a blank piece of paper and a pencil.

3. Each student should first draw a square (*A*) with each side measuring 2 inches long. It should be explained to the students that this *A* square represents A^2 or *A* times itself.

4. Each student should then draw a second square (*B*) immediately next to and touching the sides of the *A* square with each side measuring 3 inches long. It should be explained to the students that this *B* square represents B^2 or *B* times itself.

5. Now, starting in one of the corners of the *A* square and overlapping both *A* and *B* squares, a third square should be drawn with each side being the length of the hypotenuse or *C*.

6. Now, the area of the *C* square that does not overlap with either the *A* or *B* square can be filled in with the remainder of the *B* square.

7. This is the Greek mathematical proof of Pythagoras, which proves that the square of *A* (multiplying two sides of *A*, or A^2) when added together with the square of *B* (multiplying two sides of *B* or B^2) is equal to multiplying two sides of *C* (or C^2).

This is one of the most famous of the early Greek geometry theorems, and it contributed to the building of modern mathematics today.

2.11.0   ART AND CREATIVE THOUGHT

2.11.1   The Perfect Illusion of Greek Architecture

The Greeks left us no great pyramids or mummies. They left us, however, the style and motif of their architecture (Doric, Ionic, and Corinthian), which we still copy in our buildings and which you can see on almost any street in any city in the world. Although we may admire the size of Greek buildings, it is the beauty of these buildings that we love. When we think of Greece, we think of beautiful Greek columns. The tops of these columns (called capitals) tell the history of Greece and give the columns their great beauty. First in history came the Doric capital, with its strong, straight lines; second in history came the Ionic capital, with its curved scrolls; and third came the Corinthian, with its flowering capitals that were copied throughout the Roman Empire.

The Parthenon, the most famous temple in classical Greece, stands in magnificence at the top of the Acropolis in Athens and is a masterpiece of illusion—an illusion of straightness. The vertical columns are not really vertical but sloped inward and upward toward one imaginary

Illustration 2.11.1a.   *The Three Greek Capitals of Ancient Greece*

point about one mile up, in order to give the illusion of greater height. Each column is also wider at the middle than at either the top or bottom to make it appear more massive. The floor gradually slopes away from the center to increase the illusion of size and make sure the rain flowed easily away from the temple. These concepts of perspective and illusion in architecture did not appear again in Western art until the Renaissance, one thousand years later.

- **Make a Perfect Rectangle:** Horizontally, each Greek temple is a perfect rectangle. Make a square on a piece of paper and double it in one direction. This double square is a "perfect" rectangle and the exact shape of every temple in ancient Greece.
- **Comparative Columns:** Make a drawing illustrating the differences between the three different types of Greek capitals.
- **Ancient Interview:** Interview three ancient Greek architects (from your class) and have each describe why he or she thinks Doric, Ionic, or Corinthian is the best.
- **Model Maker:** Make a model of the Parthenon out of clay or cardboard.

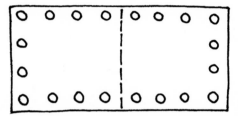

Illustration 2.11.1b.   *The Parthenon of Athens, Greece, circa 432 BCE*

- **Perfect Parthenon Perspective:** Draw a side view of the Parthenon, illustrating the perspective that all of the vertical lines of the columns of the temple will meet about one mile above the Parthenon.
- **Poet's Corner:** Describe in a poem why the Parthenon has been the "perfect" symbol of architectural beauty for more than 2,000 years.
- **Travel Poster:** Make a travel poster for the Greek government advertising the Parthenon.
- **ADV Historical Problem #1:** Ancient Greek architecture was the same throughout Greece. There was no central Greek state in ancient times. The ancient Greeks did not even have a common Greek language until after the major temples were built. Why do all the Greek temples look the same?
- **ADV Historical Comparison:** Later Gothic church architecture during the Middle Ages (500–1300 CE) was never uniform, and each church was uniquely local in design. Research this question in your library and on the Internet, and report your findings to your class.

- **ADV Historical Question #2:** We know a lot about Greek architecture today due to Vitruvius, the architect of Julius Caesar (circa 45 BCE). Vitruvius wrote a major work describing Greek architecture in detail. It remained the primary book on architecture for almost 1,500 years. Was it by the accident that his book survived, or did it survive because of the greatness of the work?
- **ADV Analyze a Quotation:** Nietzsche, the famous German thinker, once wrote: "In architecture, the pride of man, his triumph over gravitation, and his will to power assume a visible form." Look at Greek architecture and then explain what Nietzsche meant in this quotation.

2.11.2   Why did the Romans Use Cement?

The ancient Greeks (750 BCE–146 BCE) did not know how to use cement—they used only stone blocks. But the ancient Romans, by the reign of Augustus (63 BCE–13 CE), were building most of their buildings out of cement. Instead of lugging big rocks around for their buildings, as the Greeks did, the Romans crushed the rocks and made them into cement, which could be cast into all sorts of shapes. These Roman buildings might not have been as beautiful as the Greek buildings, but they were a ton (in fact thousands of tons) more practical. The best example of the use of cement by the ancient Romans was the magnificent single-domed Pantheon—which still stands in the center of modern Rome. With cement, the Romans rapidly built the world's first true cities, with cement public facilities such as communal public latrines, public baths, and trash collection bins. But, typical with many discoveries in history, the people of the Middle Ages and the Renaissance—after the fall of Rome—forgot how to make and build houses and buildings out of cement for 500 years. The rediscovery of making buildings with high-quality cement did not take place until 1780 in England.

- **Quick Write:** Look around your town. What is your favorite building? Why is this your favorite building? In a short paragraph, describe this building—its size, its beauty, and the construction materials that were used to build it. Share your thoughts with your class when you are finished.
- **T Chart:** Using a T chart, compare Greek buildings made of stone and Roman buildings made of cement. What advantages did the cement construction have over stone construction?

- **The Parthenon Versus the Pantheon:** Using photographs from the library and the Internet compare the most beautiful building constructed of stone—the Parthenon in Athens, Greece, with the most beautiful building constructed of cement—the Pantheon of Rome, Italy. Which do you think is the most beautiful and why? Be sure to share your thoughts with your class.
- **What If?** If you were an architect, which would you use in your buildings—stone or cement? Why?
- **Action Research:** Visit a nearby construction site and watch the builders pour cement. Take notes on your visit and then report to the class on each step builders must take when they are constructing with cement.

2.11.3   Roman Arches and Greek Sewers

The mainstay of Roman architecture was the cement brick, from which the Romans were able to construct round structures based on the arch, the vault, and the dome. The Greeks used round architecture only as the arch in their sewers; all classical Greek buildings had to be either square or rectangular in shape, with square mantels above every door and window. The Romans turned round shapes (such as the arch and the dome) into major architectural structures with their cement.

- **Quick Write:** In a short paragraph, pick a favorite—circles or squares—and then describe why you like one over the other.
- **Poster Power:** Make a poster illustrating the basic differences between rectangular classical Greek doorways such as the Parthenon and round classical Roman arches found in Roman monuments and buildings across the Mediterranean area.
- **Duke It Out:** With a partner in class, create a opposing list of arguments for round doorways versus square doorways. When finished, be prepared to present your argument in front of your class.
- **Diorama:** Make a diorama illustrating the basic differences between classical Greek square doorways and classical Roman arches side by side.
- **Ace Reporter:** Write a newspaper article for the *Classical Times* newspaper describing the differences between classical Greek square doorways and classical Roman arches.
- **ADV Historical Oddities Research:** As stated earlier, the Greeks always built their beautiful buildings in square shapes with square

doorways. The Greeks, however, constructed all their underground sewers with round archways. The Romans, on the other hand constructed most of their doorways for their important buildings and temples with round "Roman" arches—the same type that the Greeks used for their sewers. Search your library and the Internet to find out why this odd difference in doorways existed between the Greeks and Romans. When finished, report your findings to the class.

2.11.4   Did Tragedy Spark Creativity in 64 CE?

A great fire in Rome (64 CE) destroyed much of the city. Due to this major catastrophe, the eccentric (if not mad) young emperor of Rome—named Nero—rebuilt Rome with a frenzy of creative cement works and open patios between buildings. He also fireproofed much of Rome at the same time by tearing down wooden structures and re-building them with cement. Much of the beauty we see in the remnants of Roman architecture today is the result of Nero's rebuilding efforts. Nero died young, at the age of 30, and there are many stories about his atrocities against Christians and others—the Roman Senate also hated him. But much of the beauty of ancient Rome that we see today is due to the work of Nero.

- **Quick Write:** Have you ever been surprised by someone you did not like when they turned around and really helped you out? Write a short paragraph describing the incident and share it with your class.
- **Spin Doctor:** Almost all of the classical Roman historians writing about Nero—Tacitus, Pliny the Elder, and Suetonius—put a nega-tive spin on the young emperor. The rich landowners and senators obviously hated his high taxations, but there are hints that the poor of Rome loved him. Opposite of the negative spin we so often hear about Nero in our history books, write an editorial for the *Classi-cal Times* newspaper that gives a positive spin to Nero's work on rebuilding Rome in 64 CE.
- **ADV Historical Question:** Why does tragedy often become the spark that prompts creativity and new ideas? Discuss this question in share pairs, in teams of four, and then in a general class plenary session to share ideas on why this happens in history.

2.11.5   Japanese Architecture—Submission to Nature

Stonehenge in England, the pyramids in Egypt, and the Pantheon in Rome were all pieces of great Western architecture. They were built vertically and massively in stone for strength to withstand time and to be a symbol of human dominance over the forces of Nature. Traditional Japanese architecture is just the opposite in almost every way. Japanese architecture reflects the traditional culture and religion of Japan, which stresses the importance of human submission to the forces of Nature. Traditional Japanese temples are low, horizontal, and designed to blend into their natural surroundings (Boorstin 1992).

- **Quick Write:** Think about all of the houses in your town. Is there one small little house that is pretty and blends nicely with the surrounding trees and plants? Take a quiet moment and write a short paragraph describing this house.
- **Poet Power:** Write a small haiku poem that describes in just a few words how traditional Japanese buildings blend with Nature.
- **Viewpoint:** In American society today, old buildings are almost always destroyed to make room for new buildings or parking lots. Compare this with the traditional Japanese view of Nature.
- **Dialogue:** With a partner in the class, write and present a short dialogue between a traditional Japanese architect and a classical Western architect, comparing their buildings.
- **Personal Preference:** In a short essay, explain which type of architecture you prefer (European/American or Japanese) and why you have made this decision.
- **ADV Historical Riddle:** How can two views (European/American and Japanese) of the same thing (architecture) be so different? Research your library and the Internet to try to find the answer to this riddle of major differences between cultures.

2.11.6   Homer's *Iliad* and *Odyssey*

Homer's *Iliad and Odyssey* from ancient Greece are among the oldest written works of literature in the world. Educated ancient Greeks were required to memorize all of Homer's famous epic tales. Homer's epics were repeated orally for hundreds of years before they were formally written in Greek (circa 700 BCE). A major clue we have to the popularity of the *Iliad* and the *Odyssey* comes from Egypt. Many of the remaining ancient papyri (early paper) scrolls containing Greek writing from late dynastic Egypt are sections from the *Iliad* and the *Odyssey*. Homer's greatness lasted throughout the classical period, the Middle Ages, and the Renaissance into our own day. Homer's stories were about an ancient Trojan War and the men and women who took part in that war: Achilles, Agamemnon, Helen of Troy, and Odysseus. Homer took no side in the war, but rather tells the tale of superheroes, of regular people confronted by normal problems of love and anger, and the adventures of the very humanlike gods and goddesses. The Greek gods were powerful, but not *all*-powerful. They had weaknesses, made mistakes, and got into trouble, just like human beings. In fact, the Greek gods were patterned after humans. These gods could also be very troublesome to human beings. One-eyed monsters, sirens luring him to his death, giants, and mighty storms all tried to lure Odysseus from his path home in the *Odyssey*.

We do not know who Homer was, but we know that he was a great storyteller, as the following passage from the *Odyssey* illustrates. In the passage, a great blind singer by the name of Demodocus is led to the throne of Pontonoos, King of Phaeacia, to play for the king's banquet. Some scholars think that the passage is a reflection of Homer himself playing for the courts of the early Greek kings (Grant 1964).

(Note: The importance of Homer's work cannot be overstated in setting the model for modern literature across Europe, the Middle East, and eventually the world.)

> The crier soon came, leading that man of song
> whom the Muse cherished; by her gift he knew
> the good of life, and evil—
> for she who lent him sweetness made him blind.
> Pontonoos fixed a studded chair for him
> hard by a pillar amid the banqueteers,
> hanging the taut harp from a peg above him,
> and guided up his hands upon the strings.
> In time, when hunger and thirst were turned away,
> the Muse brought to the minstrel's mind a song
> of heroes whose great fame rang under heaven.

- **Poster Power:** Read this passage from the *Odyssey* and illustrate the images the page depicts on a large wall poster.
- **Imagine:** Imagine the ancient Greek gods depicted in the *Iliad* and the *Odyssey* as being alive today. Draw a picture of what you think they might look like.

- **Song Fest:** Create an epic song about a modern war and sing it to your class.
- **T-Shirt Logo:** Make a T-shirt logo supporting or attacking one of the Greek gods.
- **Super Hero:** Odysseus is one of the first mythical superheroes we know about in history. Make a list of his major features and then compare him to a modern superhero in a comic book.
- **ADV Literary Research:** Check out copies of the *Iliad* and the *Odyssey* from your school library or find a copy on the Internet. Read one of the stories, and then report on what it was like to read a book that is almost 3,000 years old.

2.12.0   SUCCESSES AND FAILURES OF THE ANCIENT WORLD

2.12.1   Success or Failure Quiz Show

Success or Failure? This is the competitive quiz show of the ancient era that challenges teams to list as many reasons as possible why a person, place, or thing is the most important success or failure of the classical period.

- **Pick a Name:** Each student team of four draws the name of a classical person, place, or thing from a hat. The classical names to be used can be as follows or developed from a larger list:

Hatshepsut	cuneiform	the wheel
pyramids	Parthenon	the Pantheon
Moses	Homer	Jesus
cement	Library at Alexandria	Epic of Gilgamesh
Socrates	Alexander the Great	Hammurabi
Akhenaton	Phoenicians	Aristotle
democracy	Great Wall of China	Hinduism
Tao Te Ching	Buddha	Confucius
Linear B	metal making	Roman Empire

- **Score Keeper:** Each team calls out its name, and the scorekeeper puts it on the board as the team's name. The scorekeeper will keep track of how many answers each team gives on the board.
- **Make a List:** Using any books or materials available, each student team has fifteen minutes to make as long a list as possible of reasons why the name they drew is the most important of the ancient era.

- **List Collection:** All teams must turn their lists into the score-keeper at the same time, and the scorekeeper or an assistant may read each list out loud to the class.
- **Validators:** When each team reports its reasons, the other teams should check to make sure the reasons are correct.
- **The Winners:** The team with the most number of "valid" support-ing reasons wins a free trip to the library.

2.13.0 MAJOR WORLD PROBLEMS FOR THE ANCIENT WORLD

2.13.1 The Problem of Justice—Socrates (469 BCE–399 BCE)

Does individual freedom exist? Can an individual question the reli-gious beliefs of others? Can an individual question the political actions of a state? Can the state impose its will on an individual human being? Does the state have the right to condemn one of its citizens to die? Should an individual willingly die as a martyr in support of his ideals?

These very powerful questions can all be traced back to Socrates—2,400 years ago. Today, these questions still need to be asked. Socrates was a simple scholar who asked questions about people's religious and politi-cal beliefs. The people of Athens did not like so many questions and voted to tell him to stop. He refused, and they imposed the death penalty on him. Socrates, true to his ideals of free speech and individual liberty, knowingly drank the poison he was given and died.

- **Quick Write:** People—especially politicians and religious lead-ers—often do not like to be criticized. In a short paragraph, describe what your experience has been with people who are critical of the government or religions. When finished, share your thoughts with the class.
- **What If?** Imagine Socrates in your town today. If he asked ev-erybody about their religious and political beliefs—as he did in classical Athens—how popular do you think he would be? What would happen to him?
- **Time Travelers:** With a partner in class, imagine that you were alive during the time of Socrates in classical Athens. How would you react to Socrates' speeches? What would you do when the people voted to condemn him to death for his views?

- **Action Research:** The questions of Socrates are some of the most powerful ones we can ask in a democratic society. As a class project, develop a list of Socrates' major questions and make them fit your school and community today. Ask these same questions of students and teachers in your school and of people in your community. What was the response of people to these questions? How did they react?
- **Banner Makers:** Divide the class into teams of four and have half of the teams create banners that support Socrates and the other half of the class create banners that condemn Socrates. When finished hang, the best ones across your class wall.
- **Action Plan:** Develop a community action plan to either support or condemn the ideals of Socrates.
- **Class Debate:** Socrates died for an ideal. Conduct a debate on whether or not human life is too sacred to die for an ideal.
- **Quick Skit:** Does the state have the right to impose the death penalty? In pairs, develop a short drama that illustrates Socrates' question of how much power a government has regarding the life and death of an individual. When finished, present it to the class.
- **Declaration of Liberty:** How far can individual liberty go? Was Socrates right or wrong for questioning religion and the actions of political leaders of the day? In groups of four, write up the formal declarations of individual liberties with which your group would be willing to live.
- **Plenary Session:** Does the rest of the class agree with the individual liberties of each group? How far can each group express its individual liberties before the whole class tells the group to stop? The class as a whole should discuss these issues.
- **ADV Historical Research:** Name several other people in history who willingly died for their ideals and compare them to Socrates. Research the library and the Internet for more information on how they died and the causes for which they died. When finished, report your findings to the class.

2.13.2   The Problem of Entropy—The Rise and Fall of the Roman Empire

Why do great empires (such as the Roman Empire) rise and fall? As an advanced topic of study, here is a list of questions that analyzes why great empires fall. In teams of four, carefully read each of the following questions and then carefully read about the rise and fall of Rome from library and Internet sources. From your team's readings and your own thoughts, decide which of the following questions are most important to understanding why great empires rise and fall, and report your findings to the class (see Kennedy 1987).

1. Who makes the leadership decisions to direct the empire?
2. How strong are the leaders who make these decisions?
3. Are the leaders willing and able to accept new ideas to improve the empire?
4. Do the leaders have ready sources of new information and new ideas at their disposal?
5. Do the leaders have open communication lines to all parts of the empire?
6. Does the leadership have trusted allies throughout the empire to implement new ideas?
7. What are the central ideas and strengths of the empire?
8. Where is the economic strength of the empire?
9. How secure is this economic strength?
10. Where is the empire using its economic resources?
11. Is the empire using its economic resources to improve itself and grow stronger?
12. Is the leadership of the empire seeking to constantly renew itself and adapt itself to changing conditions?
13. Is the empire spending its economic resources on luxuries rather than on the means of further growth?
14. Has entropy set into the empire with no new ideas, direction, or growth?
15. Is the leadership resistive to new ideas and changes?
16. Has the leadership of the empire lost any sense of direction and is it willing to let surrounding events and ideas take their course?
17. Is the leadership not reacting to correct obvious signs of decline in the empire?
18. Has complete entropy and inaction set into the empire as it waits to fall?

- **ADV Graph It #1:** From your readings and reports on the Roman Empire, create a graph of the major steps in the rise and fall of this great Empire.

- **ADV The Futurist:** In pairs of students, apply the same questions toward the United States today or any other country in the world. According to your analysis, what stage is this country in—Still continuing to grow, or in a stage of decline? When finished, present your findings to the class for discussion.
- **ADV Graph It #2:** From your pair's analysis of the United States, chart the current location of this great country in its rise or fall.

2.14.0 ANCIENT ERA ANTECEDENTS FOR THE FUTURE

2.14.1 Is Humankind Ready to Advance?

It is now time to judge whether or not humankind is ready to advance into the next era. Five members from around the temple grounds (the class) will state their basic viewpoints of whether or not humankind has advanced enough during the ancient era. Should humankind move forward? The five illustrious members are as follows:

1. Lidbit Betrink, the arch-conservative of the temple, believes that humankind has gone far enough with enough progress. Lidbit believes strongly that the good old days were the best and that humankind needs to hold strongly to past values and beliefs.
2. Makdak Derudzuk, one of the rising young voices at the temple, is a more moderate conservative who believes that we need to be very cautious with any change and be very sure that no harm will come to the temple if change takes place. Makdak is willing to accept some change, but only in very small amounts and only when the time is right—and he wants to decide when that time will come.
3. Pitwip Wookbot, the wishy-washy middle-of-the-roader around the temple, is willing to accept change for a few minutes after one speaker, but might have a change of mind in an instant to oppose change after another speaker has finished.
4 Yatsnurk Vatsmeer, the moderate progressive of the group is willing to support change for the good of the people around the temple. Yatsnurk is especially in favor of change that will directly benefit Yatsnurk's own family.
5. Qilmuk Varull, the radical progressive around the temple, is very willing to support any change that will move humanity away

from the drafty old Greek temple into something more modern and comfortable for humanity.

- **Pick a Position:** Each member of the temple community (students) must choose one of the five positions for humanity to take and support his or her position with evidence of what he or she has learned about human beings during the Ancient Era.
- **Plenary Session:** A vote will then be taken of all early humans around the temple community to determine whether or not humanity should move on to the next era. The consensus decision of the classic humans around the imaginary temple will determine their own future and the rest of humanity. (In reality, just such decisions by Ancient Era families were key in deciding whether humans stayed the way they were or progressed to new levels of development.)

(For more great lessons on ancient world history, also see Ron Pahl's *Breaking Away from the Textbook: Creative Ways to Teach World History Volume III*, Unit 8.)

The Middle Ages (400 CE to 1400 CE)

UNIT 3: TABLE OF CONTENTS

For more great lessons on the Middle Ages, also see Ron Pahl's *Breaking Away from the Textbook: Creative Ways to Teach World History Volume III*, Unit 8.

INTRODUCTION

The people of the Middle Ages would not have called themselves "middle people." After a moment of contemplation, they might have called themselves "the faithful," for it was an age of faith. All three major monotheistic religions from the great desert of the Middle East, "the People of the Book" (Judaism, Christianity, and Islam) grew into maturity during the Middle Ages. Monotheism, however, does not lend itself to toleration of other religions or even to different interpretations of the same beliefs. The result was a very long era of bloodshed caused by religious ideology: pogroms, burnings of "heretics," and crusades against unbelievers. Religion, however, was not the only cause of bloodletting during the Middle Ages. Hordes of invaders, from the Huns to the Mongols, swept across Asia and changed the face of Europe, the Middle East, and Asia. The centers of civilization during the Middle Ages were in Christian Constantinople, the Muslim Middle East, and Spain. Scholars in Constantinople passed the learning of the Greeks on to Muslim scholars in Baghdad. This stimulated a major flowering of scientific learning in the Muslim world. Modern medicine, mathematics, and science all can be traced to this Muslim Renaissance (circa 1000 CE). Translated by Jewish scholars in Spain and Sicily, this new Muslim science began to flow into Europe. Inspired by these Muslim thinkers, St. Thomas Aquinas (circa 1200 CE) paved the way for modern science by insisting that the church be guided by reason and not just faith. This seemingly very small step in theology was a major step during the Middle Ages and led humanity out of the Middle Ages into the Renaissance.

THEMATIC LESSON PACS

3.1.0   HISTORICAL TIME LINE

3.1.1   History Time Line of the Middle Ages

Photocopy six sets of the following thirteen names and items. Cut each name or item into a strip of paper. Place the strips of paper carefully into separate envelopes for each team and label the envelopes "3.1.1 The Middle Ages History Time Line," for later use in class.

- **Team Power:** Break the class into six teams.
- **The Envelope:** Each team should be given an envelope containing the following random thirteen names and items from the Middle Ages era:
  1. The Mongol attack of Baghdad ends the Muslim Renaissance (1258 CE)
  2. Charlemagne divides his empire into feudal states (800 CE)
  3. Muslim scholars develop modern science, math, and medicine in Baghdad (1000 CE)
  4. The Christian crusaders sack Christian Constantinople (1204 CE)
  5. Rome is sacked for the first time by the Visigoths (410 CE)
  6. Pope Urban II calls for the crusaders to retake the Holy Land from the Muslims (1095 CE)
  7. The Byzantine Emperor Justinian develops the world's first modern law code (483–565 CE)
  8. Perhaps the most beautiful piece of architecture in the world—the Alhambra Palace—is built in Granada, Spain (1250 CE)
  9. Black Death or Bubonic Plague started in China (1331 CE) and wiped out one-third of the world's population
  10. Muhammad's words from God are written into the Koran and become the center of Islam (622 CE)
  11. Dante writes *The Divine Comedy*—perhaps the first modern novel (1265 CE)
  12. Iconoclasts see all art as sinful and destroy classical statues and paintings (700 CE)
  13. The first Gothic cathedral is built in Paris, France (1140 CE)
- **Team Time Line:** The first job of each team is to correctly order the thirteen names and facts according to time, with the oldest at

the top and the most recent at the bottom. Each student should separately write the correct time line for the Middle Ages names and facts on a personal sheet of paper for later reference.

- **Team Look Up:** Once every member of the team has a Middle Ages time line on his or her own sheet of paper, each of the thirteen Middle Ages items should be divided between members of the team to find out the meaning of each item from their textbook. Once found, the meanings of each Middle Ages item can be shared with the members of the team to write on their own time lines.
- **Poster Power:** On a large piece of paper, each team should construct its own time line for the Middle Ages using the thirteen items, with descriptions and illustrations to demonstrate the meaning of each. When finished, these can be presented to the class and displayed on the classroom wall.
- **Music Mart:** Each team should pick what they think is the most important name or event in the time line and then compose and present a short song or rap about the name or event. When finished, this can be presented to the class for their approval.
- **Journal Entry:** Have each team member write a short journal entry speculating about what they now know about the development of humans during the Middle Ages—from the time line they developed—and possibly the most important things to happen during this era. When finished, students can first share their thoughts with their team and then with the class as a whole for general discussion about what they think are the most important things that happened during the era.

3.2.0 SEPARATING FACT FROM MYTH AND PROPAGANDA

3.2.1 Were the Dark Ages Really Dark?

The period after the fall of the Roman Empire has been called "the Dark Ages," but such a label obviously depends on your point of view. Would the period have been called a "Dark Age" by some of the many slaves kept by the Romans or by one of the many peoples conquered by the Romans? By 500 CE, the lights certainly might have gone out in Rome and most of Europe. The lights, however, were certainly not out in many other areas of the world, which were experiencing flowering of culture, such as Constantinople (modern Istanbul in Turkey),

Baghdad (in modern Iraq), and in Granada in Muslim Spain. The year 500 CE was the beginning of the greatness of the Christian Byzantine Empire centered in Constantinople. The rise of Islam, and with it the foundations of modern science and mathematics from Baghdad and the artistic and cultural triumphs of Muslim Spain, all took place during the so called "Dark Ages" of European history.

- **Quick Write:** In a short paragraph, compare your school with another school. Do they have a better football team? Do they have better dances? Do they have more fun? Is it fair to compare schools without really talking to fellow students from the other school?
- **Map Attack:** Using an atlas and a blank map of Europe and the Middle East, locate Rome (the former great capital of the Roman Empire), Constantinople (the capital of the Byzantine Empire), Baghdad (the early capital of the Muslim world), and Granada (one of the cultural centers of Muslim Spain).
- **Cartoonist:** Draw a comical cartoon of a poor European during the "Dark Ages" of Europe looking longingly at the splendors of culture and science of Muslim Baghdad (in modern Iraq) at the same time period of history.
- **ADV Bias Detector:** What does the use of such terms as the "Dark Ages" tell us about the bias of the writers who use the term? What would Byzantine and Muslim writers from about 1000 CE have thought of the term "Dark Ages" to describe the era in which they lived?

3.2.2   The P.R. Spin of Attila the Hun (circa 451 CE)

Few have known how to spread fear among people better than Attila the Hun (406–453 CE). His invasions and control of northern and central Europe certainly were a major reason for the rapid decline of Rome. The country of Hungary in central Europe has an interesting name, and your guess is correct. Hungary along the Danube River was the major home of the nomadic Huns starting in the 5th century, and afterward when they started settling down. Everyone was panicked at the thought of being attacked by Attila. The people in the northern Adriatic region fled into the swamps and founded the city of Venice to escape the terror of Attila during those last days of the Roman Empire. Yes, Attila's men were awesome fighters (see below 3.7.1 Attila the Hun), but they also had an excellent P.R. (public relations) team, who spread terror among the citizens of the Roman Empire. One such tale was that the Huns "roasted pregnant women alive, ate the flesh of children, and drank the blood of women." It may be hard to imagine, but cities and states across Europe and the Middle East believed this propaganda of Attila. The Romans in Italy, the Byzantines in Constantinople, and almost every other city state in Europe and the Middle East sent large sums of gold each year to Attila to keep him from attacking them. The potential enemies of the Huns, including the city of Rome itself, believed such tales and bribed Attila with huge sums of gold and silver not to attack them (Mee 1993, 22).

- **Quick Write:** Has someone scared you about something, but then you realized that he or she was just exaggerating? Write a short paragraph describing the event.
- **Spin Doctor:** As one of Attila the Hun's Advance Advertising Teams, create a wild and blood-thirsty rumor about Attila that would terrorize towns into paying huge bribes to Attila.
- **Counter Spin:** The students in your class are now an imaginary town in northern Italy threatened with attack from Attila the Hun. Develop a counter P.R. story about your town that might convince Attila not to attack your town.
- **Contingency Plan:** In case your counter P.R. plan against Attila the Hun does not work, develop a contingency plan to deal with this awesome enemy. Will you bribe him, fight him, or flee? Explain your response using a decision tree.

3.2.3   The Shroud of Turin—Myth or Fact?

The prize possession of the Cathedral of St. John the Baptist in Turin, Italy, is a long strip of tightly woven linen fourteen feet long. The piece of cloth bears the ghastly image of a bearded man who has apparently been crucified in the way the Bible says Jesus was crucified by the Romans circa 33 CE. Could it be the real thing? Everyone—believers and non-believers—calls it the Shroud of Turin. It is, without question, the most sacred relic of the Catholic Church. But, at the same time, it looks like one of the grandest fakes of all time. Which is it?

The earliest verifiable date of the Shroud in Turin is 1357. Before that date, there are a great many questions—as well as many other shrouds reported to be the one wrapped around Jesus when he was buried in 33 CE. John (20:5-7) in the Bible mentions that Peter found "linen cloth" in the sepulcher where Jesus had been buried. Did Peter lift this cloth from the grave and take it with him? We do not know. No other mention of the linen cloth is made until the Middle Ages, in 944 CE, when the Archdeacon of the Hagia Sophia cathedral in Constantinople reported holding a cloth that supposedly contained the crucified image of Jesus. He called the cloth the "Image of Edessa." In 1205, this sacred cloth was possibly stolen and taken to France by the Knights Templar during the brutal Fourth Crusades, when the Catholic Christian soldiers of Venice, the Pope, and France attacked and sacked Christian Constantinople (for more on the Fourth Crusade, see 3.7.4 below). What ever really happened to the "Image of Edessa" we do not know, but it disappeared. One hundred and fifty years later, a similar cloth called the "Shroud of Turin" appeared in Turin, Italy, in 1357.

Throughout its history, the Shroud of Turin has been called a fake by many people, including many Church officials. But the Pope in Rome and a large number of believers still consider it to be a real religious relic. In 1988, the Church allowed investigators to carbon-14 date the Shroud. The results of the test found that the cloth was sewn approximately between 1290 and 1390, or shortly before it was "rediscovered" in Turin. Other tests indicate that the image of Jesus on the cloth was painted by a very skilled artist such as Leonardo da Vinci. The Church in Rome, along with millions of believers, however, still considers the Shroud to be real. Where do you stand?

- **Quick Write:** How do you tell whether something is real or fake? In a short paragraph, describe an incident in your life when you had to make a decision about whether something was real or fake?
- **Holy Relic Supporters:** With two other Church leaders (students in class), write a short speech and present it in class defending the Shroud of Turin as being real.
- **Fake Supporters:** With two other scholars (students in class), write a short speech and present it in class supporting the position that the Shroud of Turin is a fake.
- **Poster Power:** Create a poster to hang up in class which supports your position regarding the Shroud of Turin—Real or Fake?
- **ADV Research:** Use your library and the Internet to locate more information on the Shroud of Turin and whether it is real or a fake. When finished, report your findings to the class.

3.2.4   Was El Cid Really the Hero of Spain's Christian Reconquest?

In 1616, Don Miguel de Cervantes created the first great Spanish novel *Don Quixote* based on the stories he knew about El Cid, almost 600 years before him. Christian poetry of 14th century Spain immortalized El Cid as the mighty warrior who fought to push the Muslims out of the peninsula. He was born in Burgos, the capital of Castile in Spain (1044–1099 CE). At an early age, he was given the title of *El Cid*, which in the Andalusian Arabic of southern Spain means "chief" or "lord." Now, we might ask why El Cid was given an Arabic title if he was a Christian hero against the Muslims? We find out quickly that he was respected highly by both Muslims and Christians in early Spain. In 1067, he fought for Christian Castile and captured the Moorish stronghold of Zaragosa under its leader Al-Muqtadir. Contrary to anti-Muslim mythology, El Cid asks the defeated Al-Muqtadir and his Muslim armies to join him—and they did. The rest of Zaragosa is conquered by a joint Christian-Muslim army led by El Cid. The new Christian King Alfonso VI of Castile, however, did not like El-Cid's actions and exiled him from Christian Castile. El-Cid and his army quickly joined his old enemy-ally, Zaragosa, as the leader of his army. In 1086, a large invasion of Berber and Moroccan Muslim Almoravids from North Africa invaded Spain. Alfonso and his Christian allies were soundly defeated by the Almoravids. Rejoining the Christians under Alfonso, gradually El-Cid began to concentrate his efforts on Valencia, controlled by the Almoravids. Finally conquering Valencia in 1094, El Cid ruled it through a joint Muslim–Christian administration. While reading the history of El Cid, it is easy to see why he was admired by both Christians and Muslims—but how did Christian mythology change him into just a Christian hero?

- **Tale (Christian):** Create a tall tale about a great Christian leader in Spain who conquers all Muslims in the area.
- **Tale (Muslim):** Create a tall tale about a great Muslim leader in Spain who conquers all Christians in the area.
- **Diary Entry:** Create a diary entry for El Cid, the great 11th-century Spanish warrior, which describes how he fought for and led both Christian and Muslims troops in his lifetime.
- **Banner Maker:** Create a banner for El Cid for him to carry into battle in 11th-century Spain. Display the best banners in the class in the hall in front of the class.

- **Editorial:** Write an editorial for your local newspaper, *The Daily Rag,* supporting leaders who include both Christians and Muslims in their governments and armies.

3.2.5   The First Unlucky Friday the 13th of October 1307

The Knights Templar were without question the major French warrior-monks to fight in the Christian Crusades against the Muslims in the Middle Ages. Founded after the First Crusades in 1096 to protect pilgrims visiting the Holy Land (modern Israel), the Knights Templar founded one of the first banks of Europe, as well as one of the major charities of the Middle Ages. The Knights Templar were also one of the major supporters of Cathar Christians in southern France, who—against the Pope in Rome—centered their Christian beliefs around the idea of seeing God inside themselves rather than worshiping God through the Catholic Church. In 1307, the King of France, Philip IV (the Fair) was deeply in debt to the Knights Templar. He convinced the Pope, Clement V, to proclaim the Knights Templar and Cathars to be heretics, burn them at the stake, and, of course, take all their lands and money. The infamous day of the Pope's proclamation was Friday, the 13th of October, 1307. Everybody in Europe really knew that the Knights Templar were some of the most religious and courageous people in Europe. It is amazing that, over 700 years after that date, we still take note of that tragic date: Friday the 13th.

- **Quick Write:** How has Friday the 13th been for you? Has it been an unlucky day for you? Describe something that happened to you on Friday the 13th, and share it with your class.
- **Date Check:** When is the next Friday the 13th? Set up a plan on how you will deal with this unlucky day that has been around for over 700 years. When finished, share it with your fellow classmates.
- **Time Travelers:** With a team of four students in class, go back in time to 1307 to interview Pope Clement V, King Philip the IV, and the Knights Templar. Have students role play each historical figure—including a news reporter—and create a short panel discussion about the infamous event from which the mythology of Friday the 13th originated.
- **Judge and Jury:** Individually, each student should write a report on what he or she would do on 13th October 1307. Would he or

she work to save the Knights Templar, or would he or she work to help the king and Pope? All of the students together can then hold a discussion on what the class as a whole would do if they were there in France in 1307.

- **ADV Research #1:** Using your library and the Internet, research the demise of the Knights Templar and the origin of Friday the 13th. Report your findings to your class.
- **ADV Research #2:** Wow, how can a myth (like Friday the 13th) survive for over 700 years?

3.3.0 LOCATION AND MOVEMENT

3.3.1   Global Climate Fluctuations (circa 350–450 CE)

For 100 years or more, a major drought in central Asia (circa 350–450 CE) forced the herding of the people of that region south and west into Europe. The Huns from north of the Aral Sea were the first to feel the effects of the drought. They moved into Russia (355 CE) and then across the Volga River (circa 372 CE) to attack the Ostrogoths and the Visigoths. The Ostrogoths and Visigoths then fled into the very weak Roman Empire, followed by the Huns under Attila in 451 CE. These invasions crushed the empty shell of what remained of the former Roman Empire.

- **Quick Write:** Write a short paragraph about what would happen if our planet Earth suddenly became much colder and dryer. How would this affect your life?
- **Map Attack:** Using an atlas and a blank map of Europe and the Middle East, trace the early movement of the Huns across Europe into the Roman Empire before 451 CE from the preceding description.
- **What If?** In a pair share, talk with a partner in class for one minute each about what you would do if you were a citizen of a Roman town in northern Italy, and you saw 300,000 mounted Huns on horseback coming swiftly toward your town. When finished, share your feelings with the class.
- **ADV Climate Doctor:** Look for books and articles in your library on climatic change and how climatic change has affected human history. Report to your class on your findings.

- **ADV Climate Doctor (Today):** Read about the possibilities of climatic change today. How would such a climatic change directly affect you? What if the world suddenly became warmer? What if it suddenly became colder? How would such climatic changes affect how we live on Earth? How would humans react to these changes? Develop a short presentation to the class on your findings.
- **ADV Climate Doctor (Tomorrow):** In teams of four, each team should develop two strategies for coping with climate—one for developing a plan for all humanity to adjust to the impact of global warming on the world, the other for humanity to adjust to global cooling and perhaps a new Ice Age. When finished, each team should present its strategies to all the gathered people of the Middle Ages (your class) for their deliberation.

3.3.2   The Kaaba—The Holy Stone of Islam

Since the earliest times, large stones have played a major part in the history of the Middle East. One of the most important of these is the Kaaba, in Mecca, based on Psalm 118:22–23: "The stone which the builders rejected has become the head of the corner: This is God's doing." In the corner of the large square of the Kaaba is a small meteorite, which Muslims consider to be this very stone, placed there by God. This is the holiest spot for all Muslims. Ideally, faithful Muslims travel to Mecca at least once in their lifetime to circle around the Kaaba while praying.

- **Map Work:** On a map, locate Mecca in the current country of Saudi Arabia.
- **Travel Planner:** Once in a lifetime, Muslims are to pay a visit to Mecca to worship at the Kaaba—this pilgrimage is called the *hajj*. As the imaginary travel agent of a Muslim family of six, plan all of the details of the family's trip to Mecca:
  1. The total air mileage of the trip from your town to Mecca and return.
  2. The route you will have the family travel to Mecca and back.
  3. The total cost of the trip. Call a major international airline to get the exact air fare.
  4. Present your final trip plans to your class.
- **ADV Web Search:** Using the Internet, look for pictures to see the Kaaba and the main mosque in Mecca. Be sure to share these with fellow members of your class.

3.3.3   The Dome of the Rock—Holy or Haunted?

More humans have died fighting for control of the Dome of the Rock in Jerusalem than any place on Earth—and it remains so today. All three desert religions—Judaism, Christianity, and Islam—consider this rock sacred. Four major religious traditions surround this rock: God prevented Abraham from killing his son at this rock (symbolic for ending human sacrifice), the prophet Elijah rose to heaven from this rock, Jesus died on the cross a few hundred yards from this holy rock, and the prophet Mohammed rose to heaven from the Dome of the Rock.

- **Map Work:** Find Jerusalem on a map.
- **Poster Power:** Draw a poster illustrating why Judaism, Christianity, and Islam all consider Jerusalem to be holy.
- **ADV Web Master:** Find websites and newspaper articles on Jerusalem. What is the current relationship between these three major religions in the city of Jerusalem?
- **Maimonides:** Maimonides worked hard during the Middle Ages to bring these three major religions—Judaism, Christianity, and Islam—together (see 3.6.8 below for some of his ideas).
- **U.N. Mediator:** As an imaginary United Nations command team, develop a plan for the United Nations to directly rule the holy city of Jerusalem all by itself as a way for all three religions to stop fighting over the area. Several examples of such independent city states exist, including The Vatican—the seat of the Catholic Church in the middle of Rome.

3.3.4   Constantinople—The Thousand-Year Point Guard

European history books never give enough credit to Constantinople and the Byzantine Empire. For 1,000 years, between 453 CE and 1453 CE, Constantinople ran interference for Europe from a large number of possible invasions from the East. The history of Europe and Christianity would have been much different if the massive armies of Islam had swept across a powerless Europe during the Middle Ages. Any such Muslim thoughts of invading Europe were stopped at Constantinople for a thousand years. In the reverse direction, during each of the Crusades, the crusaders from Western Europe used Constantinople as the staging point for their attacks against the Muslims in Palestine. This was, of course, before the tragic sacking of Christian Constantinople by fellow European Christians during the Fourth Crusades in 1205.

- **Map Attack:** Look on a map of the world and determine why Constantinople (modern Istanbul in Turkey) is in such a crucial location in the world in terms of East versus West relations. In a short paragraph, report your conclusions to the class.
- **What If?** In a hypothetical scenario, remove Constantinople and the Byzantine Empire from the history books between 453 CE and 1453 CE. Using a large map, plot the likely invasion route of the Muslim armies into Europe.
- **Skit Builder:** Create a short skit (a *trilogue*, meaning a discussion with three people) and present it to your class between a crusader from France, a Byzantine soldier in Constantinople, and a Muslim soldier under Saladin discussing whether or not the crusaders could have attacked the Muslims in Palestine without the assistance of Constantinople.
- **ADV T Chart:** Would early Christianity in Western Europe have survived a large Muslim invasion without the assistance of Constantinople? Using your library and the Internet as sources, compare both the pros and the cons of such a possibility on a T chart and present it to your class.

3.3.5   Mansa Musa's African Gold (1324 CE)

Mansa Musa, the king of Mali (1312–1340 CE) in West Africa, set off on a simple pilgrimage to Mecca in 1324. He started his trip in Niani, the capital of Mali, on the upper Niger river; followed the trade routes north across the Sahara Desert and modern Mauritania to Tuat, in modern Algeria, in North Africa; and then east through Cairo in Egypt to Mecca.

What Mansa Musa did on his trip, however, had repercussions far into the future. With him came 60,000 guards and attendants, all clad in expensive Persian silks. He had a minimum of at least 80 camels each carrying 300 pounds of gold. While the Emperor rode the distance on horseback, he was proceeded by 500 slaves, each carrying four pounds of solid gold. The outside world had no idea that a black king from Africa could be so powerful and so rich. He paid for everything he needed with gold—lots of gold. Never had the world seen a man with so much gold. How could one man have so much gold? Where did he get it? Mansa Musa's gold set men's eyes aflame with dreams of piles of gold. Somewhere in West Africa, across the Sahara Desert, beyond Timbuktu, was Mansa Musa's immense source of gold. It became the dream of nations across the world to find this source of gold (Ajayi and Espie 1965).

(Note from the future: Portugal's Prince Henry the Navigator would turn this dream of Mansa Musa's gold into reality in less than 100 years by starting to explore southward from Portugal down the west coast of Africa. In 1420, his sailors discovered the Madeira Islands; in 1427, the Azores; Cape Bojador in 1437; and, by 1452, the Portuguese were along the west coast of Africa purchasing gold and slaves, and minting gold coins. This was the start of Europe's age of exploration during the 15th century. It all was stimulated by Mansa Musa's famous gold-laden pilgrimage across Africa to Mecca.)

- **Map Attack:** On a blank map of Africa and the Middle East, trace the route of Mansa Musa's trip to Mecca.
- **Newspaper Reporter:** As the star reporter for the *Medieval Times* newspaper, interview people in Egypt (students) who witnessed Mansa Musa's lavish display of gold. Write an article on your interviews for the next edition of the newspaper.
- **The Gold Bug Adventure Company:** As a group of four adventurers (students), form a company starting from Fez, Morocco, and make a plan to travel to Timbuktu in Mali, West Africa, to locate and acquire some of Mansa Musa's gold. Do take into consideration, however, that a trip across the Sahara takes 114 days by camel and that large protection fees need to be paid to Tuareg guides. Ships capable of rounding West Africa and compasses to point the way are not yet in general use in Europe.

  Your Gold Bug plan must include the following:
  1. A map of how you plan to get there
  2. Your means of transportation
  3. Your method of acquiring the gold

  Present your plan to the class. The class, in turn, will rate the possibility of your company's success on a 1–5 scale (where 5 means excellent and 1 means you are very unlikely to succeed). Good luck, Gold Bugs.
- **ADV Research:** Search your library and the Internet for other examples of historical stimulation, such as Mansa Musa pilgrimage across Africa stimulating Prince Henry of Portugal into starting

the European voyages of discovery. Be sure to report your findings to your class.

3.3.6   Square Towns or Natural Towns?

Empires based on military strength, such as the Romans, built their towns in square blocks with straight streets to facilitate rapid troop movement. Most ancient nonmilitary towns of the world (such as Fez, Morocco, or Toledo, Spain), however, were natural towns with roads, houses, and buildings following a natural randomness of crooked little streets and not perfectly symmetrical buildings. With the collapse of

Illustration 3.3.6a.   Sketch of an Aerial View of a "Square" Roman Town, Timgad, Algeria, circa 100 CE

the Roman Empire, the towns of Europe gradually returned to this natural form of town, with the crooked little streets that we see in many old European towns today.

- **Map Attack:** Make two maps—one of an imaginary natural town with crooked streets, and one of an imaginary town with straight

Illustration 3.3.6b. *A Natural Town—Isle of Rhodes, circa 1200 CE*

streets and square blocks. Which type of town do you prefer and why?

- **Letter Writer:** Imagine living in such an old natural town with tight little crooked streets and houses close together. Write a letter to an imaginary friend describing what it would be like living in such a town.
- **Town Planner I:** Why are most of the towns laid out in square blocks and straight streets in the United States? Why are there very few towns in the United States with crooked little streets and houses? Why are some modern suburbs becoming more natural with circular rather than straight roads?
- **Town Planner II:** Why do many people around the world like to live in natural towns, when there is no strong government telling them to make straight streets and square houses?
- **Field Work:** Interview someone who has either visited or lived in a natural town with crooked little streets and packed-together houses. Which type of town do they prefer? Why do they prefer one type of town to the other?
- **ADV Photo Analysis:** Go to the library or the Internet to try to find pictures of old natural towns of the world, such as Fez, Morocco, or Toledo, Spain, to see all the crooked streets and houses packed tightly together. How are these cities different from your hometown? Why do you think they are so different? When finished, report your findings to the class.

3.4.0 POLITICS AND LEADERSHIP

3.4.1 Why Did Rome Collapse? (410–455 CE)

The huge border of the Roman Empire was 10,000 miles long in 410 CE and had very few soldiers to defend it. The former great thinkers of Rome had no new ideas to counter the economic and social decline of the Empire. Roman armies no longer stole treasures from other lands to run the economy of Rome. Gothic (German) slaves and soldiers now did most of the work in Rome and guarded the borders. The Roman Empire was a shell ready to break; it had declined into disorder—entropy. The population of the city of Rome fell to one-sixth its former size—from 1.5 million to 300,000 people. With the attacks from the Visigoths (410 CE), the Huns (451 CE), and the Vandals (455

CE), the greatness and riches of Rome were no more (Durant 1950, 35–43).

- **Song Writer:** Create a ballad or rap song telling the tale of the fall of Rome.
- **Poster Power:** Pick a side and then create a poster either defending the Roman Empire or supporting its demise.
- **You Were There:** Create a panel of expert witnesses (from the class) to analyze the fall of Rome. The witnesses should come dressed to fit the part, and members of the class should each have a minimum of three challenging questions to ask the witnesses about the fall of Rome. This list of witnesses should include such illuminati as:
  1. Attila the Hun, who leveled northern Italy in 451 CE
  2. Placidia, the Roman wife of Aleric, whose Visigoths sacked Rome in 410 CE
  3. Albertus, a Roman slave from Germany, who joined the Visigothic sack of Rome in 410 CE
  4. Licretius, the wife of a wealthy Roman Senator who fled Rome during the "barbarian" attacks
  5. Leo III, the Catholic pope in Rome, who convinced Attila not to attack Rome in 451 CE
- **ADV Why Did It Happen?** Research sources on the fall of Rome in your library (such as Durant 1950) and on the Internet, and then make up your own list of reasons why you think the Roman Empire fell.
- **ADV The Futurist:** With a partner from the class, discuss briefly what lessons other countries, such as the United States, can learn from the fall of Rome, and then share your ideas with the class for their consideration and conclusions.

3.4.2   Justinian (483–565 CE) — The Last Great Roman Emperor?

The magnificent mosaic portrait of Justinian and Theodora in St. Vitalis Cathedral in Ravenna, Italy, is mesmerizing. Two of history's greatest monarchs are peering back at us from over 1,500 years ago. The western part of the Roman Empire had collapsed in 411 CE with the sacking of Rome by the Goths of Alaric. It was 100 years later that Justinian and Theodora, from their Byzantine (Eastern Roman) capital at Constantinople worked hard to reestablish the whole empire. Through diplomacy and 11,000 pounds of gold, Justinian was able to

Illustration 3.4.2.   *Justinian, the Last Great Roman Emperor?*

obtain peace with the Persian Shah Khurso to the east in Iran. This treaty enabled Justinian to send his armies west toward Rome. Fortunately, they also had one of the greatest generals in history, Belisarius, who literally reconquered almost all of the old Roman Empire in the west. But, just when Justinian was ready to celebrate the reunion of the Roman Empire, one of the three largest of history's pandemics hit: Justinian's Plague (the Bubonic Plague of 541–542). It literally stopped the reestablishment of the Roman Empire. Justinian did, however, leave a major contribution to history. Under his rule, the first formal written codification of Roman law took place. Justinian's codification cut down on frivolous litigation and became the one law code of all of Europe for the next 1,300 years (see 3.5.1 below for more on Theodora and 3.8.1 on Justinian's Plague).

- **Map Attack #1:** Locate Constantinople on a map (modern Istanbul in Turkey). Determine the following:
  1. How far in miles and kilometers is Istanbul from your home?
  2. How long will it take to travel there in a jet traveling at 500 miles an hour?
  3. How long would it have taken to travel there by horse and boat during the Middle Ages, at the rate fifty miles a day?
- **Map Attack #2:** On a blank map of the Mediterranean Sea area, identify the following strategic people and places affecting Justinian's Byzantine Empire of the mid 6th century CE When finished, with two fellow generals from class, create a strategic plan for Justinian to reconquer the western part of the Roman Empire by military or diplomatic means, and present this plan to the class:
  1. Constantinople, Justinian's capital of the Byzantine (Eastern Roman) Empire
  2. Khruso, the Shah of the powerful Persian Empire (modern Iran)
  3. The Ostrogoths (eastern Goths) who, before Justinian, had captured Rome and conquered all of Italy from their capital at Ravenna
  4. The Visigoths (western Goths), who controlled most of Spain and North Africa from Carthage in modern Tunisia before Justinian
- **Quick Write:** Think for a moment and then describe a law you would like to see enacted. Imagine what your law would look like 1,300 years later.
- **Pair Share:** Share your law with your partner.
- **Plenary Session:** Share your laws with the class. As a class, decide which laws you like best and which might last 1,300 years—as Justinian's Law Code did.
- **ADV Historical Research:** Using your library and the Internet, read about the law code of Justinian and its impact on our law codes today. When finished, report your findings to the class.

3.4.3   Did Charlemagne Invent Feudalism? (circa 800 CE)

There was not much to Europe in 800 CE. The Roman Empire was long gone, and even the 5th-century invaders who toppled Rome were either gone or had settled down. Only one man had big ideas in 800 CE Europe—Charlemagne (Charles the Magnificent). With very little opposition, he conquered most of western Europe and declared it the Holy

Roman Empire. Although a good fighter, he did not know how to read or write, and he knew he did not have the power to hold his empire together for long. He solved this problem by giving land and people to his loyal vassals, so that they would rule in his name. Each vassal, in turn, would pay a yearly tribute or tax to him in soldiers, servants, sheep, or grain. Was feudalism an original idea of Charlemagne?

No. This idea of loyal vassals controlling the land in the Emperor's name was not original, but first came from Shah Khusro, the Emperor of Persia (Iran) during the 6th century CE.

In adopting this Persian system of rule, Charlemagne created a *feudal* system that would dominate Europe for almost 500 years—until the Black Death during the 13th century.

- **Quick Write:** If you were king or queen of your school, write a short paragraph describing how you would rule your kingdom. Are you strong enough to rule the kingdom by yourself? If not, which of your friends would you have help you to rule, and which areas of the kingdom would you have them rule?
- **Time Machine:** If you were king or queen of an imaginary feudal state of Morania during the Middle Ages, describe the feudal organization of your realm. Who were your vassals? What kind of tribute did they pay to you? Where was your castle? How many knights did you have? How many peasants and serfs worked your fields?
- **Map Attack:** Draw a map of your imaginary feudal kingdom of Morania, indicating your castle, the feudal lands held by your vassals, where the peasants and serfs lived, and the lands they tilled in your service.
- **Model Maker:** Create a three-dimensional diorama of your castle in the feudal kingdom of Morania. Label all the important parts of the castle—moat, keep, drawbridge, and living quarters. Also label where serfs and peasants lived and worked.
- **What If?** What if you were a serf in the feudal kingdom of Morania, toiling in the fields of the king? What aspirations would you have as a serf? Would you ever hope to be anything other than a serf? How would you improve yourself? What if the king opposed the idea of your improving yourself? What would you do? Write a description of what it would be like to be a serf, and what you would change if you were a serf. When finished, present your ideas to the class.

- **ADV Historical Research:** Using resources in your library and on the Internet, examine Charlemagne's life and how he attempted to rule Europe through feudalism. In a short research paper, describe whether you think he was successful or not, and report your findings to the class.

3.4.4   How Important Is the Magna Carta? (1215 CE)

The first successful rebellion against feudalism was mounted by the vassals of King John of England in 1215 CE. At swordpoint, the vassals forced him to sign a paper called the Magna Carta, which guaranteed their rights against unjust actions by the king. This was the first time in history that people demanded the right to stop those actions of the king that they did not like. A few examples of the 63 basic rights listed in the Magna Carta of 1215 are as follows:

- Number 1: ". . . the English Church shall be free. . . ."
- Number 7: ". . . A widow, after the death of her husband, shall forthwith and without difficulty have her marriage portion and inheritance."
- Number 30: "No sheriff or bailiff of ours, or other person, shall take the horses or carts of any freeman for transport duty, against the will of the said freeman."
- Number 39: "No freemen shall be taken or imprisoned or disseised (deprived) or exiled or in any way destroyed, nor will we go upon him nor send upon him, except by the lawful judgment of his peers or by the law of the land."

(Note from the Future: The Magna Carta became the first step in what we now call *human rights* against the arbitrary rules of kings and governments.)

- **Quick Right:** Which, in your view, is the most important human right we have? Write a paragraph describing your view.
- **Create a Skit:** Develop a skit with four members of your class demonstrating the forced signing of the Magna Carta by King John.
- **Newspaper Reporter:** As a reporter for the *Medieval Times* newspaper, write a front-page headline story about the signing of the Magna Carta.

- **What If?** What if Thomas Jefferson, in 1776 one of the founders of the concept of human rights, traveled back in time to be with the vassals and King John in 1215? What would he say to King John? What would he say to the vassals?
- **ADV Bill of Rights:** Using the library or Internet, compare three of the basic rights guaranteed by the Magna Carta of 1215 with the Bill of Rights of the United States. What similarities and differences did you find?
- **ADV Basic Human Rights:** Using your library or the Internet, compare the Magna Carta with the basic human rights listed by the United Nations. Which of these basic human rights are being violated by major countries of the world, including the United States? What actions are needed to ensure that all nations follow these basic human rights of the United Nations?

3.4.5   Roger II's Kingdom of Sicily—Christian, Muslim, and Jew United Together

Who was the greatest monarch of the Middle Ages? Was it King Roger II of Sicily (1095–1154 CE)? How can the son of a Viking (Norman) invader of southern Italy possibly be called the greatest monarch of the Middle Ages? It was a period of intense hatred among Christian, Muslim, and Jew. The Christian Crusades were just starting to take the Holy Lands (Israel) from the Muslims and their Jewish allies (yes, at this time, Muslim and Jew were united against the Christians in the Middle East).

But what was different about the reign of Roger II in Sicily (which then consisted of the island of Sicily and southern Italy up to and including Naples)? The description by the Muslim scholar Ibn Jubair, in 1184, gives strong evidence of what Roger II brought to the Middle Ages: "The Christian women's dress in Palermo is the dress of Muslims. They are eloquent speakers of Arabic and cover themselves with veils. They even appear at their churches bearing all the finery of Muslim women in their attire, henna, and perfume."

Roger II employed Christians, Muslims, and Jews in his administration based on their ability, not their religion. The word *Admiral* (*emir* in Arabic) for the chief officer of the navy comes from Roger II. His gold coins had the words "Jesus Christ Conquers" in Greek on one side and "By the Grace of God" in Arabic on the other. Roger II brought in scholars from all across the Mediterranean Sea to translate many of the Greek thinkers, such as Plato, Aristotle, and Ptolemy from Greek and Arabic into Latin. A major Arabic scholar under the employment of Roger II was Al Idrisi, the constructor of the first "modern" map of the world.

How many leaders of the world in history and today are known for bringing people together, rather than trying to conquer them militarily? Roger II was one of these kings. That is why many consider him to be the greatest monarch of the Middle Ages (Astarita 2005).

- **Quick Write:** In your mind, who is the greatest ruler of all time? Write a short paragraph about why you think this leader is so great. When finished, present your thoughts to the class.
- **Art Mart:** Create a drawing or painting of Roger II, the 11th-century Holy Roman Emperor, in all his glory and riches.
- **Newspaper Interview:** Traveling back in time to the 11th century of Roger II in Sicily, interview people on the street—Christian, Muslim, and Jew—who lived peacefully together under his rule.
- **Travel Brochure:** Create an 11th-century travel brochure describing Sicily under the rule of Roger II and especially the variety of people who lived peacefully together there.
- **ADV Research:** Look up on the web both the history of the island of Sicily and of Roger II. Find out what is so special about this leader and his home during this era, the 11th century, which was so full of hatred and bitter fighting during the Crusades in the Middle East.
- **ADV 21st Century Comparison:** What if Roger II came by time machine to the 21st century? How could he help the world today? What advice can we give world leaders today, based on the rule of Roger II?

3.5.0   SOCIAL AND ECONOMIC LIFE

3.5.1   Theodora, Empress of Byzantium (483–565 CE)

Justinian was a wimp! He might have been the greatest Byzantine emperor in history, but whenever the going got tough, Theodora, his wife, was there to push him on to crush rebellions, build one of the major churches in the world (the Hagia Sophia), and to codify Roman law. In turn, Theodora, daughter of a lion tamer, empress of the Byzantine

Empire, became one of the most powerful women in history (see Severy 1983).

- **Gossip Column:** Make up a ridiculous story for the *Medieval Times* newspaper of how a lion tamer's daughter became one of the most powerful women in history and completely controlled her husband, the emperor. (The problem with this story, however, is that it was true!)
- **Bumper Sticker:** Create an appropriate bumper sticker for Theodora to stick on the back of her human-drawn carriage.
- **Time Travelers:** With a partner, go back to the Byzantine Empire in 560 CE. You have been granted an audience with Empress Theodora. Make a list of questions you plan to ask her, and present a list of the answers you think that she will give to your questions.
- **Quick Skit:** With a team of four student actors from the class, create a short skit that illustrates how Theodora and Justinian might have ruled the Byzantine Empire together.
- **ADV Rank Them:** After searching the library and the Internet, who do you think are the three most important women in history? Rank them in order of their importance and describe why you think they are important. When finished, report your findings to the class.

3.5.2   The Church's Ban on Education During the Middle Ages

Early Christian leaders, such as Pope Gregory I (circa 540–604 CE), believed that the general public—both children and adults—should not be educated. These early leaders of Christianity believed that people, if they knew how to read and write, might read things that were anti-Christian. These early church leaders believed that education was only for the priests, so that they could read and write about their God. Under this religious system, only the priests would have access to the word of God, and the people would have to come to the priests to hear the word of God or be sent to hell. The result, during the Middle Ages, was that the general public was uneducated, and the priests had a monopoly of access to the Christian God, as well as a near-monopoly on education, including such basics as reading and writing (Boorstin 1992, 245).

- **T Chart:** With a T chart, list the advantages and disadvantages that the early church gained by having only the priests read or write, and an entire population of people who could not read or write.

- **Time Traveler:** Imagine Pope Gregory I visiting the United States today. What would he say about an educational system for everyone? Write a speech for the pope concerning education in this country.
- **Quick Skit:** Write and present a short skit with four student actors from your village (the classroom) discussing education in Europe during the Middle Ages. The four imaginary people are as follows:
  1. Magdalena, a devout, illiterate churchgoer who faithfully follows what the local priest tells her to do
  2. Giotto (Joseph), the local Christian priest
  3. Johannis, a servant boy who wants to learn how to read and write
  4. Heloise, the daughter of a local wealthy merchant who secretly learned how to read and write
- **ADV Amicus Curiae:** As an imaginary trusted advisor to the pope during the Middle Ages, write a position paper (*amicus curiae*) outlining the directions in education you think the church should take.
- **ADV Research:** Read about Abbess Hildegard von Bingen, who became one of the great female authors and church leaders during the Middle Ages—highly respected by all—who but did so by defying many church practices of the Middle Ages. (See Pahl, Volume III, Unit 8 for a specific lesson on the great Abbess.)

3.5.3   Eleanor of Aquitaine—Wow, What a Woman!

She has been called "a bad wife," "a bad mother," and "a bad queen"— and also "Wow, what a woman!" Eleanor of Aquitaine (1122–1204 CE) was born into a man's world, but became one of the great women of history by marrying the kings of both France and England. It is certain that her first husband, the boring King Louis VII of France, wished that she had stayed at home and knitted while he was off fighting the Second Crusade (1147) in Palestine; instead, she followed his French army into battle with her own entourage of ladies-in-waiting and troubadours. Bored with Louis, she convinced the Pope to accept a divorce between them, and then she married the future king of England, Henry II. Both Eleanor and the younger Henry had hot tempers and passionate beliefs, and they clashed about everything. Fed up with his high-strung queen, Henry finally confined Eleanor to house arrest for sixteen years, so that he could rule England by himself. Troubadours sang with sorrow over poor Eleanor, and their five sons fought to dethrone their father and free their mother, Eleanor. Henry II died in 1189, after being wounded in a joust. Their son, Richard the Lionhearted, became king and promptly went off to fight the Third Crusade against Saladin. Eleanor in effect ruled England as Regent of England while he was gone. In 1199, Eleanor's fifth son, John, became King of England. While John signed the Magna Carta in 1215 and maybe fought with Robin Hood, Eleanor retired to a convent in France, where she died as a nun at the age of eighty-two. Wow, what a woman (Durant 1950).

- **Quick Write:** In a short paragraph, imagine what it would be like to meet a woman who went off to help fight in a foreign war and then marry the kings of two different countries. When finished, share your thoughts with the class.
- **Rumper Sticker:** Create an appropriate rumper sticker to place on the back of Eleanor of Aquitaine's horse.
- **Poster Power:** Create a poster that illustrates the extraordinary life of Eleanor of Aquitaine.
- **Medieval Gossip Columnist:** As an imaginary gossip columnist for the *Medieval Times* newspaper, write an ever-so-revealing column from unnamed sources about the simply scandalous behavior of Eleanor of Aquitaine. Why won't she just stay at home in the kitchen raising children?
- **Front Page:** With a team of reporters (students from the class) from the *Medieval Times* newspaper, create a front-page edition focused on an exclusive interview with Eleanor of Aquitaine. Be sure to add a drawing of what she might have looked like, as well as a discussion about her marriages to two kings and going on the Crusades.
- **Women's Liberation:** Women's liberation is a recent phenomenon, but Eleanor of Aquitaine from the Middle Ages certainly fits the model of the liberated woman. Imagine Eleanor of Aquitaine visiting your hometown today. Discuss with a partner what you think she would tell the students in your school and then share these ideas with your class.
- **ADV Historical Comparison:** Using the resources in your library and on the Internet, look for other great women in history and compare them to Eleanor of Aquitaine. When finished, present your findings to the class.

3.5.4   Medieval Pollution: Ugh!

Many of the people of Europe during the Middle Ages lived in walled towns for protection—but these towns did not have any toilets, sewers, or garbage collection services. People dumped their human waste and garbage out the window into the street or river. The pigs, chickens, and fish then ate the human waste and garbage—and guess who ate the pigs, chickens, and fish? When the streets became so bad nobody could walk in them, everybody would dump the human waste and garbage over the city wall. Piles of human waste and garbage then accumulated for years on the outside of the city walls. During the Middle Ages, many towns were defeated in battle because the enemy was able to walk up the piles of human waste and garbage, over the city wall, and into the city (Durant 1950).

- **Quick Write:** In a short paragraph, quickly describe the sight and smell of a pile of old garbage and human waste.
- **Time Travelers:** With a classroom partner, imagine you are visitors to a town during the Middle Ages, and describe to each other the sights and smells of pollution you witness.
- **Poster Power:** Create a poster that illustrates the major pollution problems of cities during the Middle Ages.
- **Bumper Sticker:** Create a bumper sticker for wagons during the Middle Ages to encourage people to dispose of their garbage and human waste outside of town.
- **Citizen's Action Council:** As the Citizen's Action Council of four students representing a neighborhood of a small city during the Middle Ages, what rules would you make regarding pollution? How would you ensure that your policies were implemented?
- **Town Council:** When the Citizen's Action Councils representing each Medieval neighborhood are finished, the Town Council (the whole class) can meet to see what actions can be taken regarding cleaning the town's immense pollution problems.
- **ADV Comparative Research:** Using your local library and the Internet, compare the pollution problems in your own town to the pollution problems during the Middle Ages.

3.5.5   Why Didn't Christians Take Baths?

Whoever said "Cleanliness is next to godliness" did not live during the early years of Christianity. The ancient Romans were very fond of their daily baths, but anything the ancient Romans did, the early Christians saw as evil—including bathing. Early Christians also had a major model of an unwashed holy man in James, the brother of Jesus—who never washed or cut his hair (Josephus 1988). As a result, the early Christians throughout Europe saw bathing as sinful. An average person on the street might take a bath only once or twice in a lifetime. The idea of taking baths reentered Europe with the crusaders, who rather enjoyed the old Roman/Turkish baths they found in Constantinople and the Middle East. As late as 1588, however, bathing was still not very popular in Europe. In that year, Queen Elizabeth I of England issued a rule that required that members of her royal court take baths at least once a year—whether they liked it or not. Royalty during the late Middle Ages began to add perfume to each article of clothing to counter their own body odors.

(Note: We can only imagine today—with horror—the smells of a crowded room during the Middle Ages.)

- **Quick Write:** In a short paragraph, describe the smell of someone who has not taken a bath in several days.
- **Poet's Corner:** Create a poem or song about the rather strong smells of the Middle Ages.
- **Pro and Con:** Write a short paragraph as an early Christian during the Middle Ages arguing that bathing is against the will of God. When finished, take the opposite position as an ancient Roman, writing in a short paragraph that bathing daily is great and smells much better. When finished, share these arguments with your class, and vote on which ones are best.
- **What If?** If you had to live during the Middle Ages, what steps would you take to ensure the survival of your nose?
- **Role Play:** If you were a king or queen during the Middle Ages, what requirements of cleanliness would you require for your subjects? What penalties would you establish for subjects who disobeyed you?

3.5.6   Ye Olde Medieval Faire

- **ADV Middle Ages Recreation:** Attend a Medieval Faire in your area or put one on for your school. Everyone must dress up for the faire as fair maidens, knights, nobles, peasants, and perhaps even a medieval dragon or two. Be sure to have grog (punch) to drink, archery contests, medieval music on CD, and a drama based on the Middle Ages. And do not forget, have fun.

3.6.0 RELIGIOUS THOUGHT

3.6.1 Defining the Christian God in Nicaea (325 CE)

The meeting of Church Bishops in Nicaea (in modern Turkey, south across the Bosporus Straits from modern Istanbul) in 325 CE had a major argument on its hands: Who was Jesus? Was he God, or was he human?
There were many different views of Jesus:

1. Was he a Jewish political/religious rebel and "King of the Jews" who sought to overthrow the Roman rule of Judea? This was certainly the view of the Romans and likely the reason for his execution (circa 30 CE).
2. Was he the promised political/religious Messiah (savior) of the Jews who was not God—but who rose to heaven, as had Moses and Elijah? This was the view of James, the brother of Jesus, the disciples, and the early Jewish Christians (circa 40–70 CE).
3. Was he a man whom God raised from the dead to become the Son of God? This was the view of St. Paul, an early Christian leader (see Romans 1:1–10 and Galicians 1:1–10), circa 50 CE.
4. Was he a follower of John the Baptist who was made the Son of God by the Holy Spirit when he was baptized? This was the view of St. Mark (see Mark 1:9–11), an early Christian writer (circa 60 CE).
5. Was Jesus the Word of God from the beginning of time who came down from heaven to become human for a short time before returning to heaven? This was the view of John (see John 1:1–18), an early Christian writer (circa 120 CE).
6. Was he the highest level of human, but not God? This was taught by the Egyptian Christian priest named Arius (circa 318 CE) and his followers called Arians.

To resolve these differences, the Roman Emperor Constantine called all the Christian Bishops to the town of Nicaea (in 325 CE) for a church council to decide on the relationship between Jesus and God. Of the 1,800 bishops who were invited, only 318 showed up.

- **Time Machine:** Your whole class has now boarded a time machine back to that famous Council of Nicaea in 325 CE.
- **Time Warp:** Wait a moment for everyone to get over their sense of time warp—it can be very dizzying at times.
- **Role Play:** The teacher is now the Emperor Constantine, and the class is divided into six groups each representing one of the above six positions.
  1. Each student should now stop and think about the position he or she is about to take. In a Quick Write, describe one or more reasons for supporting this position.
  2. Each group should then get together to develop an argument in front of the class supporting their position.
  3. Each group of "church leaders" should then present their argument in front of the Council of Nicaea (the class).
  4. The Council should then vote to determine what beliefs Christians should have about Jesus and God.
  5. The vote of the class Council of Nicaea can then be compared with the real Council of Nicaea of 325 CE (see below).

(Note: The Council of Bishops voted 313 to 2 in favor of a Nicene Creed, which saw Jesus as one-third of a three-part Christian God—Father, Son, and Holy Ghost. The Arian view that Jesus was just a normal human being—and not God—lost overwhelmingly. The 318 bishops attending the meeting were mostly from Asia. Most of the Western European, Roman, and Egyptian bishops supporting Arian and other views did not come, or were not able to make the Council meeting. Poor Arius of Egypt, the main speaker for Arianism, never made it to the meeting—his chariot broke down. It was the only time in history when a chariot breakdown changed the course of a major religion forever [see Durant 1950, 658–660].)

3.6.2   The Real Beginning of the Middle Ages

The Council of Nicaea (325 CE) was the real beginning of the Middle Ages. Christianity was rapidly growing, and old Greek and Roman gods were disappearing. The religious leaders of Christianity were also confident enough of their growing power to become intolerant of different ways of belief. The council decided that all other Christian teachings should be burned and teachers of other religions and beliefs killed. The classical Greek and Roman belief in reason was rapidly being replaced by an intolerant "faith" in one set of religious ideas (Durant 1950, 658–660).

- **Quick Write:** The word "intolerance" is an important word to understand. Try to define it and give an example from your own personal experience.
- **Concept Web:** The class can compare their examples of intolerance using a Concept Web on the board.
- **Role Play:** The class should be divided into five groups: snow boarders, skiers, in-line skaters, skate boarders, and couch potatoes.
  1. Each of the five groups should make its list of intolerant demands to try to impose its belief on the others.
  2. Each group should also state which penalties should be imposed on other groups.
  3. The intolerant demands and penalties of each group can then be presented to the class.
  4. The class, as a whole, should then examine these intolerant demands and come to an agreement on how to resolve the differences of belief between these groups.
  5. In a concluding essay, each student should describe his or her personal experience with intolerance and make suggestions on how it should be stopped across the world.

3.6.3   Faith Versus Reason—The Real Battle of the Middle Ages

St. Augustine (354–430 CE) set the transition point between the era of classical Greece and Rome and the following Middle Ages, which he described as the difference between reason and faith. He taught that "goodness" did not come from humans but from God. To Augustine, "reason" and "bodily pleasure" were evil. If left alone, said Augustine, the "free will" of humans would lead them to evil. The only way humans could become free of evil, said Augustine, was by a faith in God—and faith in God was given to humans only by the grace of God.

The teachings of Augustine ended a thousand years of Greek and Roman belief in the supremacy of reason. With Augustine, Western Europe rejected the ideas of great thinkers from ancient Greece and Rome, such as Aristotle and Plato, and put its faith in the new Christian God. The importance of reason would not reemerge for almost another thousand years in Western Europe. The same argument between faith and reason also took place during the Middle Ages within Judaism and within Islam.

(Note from the future: The beginnings of the Renaissance [see Unit 4, below] during the 14th and 15th centuries are in large part a revival of the classical Greek and Roman trust in reason. The Augustinian position of the supremacy of faith over reason, however, reappears in the early 16th century in the Protestant Reformation of Martin Luther [see Durant 1950, 64–79]. Also, for more on St. Augustine and "reason," see Pahl, Volume III, Unit 8.)

- **Quick Write:** In a personal statement that you do not have to reveal to anyone, write down whether your basic trust is in *faith* or *reason*.
- **Bumper Sticker:** If St. Augustine needed a bumper sticker for the back of his chariot, what do you think it would say?
- **Ace Reporter:** As the ace reporter from the *Medieval Times* newspaper, go back in time to interview St. Augustine concerning his views on reason and faith. Write up your interview as a newspaper feature article for the front page.
- **Roman Rebuttal:** As a former Roman senator from an old and noble family, write a rebuttal to St. Augustine's belief that faith is more important than reason, to be published in the next edition of the *Medieval Times*.
- **Editorial:** The *Medieval Times* newspaper has asked you to write an editorial defending either the importance of faith or the importance of reason.
- **ADV Research Essay:** Using information from your library and the Internet, compare the battle between faith and reason during the early Middle Ages with the same battle today, over issues such as abortion rights. Be sure to share your findings with the class.

3.6.4   Why Did the Churches Split? (circa 730 CE)

By 700 CE, and following the Bible verse Exodus: 20:4 "Thou shall not make for thy self an idol" the Christian iconoclastic movement was in full swing, destroying many ancient Greek and Roman statues and books. Many Christians in Western Europe, however, began to follow and believe in another biblical passage (Genesis 1:27): "God created man in his own image." These Christians in Western Europe started making statues and paintings of Jesus to "see the image of

God." The Byzantine Emperor Leo III (717–741 CE) in Constantinople was enraged to think of Christians making statues and paintings, and he began to destroy as many of such images as he could find. The Western churches, led by the pope in Rome, strongly opposed Leo III's destruction of Christian art. This friction over the meaning of two biblical verses was the beginning of the long split between the Eastern Orthodox Church in Constantinople and the Western Roman Catholic Church in Rome. The split between these two churches still exists today.

Two of the great religions of the world—Judaism and Islam—are also iconoclastic and believe that there should be no "graven images," either sculptured or painted. Christianity (circa 700 CE) came very close to becoming a religion without any painting and sculpture, and the shadow of the iconoclasts still hangs over the Eastern Orthodox Churches 1,200 years later. Icons (images of holy figures) are the only acceptable forms of art, and then are only to be displayed in front of the church altar. Any three-dimensional art, such as a statue, is still strictly forbidden by the Eastern Orthodox churches (Boorstin 1992, 189).

- **Quick Write:** In a short paragraph, describe your favorite statue or work of art. What if someone deliberately destroyed this work of art? What would you think of that person? What do you think should happen to that person? When finished, share your thoughts on this topic with a partner in class and then with the class as a whole.
- **Take a Stand:** Are you pro-iconoclast or anti-iconoclast? Write a short position paper either attacking or defending iconoclasts.
- **Mock Argument:** With a partner in class, stage a mock argument between a Christian iconoclast and a Roman patron of the arts (circa 700 CE). Outline the major arguments of each side and then present the mock argument to the class.
- **What If?** What would happen if Christians had continued to follow the iconoclastic movement—where would art be today? Do a Quick Write, Pair Share, and Room Share on this topic.
- **Field Trip:** Visit a Roman Catholic and an Eastern Orthodox Christian church in your community and compare the artwork displayed in each.
- **ADV Mock Ecumenical Council:** To our thinking today, it is incredible that a simple argument about art could lead to a major 1,200-year split in the Christian church. In your class, convene

a small mock ecumenical council and try to resolve the basic iconoclastic argument between the churches—first with pairs of students, then in groups of four, then with the whole class.

(Note from the future: Another wave of Christian iconoclastic thinking took place during the 16th century during the Protestant Reformation against the Roman Catholic Church [see unit 4 below, and Pahl, Volume III, Unit 9].)

3.6.5 The Poor Arab Orphan (569–622 CE)

How could a poor illiterate Arab orphan rise to be the founder of one of the world's great religions? His hometown of Makkah (Mecca) was a center of idol worshipers, but Mohammad was more influenced by the monotheists around him—both Jewish and Christian. In 610 CE, he had a vision in which the angel Gabriel proclaimed that he was the prophet of God (Allah). Over the next years, he continued to have visions in which God dictated to him. Close followers then wrote down his visions, which formed the Koran (Qur'an). Many of the Jews and Christians in Makkah became his early followers (Sardar and Malik 1994).

- **Quick Write:** Have you ever heard of someone having been visited by an angel? In a short paragraph, describe the story you have heard, and then share it with the class.
- **Ace Reporter:** Imagine you are the ace reporter for the *Medieval Times* newspaper and Mohammad has just come to you with a story of the angel Gabriel appearing to him. Write a newspaper article describing this vision of Mohammad for the next edition of your paper.
- **Skeptics:** In a team of four students, develop a short skit that illustrates the opposition Mohammad received from some of the people of Mecca (students in the class) who were skeptical of Mohammad's new teachings and of his seeing an angel.
- **Letter to the Editor:** As one of the early believer of Mohammad's visions, write a letter to editor of the *Medieval Times* describing what happened to Mohammad.
- **ADV Research Topic:** Do you think that the conditions in Arabia in 622 CE made it possible for Mohammad to create a new religion? Or, do you think that it was the personal abilities of Mohammad that enabled him to form this new religion? Use the resources

in your library and on the Internet to research and discover what you can find on this topic. When finished, report your findings to the class.

3.6.6   The Koran (Qur'an)—The Light of Allah

The words of the Koran, said Mohammad, were not his words, but the very words of God. The words of the Koran, according to Mohammad, were not created. They were the words directly from God and therefore the Koran is God. This became the simple central belief of Islam. To become a Muslim is simple—declare belief in the Koran as the word of God and acknowledge that Mohammad is his prophet. It is clear that the Koran was intended to convert the "People of the Book" (Jews and Christians) to Islam: "People of the Book (Jews and Christians)! Our Messenger has come to reveal to you much of what is hidden in the Book (the Bible), and to forgive you. A light has come to you from Allah (God) and this light is the Clear Book (the Koran)" (see the Koran, chapter 5:15).

- **Quick Write:** From your own experience, how easy is it to convert someone from one religion to another religion? Write a short paragraph on your thoughts about this topic and share them with a partner in class. The class as a whole can then come to its own conclusions on how easy it is to change religions.
- **People of the Book:** In groups of four, study the above passage from the Koran and role-play People of the Book (Jews and Christians) who are reading the Koran for the first time. Create a short skit that illustrates your reaction to this passage and present it to the class. The class as a whole can then speculate if they think that the People of the Book converted to Islam because of this passage.
- **ADV Read and Report:** Find a copy of the Koran in your library or on the Internet (http://www.mosque.com) and read a section from it. Describe to your class the section of the Koran you read and discuss its meaning.
- **ADV Comparison I:** Review (see 2.6.6) the concept of Logos— the word is God—of Philo of Alexandria (circa 25 BCE) and compare that with the teachings of Mohammad.
- **ADV Comparison II:** Using your library and the Internet, compare the Koran to the Bible. What similarities and differences did you find? Be sure to share your findings with your class.

3.6.7   Are These Verses Jewish, Christian, or Muslim?

Believers in Judaism, Christianity, and Islam often do not realize how similar their desert religions are. From the following list, pick out which are from the Jewish Bible (Old Testament), the Christian Bible (New Testament), or the Muslim Bible (the Koran). Mark your answers with a "J," "C," or "K."

1. _____ And We said: Oh, Adam! You and your wife dwell in the Garden, and eat freely of its fruits, but do not come near this tree or you will become wrong doers.
2. _____ O Children of Israel! Remember that I favored you and preferred you above all creatures.
3. _____ And when Moses spent forty nights in solitude, you chose the calf when he had gone from you, and in so doing were wrong doers.
4. _____ And when the angels said: O Mary, verily God hath chosen thee and purified thee above all other women.
5. _____ The Messiah, Jesus, son of Mary, is only the messenger of God, and his word which he cast upon Mary came from the spirit within him.

(Answer: All of the above five verses are from the Koran.)

- **Quick Write:** Why are you surprised that all of these verses are from the Koran? Write a short paragraph describing your thoughts on this and then be prepared to share them with the class.
- **Pair Share:** With a partner, compare your reactions to each of these verses from the Koran.
- **Room Share:** Pairs should then share their reactions with the whole class.
- **ADV Class Discussion:** With Moses, Jesus, and Mary being holy people in the Koran, what does this tell us about the Muslim religion?
- **ADV Problem Analysis:** With Moses, the holiest man in Judaism, and Jesus, the holiest man in Christianity, both revered in the Koran, why have there been such major battles among Jews, Christians, and Muslims over the past thousand years?

(Note: After some reflection, the discussion of this major historical problem can be continued in 3.6.8 below.)

3.6.8   The Three Religions of Maimonides (1135–1204 CE)

Jews, Christians, and Arabs have always fought each other—correct? Wrong! Maimonides, a Jew from Cordova in Spain, accepted that Jews, Christians, and Muslims all worshiped the same God in different ways and should tolerate one another. Although Jewish, he wrote in Arabic and was the family physician of Saladin, the Muslim leader during the Crusades. He simplified Jewish Law and became the main source of information about medical practices from classical Greece. Maimonides certainly holds the distinction in history of being called a heretic and having his books burned by Jews, Christians, and Muslims all at the same time—because he believed that religions should be practiced with careful reason, not blind faith (Durant 1950, 408–416).

- **Quick Write:** Why do you think religious leaders from Judaism, Christianity, and Islam would all burn the same man's books? What could he have said that got or made all three religions mad at him?
- **Bumper Sticker:** Create a bumper sticker that either supports or opposes the ideas of Maimonides.
- **Poster Power:** Create a poster that illustrates the major ideas of Maimonides and the strong opposition he faced from Jews, Christians, and Muslims alike.
- **Press Conference:** Go back in time and stage a press conference with Maimonides (a student dressed up in a robe and turban). Leaders from all three religions have just burned his books. Have reporters (students) read about Maimonides (above) and then prepare at least three questions each to ask of him.
- **ADV Peace Plan:** In teams of four, read more about Maimonides from the library and the Internet. When finished, develop a peace plan for all three religions—Judaism, Christianity, and Islam— based on the teachings of Maimonides.

3.7.0   CONQUEST AND WARFARE

3.7.1   Attila the Hun—Almost Invincible (450 CE)!

In 450 CE, Attila and his 300,000 Huns swarmed into Western Europe. The Roman Empire was built with large numbers of foot soldiers who fought at close quarters with swords. The Huns were just the opposite.

They were mounted on fast ponies and fought their battles at a hundred yards with a secret weapon—the powerful composite bow and arrow. The combination of large numbers, superior weaponry, and speed on horseback made the Huns of 450–453 CE almost invincible—especially to the slow-moving Roman foot soldiers (Mee 1993).

- **Quick Write:** Take your pick—would you rather be a Hun mounted on a fast pony with a bow and arrow or a heavily armored Roman foot soldier? In a short paragraph, describe the reason for your choice and then share your opinions with the class.
- **Poster Power:** On a large piece of paper, illustrate the differences between the fighting styles of the Romans and the Huns. Label the important major differences.
- **Eyewitness:** As a Roman living in northern Italy in 451 CE, write a letter to a friend in Rome describing an attack by the Huns that you recently witnessed.
- **Battle Plan:** If you were the commander of a Roman army, what preparations would you make for a battle with the Huns?
- **Oral Tradition:** As an old man and the last remaining Hun who attacked the Roman Empire in 451 CE, retell for your family and friends (the class) how you attacked the Romans with your friends under the leadership of Attila.
- **ADV Historical Comparison:** Using resources in your library and on the Internet, make a chart comparing the fighting styles of the Huns of 450 CE and the Plains Indians of North America in the 1870s.

(For more on Attila the Hun and the fascinating reason why he did not attack Rome directly see Pahl, Volume III, Unit 8.)

3.7.2   Muslim Conquests—From Spain to Iran (700 CE)

By 700 CE, the armies of Islam conquered virtually all of the Middle East (from Saudi Arabia to Iran) and North Africa (from Egypt to Morocco), an area larger than the Roman Empire. In 711 CE, a Muslim army under Tariq crossed the Straights of Gibraltar (translated from Arabic: *Gibr-al-Tariq,* the Rock of Tariq) from Morocco and conquered Spain. The Islamic "conquests" were often quite easy because of the constant battles Christians had with each other over endless religious questions, such as "Was Jesus God or man?" or "Was Mary, the mother of Jesus, holy or not?" Many Christians, as a result, did not offer much resistance to the new Muslim conquerors and willingly followed the much simpler beliefs of Islam. The Muslim armies, however, never had enough power to conquer Europe. A major roadblock was in their way for a thousand years—Constantinople. (For more on the historical roadblock of the Byzantine Empire, see Pahl, Volume I, TLP 3.3.4 above and Durant 1950.)

- **Map Attack:** Using an atlas and a blank map of the world, illustrate the swift conquests of the Muslim armies from Mecca and Medina (in modern Saudi Arabia) eastward to Persia (modern Iran) and westward to Morocco and Spain.
- **Rumper Sticker:** Create a rumper sticker for Tariq's horse as he crossed the Straights of Gibralter (Gibr-al-Tariq) by boat from Morocco to conquer Spain.
- **Poster Power:** Create a poster advertising Tariq's conquest of Spain in 711 CE.
- **Map Analysis:** Using an atlas and a blank map of the world, indicate why the Muslims (in the Middle East) were not able to conquer central and northern Europe. (Clue: Be sure to note the location of Constantinople.)
- **ADV What If Analysis?** What would the world be like today if all of Europe had been conquered by Muslim armies circa 800 CE? Would Christianity exist today as a major world religion if this had happened? Use the resources in your library and on the Internet to research this problem and then report your findings to your class.

3.7.3   Were the Crusades (1095–1291 CE) One of the Biggest Flops in History?

The Crusades have been called one of the biggest flops in history. The First Crusade was called by Pope Urban II in 1095 CE to free Jerusalem from Muslim rule. With the blessings of the Church, the kings of Europe sent armies of young men to recapture the Holy Land around Jerusalem. Millions of people died in endless battles, in which Muslims and Jews united to fight the Christian warriors from Europe. European armies tried four times to conquer the Holy Land but failed to hold it very long. The effects of the Crusades, however, have been long-lasting and still echo loudly in the tensions among Christian, Muslim, and Jew in the Middle East today.

- **Quick Write:** As a Christian knight riding off to fight in the Crusades, write a letter to your true love describing what it feels like to ride off to battle to fight for a noble cause—the freeing of the Holy Land for Christianity.
- **Troubadour:** Compose a ballad for the Crusades (and sing it)—in good medieval fashion—about how noble it is to go and fight (and die) in battle with a true love at home waiting for that knight in shining armor who might never return.
- **Crusader Spin Doctor:** With a partner in class, write and put on a short skit of a knight in shining armor riding off to fight in the Crusades to save the Holy Land for Christians.
- **Muslim Counter Spin:** With a partner in class, create a short skit that illustrates a Muslim knight with his friends describing the valor of fighting alongside Jewish soldiers against the Christian crusaders to defend the Holy Land in the name of God against foreign invaders.
- **Jewish Counter-Counter Spin:** As a Jewish fighter with his friends, describe the valor of fighting alongside Muslim soldiers against the Christian crusaders to defend the Holy Land in the name of God against these foreign Christian invaders from Europe.
- **Front Page:** In a team of four ace reporters from your class, create a front-page edition of the *Medieval Times* newspaper, focusing on the horror of seeing thousands of people either killed or wounded during the Crusades.
- **The Big Question:** Be sure also to see TLPs 3.7.4 and 3.7.5 on the positive and negative results of the Crusades. Then you can answer the big question: What do you think? Were the Crusades one of the biggest flops in history? Write a short essay defending your position and then share this major question with your class.

3.7.4   The Positive Results of the Crusades

Before the Crusades, most of Western Europe was a vast forest dotted with small feudal kingdoms full of poor, illiterate peasants and serfs, ruled by a small class of nobles. Western Europeans during the Middle Ages did not shave or bathe. The Crusades changed all that. The strange "new" ideas from the East of shaving, bathing, and toilets became popular again—as in ancient Rome. In reality, these old Roman customs had never died out in Byzantine cities such as Constantinople. Other new ideas acquired from the Muslims included gunpowder, the compass, printing, window glass, spices, and citrus fruit. The idea of economic trade suddenly became important. Former feudal serfs who fought in the Crusades now moved to rapidly growing towns and became merchants and craftsmen. The Church grew in wealth from the lands it inherited, but diminished in power as people began take greater interest in money, worldly pleasures, and greater knowledge through reading and writing (Durant 1950, 609–613).

- **Quick Song:** As a crusader from Western Europe who is the first one in his family to take a bath, compose a song (and sing it to the class) of the great joy of bathing and being squeaky clean.
- **Advertising Campaign:** In a team of four students who happen to represent the first advertising team during the Middle Ages, develop an advertising campaign to introduce the new Persian fruits of apples, oranges, apricots, and grapefruit to Western Europeans. Remember, these new foods were first introduced into Europe by the returning crusaders, who acquired them from Muslim merchants. When finished, present your ad campaign to your class.
- **Quick Skit:** In a group of four students, create a short skit for your 13th-century European town (your class) in which the participants are arguing over which was the most important new discovery from the Crusades: gunpowder, paper, window glass, or the compass.
- **Board Games:** The board game of chess also became popular in Europe after the Crusades. The game originated in Persia, where the King is called the Shah. The German language still retains the original Persian title in their name for chess: *schach*. Next time you play chess, remember that the Crusaders carried it from the Middle East back to Europe were it became an instant hit—and still is today.

3.7.5   The Tragic Results of the Crusades

The tragic effects of the Crusades are still being felt today around the world.

1. The Crusades lasted for 150 years (1095–1245 CE) and caused untold hardship and death to millions of Christians, Jews, and Muslims.

2. The antagonism between the Muslim Middle East and the Christian West today comes largely from the extended fighting and hatred generated during the Crusades.
3. The bigotry, ignorance, and hatred the Crusaders showed to the Jewish folk continued down to 20th-century Nazi Germany and Soviet Russia.
4. The pillaging of Constantinople by the crusaders in 1204 CE permanently ended any possibility of reuniting the eastern and western Christian churches.
5. The illiterate Christian European knights of the Fourth Crusades burned libraries in Constantinople containing the priceless last remaining copies of thousands of ancient Greek plays, essays, and scientific descriptions.
6. The sack of Constantinople by the Crusaders in 1204 CE greatly weakened the thousand-year-old Byzantine Empire and opened it to a final conquest by the Muslims. It no longer provided the strong Eastern shield of protection for Europe from Muslim conquests. Only a new Mongol threat from the East enabled Constantinople and Europe to be safe from Muslim attacks for several hundred years more (see TLP 3.7.6 below).

- **Rumper Sticker:** Create a rumper sticker for horses during the Middle Ages reminding Crusaders not to pillage, steal, and rape.
- **Poet's Corner:** Compose a sad poem about loved ones lost during the Crusades.
- **Newspaper Reporter:** As a reporter for the *Medieval Times* newspaper, interview Jews, Christians, and Muslims (students) who experienced the mass destruction of the Crusades and write an editorial regarding the Crusades for your newspaper.
- **ADV Pro and Con:** Conduct a class symposium on the pros and cons of the Crusades. Were they more beneficial than harmful, or were they more harmful than beneficial? Teams of four students should conduct their own research in the library and on the Internet, come to their own conclusions, and then present their findings to the whole class.

3.7.6   The Terror of Genghis Khan (circa 1160–1227 CE)

The recent 20th century was certainly a bloody century — but so was the 13th century. The Crusaders killed as many people as they could in the

Middle East, but they were quickly followed by the Mongols of Genghis Khan. As the close relatives of the Huns, the Mongols used good leadership, superior organization, fast ponies, and excellent skills in archery to quickly conquer China and central Asia in a few short years. The Mongols had all of Asia and the Middle East frightened. Beijing, the capital of China, was founded by the Mongols. The Great Wall of China was constructed to prevent further Mongol invasions. Hulagu, grandson of Genghis Khan, sacked Baghdad for a week (1258) and ended the great cultural flowering and military strength of the Muslims for several hundred years (see Edwards 1996, 5–37).

(Note from the future: Europe's eastern shield, Constantinople, was no more than a shell after the crusaders attacked it in 1204. Constantinople, and possibly Europe, could have easily fallen to Muslim conquest, but the Byzantines and Europeans were lucky. The Mongols began to attack the Middle East in 1218 and even captured the capital of Islam—Baghdad—in 1258. After the Mongol attacks, it took 200 years for the Muslims to recover their strength and finally capture Constantinople in 1453.)

- **Quick Write:** As a Muslim standing on the city wall of Baghdad in 1258, describe your terror as you see the massive Mongol armies approach your city.
- **Rumper Sticker:** Create a rumper sticker for the backside of Hulagu Khan's horse.
- **Graffiti:** On a piece of paper, create a wall graffiti that urges Muslim warriors to fight their best against the armies of Hulagu Khan.
- **Mongol Marksmen and Markswomen:** Mongol men and women were excellent marksmen, firing arrows from bows while traveling at full speed on ponies. With the archery equipment at your school, have your whole class practice shooting arrows at a fixed target.
- **Role Play:** As a male or female Mongol warrior, describe what it feels like to ride full speed on a pony and shoot an arrow at a target behind you. Imagine 10,000 mounted Mongols attacking all at the same time.
- **You Were There:** As the television anchorperson for the hit show "You Were There," interview several witnesses (students) to the Mongol capture of Baghdad in 1258:

1. Fatima, the rich first wife (one of twenty) of the sultan of Baghdad
2. Ali, a Muslim solider who saw the main Mongol attack and escaped alive
3. Suliman, a Muslim merchant who saw Baghdad being burned to the ground
4. Ibn Sina, a scholar who saw the great scientific, medical, and mathematical writings of Islam going up in flames
5. Tamarin, a strong female Mongol warrior who participated in the attack on Baghdad

• **ADV Mongol Map Attack:** Using your library and a historical atlas, use a blank map of Asia and the Middle East to trace the routes of the Mongol attacks on the rest of the world (see Edwards 1996, 6). Measure in miles or kilometers the great distances covered by the Mongol armies and compare these distances with distances between major cities in the United States.

3.7.7   Islamic Civilization Saved at 'Ain Jalut

By 1200, the Islamic Renaissance was at its height in Baghdad, Iraq, Spain, and in Cairo, Egypt, with a flourishing of art, science, and literature while Europe was just emerging from the Dark Ages. Unfortunately, in 1253, the Mongols under Hulegu massed 300,000 well-trained horsemen armed with powerful compound bows and one million support personnel, all ordered to conquer the Middle East. They almost succeeded. Starting in Persia (modern Iran), the Mongols were unstoppable. They sacked Baghdad, the capital of the Islamic Renaissance, in 1258. They then swept across Iraq, Jordan, and Syria to capture Damascus. Hulegu began to move south to capture the last remaining Islamic center in the Middle East—Cairo in Egypt. Fortunately for Cairo and the rest of the Muslim world, the Great Khan Mongke (grandson of Genghis Khan) died and Hulegu had to return to Mongolia to elect a new Khan. Hulegu expected to easily conquer Cairo and left a small force of 20,000 to do the job, while he and most of his troops returned to Mongolia.

Jerusalem had only recently been retaken, in 1244, by the Muslims from the Christian Crusaders of Europe. Although still exhausted from the Crusades, Qutuz, the Mamluk leader of Egypt, was able to rally his troops and allies to fight the remaining Mongol forces. At

Illustration 3.7.7. *Mongol Conquests circa 1209–1258*

'Ain Jalut, in 1260, north of Jerusalem, the Egyptian Muslim forces under Qutuz were able to trap the Mongols and then quickly routed them from the rest of the Middle East. The battle became one of those turning points in history. Without the defeat of the Mongols at 'Ain Jalut, Islam might have ceased to be the major religion of the Middle East, and Mongol might have become the major language of the region (Tschanz 2007).

- **Hinge Point:** A *hinge point* in history is an event that changes the course of history. Describe something in your life that really changed the way you thought or acted—a personal hinge point. Share your thoughts with the class.
- **Map Attack:** On a blank map of the Middle East, using arrows and indicated years, trace the route of the Mongol invaders of 1253 under Hulegu and the devastation they caused to the Muslim Renaissance of the era. Be sure to include the sacks of Baghdad and Damascus. Be sure also to put a star at 'Ain Jalut, north of Jerusalem, where the Muslims under Qutuz finally defeated the Mongol forces.
- **Poster Power:** Create a Muslim poster celebrating the victory of 'Ain Jalut over the Mongol forces in 1260 CE.
- **What If?** What if the Mongols had conquered all of the Middle East and won the battle of 'Ain Jalut in 1260? Write a brief description of what you would think today's Middle East—Saudi Arabia, Iraq, Iran, Syria, and Israel—would be like if their rulers would have been Mongol rather than Arab and Muslim. Be sure to share your thoughts on this "What If?" with the rest of your class.

3.8.0 TRAGEDY AND DISASTER

3.8.1 Justinian's Plague of 541–542 CE

Justinian (see 3.4.2 and 3.5.1 above), the Emperor of the Byzantine Empire in Constantinople had, in 541, just reconquered most of the ancient Roman Empire under the leadership of his great general Belisarius. For a very short moment, he could have been crowned the Emperor of the whole Roman Empire—which might have lasted for another 1,000 years—but it did not happen. The Byzantine Empire at that moment was hit with one of the worst pandemics in history—ironically called Justinian's Plague. It was almost identical to the Bubonic Plague that hit Europe in 1347 (see 3.8.3 below). Approximately 10,000 people a day died in Constantinople. Four million died across the empire during the first two years. Before the Plague, Justinian ruled over 26 million subjects. By the end of the century, the population of the Byzantine Empire was 17 million people. Justinian, himself, became sick with the plague, but recovered. The greatness of his empire, however, crumbled as the plague would not go away. Every spring when it warmed up, plague-carrying fleas would reinfect the rats that carried the disease through every village and town. Justinian's Plague persisted throughout Europe and the Middle East for 52 years, and it took over 300 years for this area of the world to recover from this disaster. When looking at the effects of Justinian's Plague, the term "Dark Ages" is appropriate.

- **Quick Write:** Describe a time when many of your family and friends were sick. What did it feel like? What did you do to counter the effects of the sickness?
- **Morticians Anonymous:** In teams of four students each, imagine you are the morticians who must deal with 10,000 dying each day in Constantinople during the plague. How would you deal with this massive problem? Present a plan to the class for discussion.
- **Decision Tree:** Develop a decision tree (from bottom to top) to plan the best course of action for the Byzantines to deal with this devastating plague:
  4. Summation at the top of the tree: After debating which is the best way to solve the problem, write your answer at the top of the tree.
  3. Add two limbs to each branch: One limb for a positive response and one limb for a negative response.
  2. Add three branches to the tree: Three Alternative Courses of Action
  1. Tree Trunk at the bottom: State the Problem
- **Just Imagine:** What if your town suddenly had 10,000 fewer people? What would happen? How many businesses and restaurants would close from the lack of customers? How many schools would close? With two fellow students, make a list of things that would happen to your town with 10,000 fewer people.

- **ADV Research:** Search your library and the Internet for more information on Justinian's Plague and the devastating consequences it had on the Byzantine Empire in 541.

3.8.2   A Jewish Holocaust of 1095–1096 CE

On the way to the Crusades, Christian armies from Europe often killed the Jews that they found in towns along the way. Why? They did so, they said, because the Jews killed Jesus. In reaction to this holocaust, Jewish soldiers joined with the Muslims to fight against the Christian invaders of the Holy Land during the Crusades.

(Historical Correction: The Romans, not the Jews, killed Jesus [see Mark 15:16–20]. Josephus [1988, 264], the major historical source of the era, states specifically: "Pilot condemned him [Jesus] to be crucified and to die." The ancient Jewish death penalty for religious reasons was stoning to death. The ancient Roman death penalty for rebels against Roman rule was crucifixion. Few, if any, of the Crusaders of 1096 knew how to read or write—only priests were allowed to do this. If the Crusaders knew how to read, they could have read the Bible themselves to verify who killed Jesus. They, however, did not do so and let their prejudice overrule their reason.)

- **Poster Power:** Make a poster and a slogan illustrating why it is dangerous to believe a rumor without checking whether it is accurate or not. Example: "Don't Act! Check your facts!"
- **Diary Entry:** As a Jewish teenager in medieval France, describe the terror of seeing your friends and family being killed by the Christian crusaders. When finished, share your diary entry with your class.
- **Pair Share:** With a partner from your class, discuss for one minute each why it is dangerous for people (like the Crusaders) to *not* know how to read and write.
- **Fighting Prejudice:** In a team of four students, devise a plan to help students at your school stop negative rumors about other students. Share your ideas with the class and the whole student body.

A sad historical irony: During the Crusades of 1095–1204 CE, Muslims and Jews fought on the same side to defend the Holy Land (Israel/Palestine) against the Christians. During the 20th century, Jewish forces—with American Christian support—fought Muslim forces for the control of the same land.

3.8.3   The Black Death (Bubonic Plague) of 1331–1369 CE

The Black Death (bubonic plague) of the late Middle Ages killed about 25 million people. It first broke out in China in 1331 and killed half of its population. Venice, after the Crusades, controlled the trade between Europe and Asia. The plague hit Venice first in 1347 and spread northward during 1348 to 1349. Subsequent outbreaks occurred in 1361–1362 and 1369. Milan (in Italy) was spared. Bristol in England was nearly wiped out. Nearly one-third of Europe's population perished. The plague quickly ended feudalism in many places—there was no one left to till the fields for the nobles. Anybody who survived the plague fled to the growing cities of Europe, such as Venice, Florence, London, and Paris (McNeil 1977).

The only people who seem to have survived the bubonic plague of the late Middle Ages in any substantial numbers were the Jews, because of their house-cleaning rituals of Purim before Passover, which discouraged plague-infected rats from entering their homes just before the outbreak of the plague each spring.

- **Quick Write:** Imagine if one-third of the people around you suddenly died of an unknown cause. How would you feel? What would you do?
- **Medieval Artist:** As the major artist in your town during the Middle Ages, record for history the horrid scene of so many people dying of the plague.
- **Playwrights:** With four other students, write and present a short skit to your class that depicts the bubonic plague infecting a town.
- **Medieval Rumor Mill:** Fear creates rumors, and rumors create more fear. The teacher can start a rumor in class by whispering the name of a popular student to one student and then have the rumor spread across the room—that person in the class caused the bubonic plague. A class discussion should follow the spread of the rumor using the following questions:
  1. Is the rumor true? (Of course it is not!)
  2. Why do people believe rumors or want to believe rumors?

3. Why are ethnic minorities and old people often the target for such rumors?

4. What can be done to stop such rumors?

- **What If?** In teams of two, imagine that you are medical doctors from the Middle Ages. What would you start looking for as the cause of the Black Death? What would you do to aid people who suddenly fall ill with the bubonic plague? What would you begin to do to prevent further spread of the plague? Share your ideas with the other medical doctors (students) in the room.

- **ADV Epidemiologist:** Research the background of the causes and cures of the bubonic plague of the mid-14th century. Compare this epidemic with other large world epidemics, such as the Spanish Influenza of 1918. Report your findings to the class.

3.9.0   EXPLORATION AND DISCOVERY

3.9.1   Marco Polo (1254–1323?) — Real or Fake?

A story from a prison in Genoa (Italy) in 1298 fired the imagination of Europeans in the late Middle Ages. It was written in French by a prisoner named Rustichello. A fellow prisoner by the name of Marco Polo had told him the tale of his travels to China, where he had lived some seventeen years in the service of Kublai Khan, the Mongol emperor of China. Rustichello knew how to embellish a story and make it exciting; as a result, *The Travels of Marco Polo* became a best seller of the Middle Ages. It was laboriously hand-copied into almost every major language of the time (Boorstin 1983, 134–138). Some recent scholars believe that Rustichello, and perhaps Marco himself, made up all or large parts of the story (see Wood 1996). Whether true or not, Marco Polo's story had a tremendous influence on the history of the world. Kings and adventurers across Europe had the story read to them and burned with desire to explore new lands.

(Note from the future: Virtually every explorer of the 15th century read the book or had it told to him. Even Columbus had his own copy, in which he took notes. In 1477, *The Travels of Marco Polo* became one of the first books, after the Bible, to be printed. Today, after 700 years, the book still remains very popular — even if it is a fake.)

- **Adventure Writer:** Think of the most exotic place you would like to visit in your lifetime. Write down the name of this place and why you would like to travel there. (People during the late Middle Ages considered Marco Polo's trip to be the most exotic adventure possible.)
- **Map Attack:** On a blank map of Asia, trace the route of the Silk Road traveled by Marco Polo and his brothers from Constantinople through Samarkand (Uzbekistan) to the Mongol capital of Karakoram.
- **Pair Share:** With a partner, describe the most important book you ever read, and then share your discussion with the class.
- **ADV Research:** How can a simple, possibly fictional, book have stimulated humans to begin exploring the world and think about their planet in a whole new way? Conduct interviews with people you know and research this topic in your library and on the Internet. When finished, present your findings to the class.

3.9.2   Ibn Batutta (1304–1369 CE) Ran Circles Around Marco Polo

Why is so much written about Marco Polo, when a contemporary of his from Tangier (Morocco) traveled over 75,000 miles across the globe in twenty-nine years? This was over three times the distance traveled by Marco Polo—if his travels were real. Ibn Batutta traveled to Mecca in 1325, became a Muslim judge, worked his way to India, then China, then back to Mecca, and back to Morocco, where he traveled north to Muslim Spain and then south across the Sahara Desert to Timbuktu, and then returned to Fez, Morocco, where he retired to write an account of his travels in 1354. No one questions whether Ibn Batutta's travels are real—the original manuscript of his travels, written in Arabic, still exists today in the Bibliotheque Nationale in Paris, France (Abercrombie 1991, 2–49). Now, why is Ibn Batutta not in every one of our history books?

- **Travel Wish List:** Make a list of ten places in the world you would like to visit, and then, using a blank map of the world, show how you could visit each place in one long trip.
- **Travel Log:** When finished, measure the mileage you plan to travel to see if it is greater than the 75,000 miles traveled by Ibn Batutta during the 14th century.

- **Map Attack:** On a blank map of the world, trace the major routes of Ibn Batutta's 14th-century journeys from the above description. Start with his home in Tangier, Morocco, and end it 75,000 miles later at Fez, Morocco. Be sure to label the major places he visited.
- **ADV Research:** If Ibn Batutta traveled three times as far as Marco Polo, and there is no question that he really did travel to all these places, why did Marco Polo become famous, and only a few historians know about Ibn Batutta? Research your library and the Internet to try to find the answer to this problem. When finished, present your findings to your class. (Hint: Could it be an ethnic bias, such as that Marco Polo was a European Christian and Ibn Batutta was a Muslim from Morocco, North Africa?)

3.9.3   Did Saint Brendan of Ireland Sail to America in 800 CE?

Today, there are 120 surviving early Latin manuscripts entitled *Navigatio Sancti Brendani Abbatis* or *The Voyage of Saint Brendan*. All of these early manuscripts are very similar in that they describe the fascinating sailing voyage of Saint Brendan of Ireland in approximately 800 CE to a place he called "The Promised Land" and that many now consider to be Newfoundland in North America. Saint Brendan and his seventeen fellow monks traveled across the northern Atlantic and back in seven years in a small wooden sailboat covered with leather. The *Navigatio* is full of fantastic tales of camping on the back of a whale, fire-breathing monsters, an island made of crystal, an island full of fire laden rocks, and finally, after many other exciting adventures, their return home to Ireland.

Did Saint Brendan of Ireland make it to North America long before the Vikings and Columbus? Much of his *Navigatio* is full of mythology, as are Marco Polo's travels to China. But much of his voyage also makes sense—the area is full of whales, Iceland is definitely a volcanic island, and icebergs frequent the area south of Greenland near Newfoundland. It certainly would have been a most difficult voyage in some of the roughest ocean in the world—but it is possible that he made it. There are indications that the Vikings might have gotten their idea to travel west to "Vineland" or North America from Saint Brendan. There are records of Columbus visiting Ireland before he traveled across the Atlantic—he also might have been inspired by Saint Brendan. Just to test the possibility that the voyage of Saint Brendan might have been true, an adventurous sailor named Tim Severin built a leather-covered replica of Saint Brendan's twenty-one-foot sailboat and successfully sailed and rowed it with his crew across the rough north Atlantic Ocean in 1976 (Severin 1978).

- **Quick Write:** If Saint Brendan asked you to join him on his voyage to "The Promised Land" in 800 CE, would you have accepted the invitation? Write a short paragraph describing why or why not.
- **Quick Skit:** With four members of your class, write and present a short skit in which Saint Brendan and three of his monks, Ennis, Norris, and Plenarny, present their version of their fantastic voyage.
- **Pair Share:** With a partner in class, develop a dialogue debating whether Saint Brendan's voyage was a mythological legend or a real description of perhaps the earliest voyage to the Americas from Europe. When finished, present your dialogue to the class, along with your conclusions.
- **Plenary Session:** After the Pair Share presentations are finished, the class as a whole can debate and make their own conclusions as to whether Saint Brendan's voyage was myth or history.
- **ADV Internet Research:** Search Saint Brendan's name on the Internet to find out more information about this fabled Irish monk and whether his story is real or imagined. Be sure to report your findings to the class.

3.10.0   INVENTION AND REVOLUTION

3.10.1   The Power of Zero

The numbers 1 through 9 first appeared in India 2,000 years ago, but without any place value and without the concept of zero. Sometime around 400 CE, Indian scholars began to use a dot or zero as a place-holder to indicate nothing. For the first time in history, it was easy to add, subtract, multiply, and divide by 10, 100, or 1,000. In 773 CE, an ambassador from India brought the gift of numbers and calculation to the Muslim Caliph Mansur in Baghdad. Arab scholars in Caliph Mansur's court immediately recognized the importance of this gift and studied it intensely. Within a few short years, an Arab scholar named Al-Khwarizmi (circa 780–850) wrote the first major book about mathematics, *The Book of Addition and Subtraction by Indian Methods.* The book was translated into Latin in Muslim Spain and quickly spread to Europe. Al-Khwarizmi, as a result, became recognized as the father of modern mathematics. The modern mathematical word "algorithm" is based on Algorismus, Al-Khwarizmi's Latin name (Guedj 1996, 45–54).

- **Roman Math:** Add together XIII plus CIX (Answer: CXXII). Is that tough to do? Now try 13 + 109 (Answer: 122). Why is this Indian/Arab method so much easier? (It's the use of place values 10 and 100, along with the concept of zero, that makes it easy.)
- **Arab Numbers:** Write the numbers from 0 to 10 in Arabic numbers. For a hint, see illustration 3.10.1—and remember that zero in Arabic numbers is a dot and that Arabic is read from right to left.
- **T Chart Comparison:** What differences do you see between Arabic numbers and the numbers we use today? Using a T chart, write modern numbers from 0 to 10 down the left-hand side of the T chart and the parallel Arabic numbers down the right side. Looking very carefully at the Arabic equivalent of each, describe how each Arabic number is different from our modern numbers.

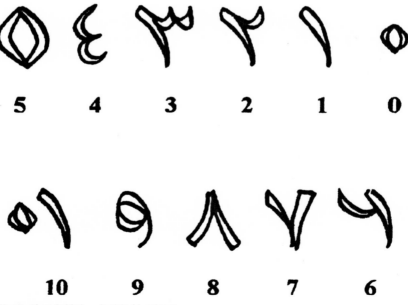

Illustration 3.10.1. *Arabic Numbers*

- **Arabic Mathematician:** Now that you are a scholar in Arabic numbers, write the current year using Arabic numbers and then write down the year you were born in Arabic numbers. (Remember that Arabic is written from right to left.) When finished, share your work with the class.

3.10.2   Islamic Medicine

Good Christians during the Middle Ages never washed. Cleanliness was sinful. A person was sick because of the evil deeds committed by that person. These were major Christian beliefs during the Middle Ages in Europe. Little wonder the age was considered the "Dark Ages." Muslim physicians in the Middle East, on the other hand, conducted major studies of ancient Greek medicine and made great progress in improving Greek medical practices. Muslim and excommunicated Nestorian Christian doctors at Jundisharpur—the major medical school of the Middle Ages—made major medical improvements. Al-Rashid (786–809) and his son Al-Ma'Mon established a translating bureau to translate Greek works into Arabic. By the end of the 9th century, all of the major Greek medical works were translated into Arabic. Some of the more notable achievements were as follows (Tschanz 1997):

1. Al-Rashid established the first modern hospital circa 805 CE.
2. Al-Razi (841–926 CE) wrote more than 100 medical books, including *The Diseases of Children* and a twenty-five-volume encyclopedia of medicine.
3. Ibn Sina (980–1037) (Avicenna in Latin) wrote the million-word *Canon of Medicine*, which codified all existing medical knowledge from Greece, Syria, Persia, and India.

(Note from the future: The medical works of Al-Rashid, Al-Razi, and Ibn Sina became the medical bibles for the Middle East and Europe for 400 years.)

- **Quick Write:** Imagine, for a moment, what life would be like without modern medicine. In a short paragraph, describe what you think it would be like if superstition was used instead of modern medicine.
- **Poster Power:** Create a poster that illustrates the power of modern medicine, introduced into Europe at the end of the Middle Ages by the major Arab medical doctors.

- **Music Mart:** Compose a medieval ballad praising the work of the early Arab medical doctors for bringing modern medicine to the rest of the world.
- **You Were There:** As the host of this top TV show of the Middle Ages, your guests for today's show are three of the great Muslim medical doctors from Baghdad: Al-Rashid, Al-Razi, and Ibn Sina (students dressed up as Muslim scholars). Be sure the members of your studio audience (students in class) have three questions each for these honored guests from the Middle Ages.
- **ADV Historical Research:** Using resources in your library and on the Internet, discover what else you can find out about early Arabic medicine and scientific research, during a time when little or none of it was being conducted in Europe.

3.10.3   Jewish Translations of Arabic to Latin (1000–1200 CE)

The flowering of the Renaissance in Europe during the 15th century might not have happened if it were not for the intellectual enlightenment and religious toleration among Jews, Christians, and Muslims practiced by two very small Christian kingdoms during the Middle Ages. In an era known for its ignorance and religious bigotry, the kingdoms of Toledo in Spain under Alfonso X and the kingdoms of the Two Sicilies under King Roger II in Salerno provided the crucial intellectual background and tolerant climate needed to stimulate Europe's long, slow road out of the Middle Ages (see TLP 3.4.5 above for more on King Roger II).

In Toledo, King Alfonso X had the great wisdom to sponsor a school to translate major Greek and Arabic scientific, mathematical, and medical books from Arabic to the dominant language of Europe—Latin. The translation work in Toledo from Arabic to Latin was done primarily by Jewish scholars under Gerard of Cremona (1140–1187), who were fluent in both Arabic and Latin. Some of the major works translated at Toledo were commentaries on Aristotle by Ibn Rushd (Averroes), works on algebra and mathematics by Al-Khwarizmi (from whose name we get the mathematical term algorithm), and *The Canon of Ibn Sina* (Avicenna), which became Europe's medical standard for 500 years. These works by the school in Toledo under the tolerant Christian ruler Alfonso X were to become the backbone of the intellectual growth of the Renaissance in Europe.

In Salerno, Sicily—in the Cloister of Monte Casino—under the tolerant and enlightened Christian King Roger II, major translation work from Arabic to Latin was also done by such Muslim scholars as Leo Africanus (1020–1087). In both kingdoms, Arabs, Christians, and Jews were openly accepted and worked closely together to translate the crucial new medical and scientific information from the Middle East that would eventually awaken Europe from its long intellectual slumber (Abercrombie 1988).

- **Map Attack:** Use an atlas to locate Toledo, Spain, and Salerno, Italy, on a map of Europe. On a blank map of Europe, put large stars next to these cities because of the important work these towns did advancing science and encouraging tolerance in Europe.
- **Quick Write:** Using your knowledge of the locations of the translation schools in Toledo and Salerno, describe in a short paragraph the importance of the location of these two towns between the Muslim world in southern Spain and North Africa and the European Christian world to the north.
- **Bumper Sticker:** Create a bumper sticker cheering on the work being done in Toledo and Salerno during the Middle Ages.
- **Poster Power:** Create a poster that illustrates the importance to history of the translation work done at Toledo and Salerno during the Middle Ages.
- **What If?** With a partner in class, discuss for one minute what would have happened to European history if the translating schools in Toledo and Salerno never existed. When finished, share your ideas with your whole class for their consideration.
- **ADV Translator:** With the help of a student in your classroom who knows a language other than English, work to translate a short poem from that language into English. Describe in a Quick Write how difficult the task of translation from one language to the next can be.
- **ADV Historical Research:** Using resources from your library and the Internet, research the question why Christian Europe had so much to learn from the Muslim Middle East in terms of science and medicine. Why did Christians in Europe at the same time develop so much hatred against the Muslims that they attacked them repeatedly during the Crusades after 1095 CE? When finished, report your findings to your class.
- **ADV Interpretative Research:** Why are the translating schools of Toledo and Salerno rarely mentioned in many textbooks of

European history? Search your school library and the Internet to see if you can find any information on this question. When finished, share your findings with your class for their general discussion.

3.10.4   St. Thomas Aquinas (1225–1274 CE)

One of the most powerful thinkers to emerge during the thousand years of the Middle Ages was Thomas Aquinas. Benefiting from the Arabic to Latin translations done at Toledo and Salerno, he pulled all of the great Jewish and Muslim thinking of his age from writers such as Maimonides and Avicenna together and concluded that the ancient Greeks, such as Aristotle, were correct. Humans must use their brains to understand the world around them. Weaker men would have been burned at the stake by the Church, but Aquinas survived. Aquinas applied the classical Greek thinking of Aristotle to Christianity and accepted rationalism along with faith. This was the beginning of modern science. With St. Thomas Aquinas, Europe began to move out of the Middle Ages and into the Renaissance.

(Note from the future: As a result of his stand on reason, Thomas Aquinas is considered an early father of the Renaissance, which was still 100 years into the future. The Church also began to change and sainted him in 1323; however, it was nearly 600 years later—in 1921—that Church leaders finally declared his teachings to be part of Church philosophy [Durant 1950, 961–978].)

- **Quick Write:** Describe an example from your life when you wish you had used your brain rather than your emotions. Why is it better to stop and think for a moment rather than act on pure emotion?
- **Pair Share:** Share your regret not to use reason with a partner and then with the class as a whole.
- **Rumper Sticker:** Create a medieval oxen rumper sticker supporting Aquinas during the Middle Ages.
- **Art Mart:** Create a drawing or painting that illustrates Aquinas's contribution to world history.
- **Quick Skit:** With a team of four students from your class, develop and present a short dramatization that illustrates Aquinas's trust in reason and the reluctance of the Church to accept anything other than religious faith.

- **ADV Research Report:** Using your library and the Internet as resources, research in more detail the influence Aquinas had on the Middle Ages. When finished, report your findings to the class.

3.11.0   ART AND CREATIVE THOUGHT

3.11.1   Hagia Sophia (537 CE)—The Masterpiece of the Early Middle Ages

The masterpiece of the Early Middle Ages was the Hagia Sophia church, dedicated by Justinian and Theodora in 537 CE. It was built by Justinian and Theodora following the Nika revolt and burning of Constantinople in 532 CE—an example of catastrophe inviting innovation. Key to the architectural design of the Hagia Sophia is the balancing of a dome over a square structure; this feature became the great contribution of Byzantine architecture. The major problem with the Hagia Sophia was that the Byzantines had forgotten how to cast in cement—a technique that had enabled Rome to build magnificent domed structures only 300 years before. As a result, the Hagia Sophia was constructed out of stone, brick, iron, and lead—magnificently well done, but not anything like the grand elegance of the Pantheon of Hadrian 400 years before.

(Historical irony from the future: Ironically, in 726 CE, the great mosaic images of the Hagia Sophia were plastered over for a time until the fury of the iconoclasts passed—this aided in their preservation. The Muslim Turks aided its preservation in 1453 CE by again plastering over the great mosaics and turning the great structure into a *masjid* [mosque]. The enlightened Turkish government turned the Hagia Sophia into a museum in 1935, and now we all can see the remnants of the great Byzantine mosaics of 537 CE Istanbul in all their splendor. For more on Justinian and Theodora and the Byzantine Empire see 3.4.2, 3.5.1, and 3.8.1 above.)

- **IQ Test:** In a short paragraph, describe how to put a round object on top of square walls. (This was the basic problem of designing the Hagia Sophia church in Constantinople.)
- **Modeling:** Make a model or diorama of the Hagia Sophia church out of cardboard.
- **Mosaics:** Gather many pieces of colored paper from old magazines and cut them into small half-inch squares. With a glue stick,

make a picture of a friend or someone you admire using these small squares of colored paper, using the technique of Byzantine mosaics.

- **Field Work:** Find the oldest building in your town. How old is it? Is it being maintained for history? Imagine what it will look like in 1,500 years. Create a plan to have this building restored, and present it to your class and city council.
- **ADV Historical Research:** Using the resources in your library and on the Internet, examine in more detail the contributions of Byzantine in the fields of art and architecture.

3.11.2 The Joyful Songs of the Medieval Troubadours

Although frowned on by the Church, music continued to flourish outside of the Church during the Middle Ages. A major musical medium outside of the Church was the troubadour. Singers and musicians from the poorest peasant to the most noble of princes performed the songs of the troubadours during the Middle Ages. Over 2,500 such songs and poems still exist. Such troubadour songs and verses were extremely popular in that they were sung in local languages, such as early French and early German. In many cases, these early troubadour songs and verses represent the first written evidence of languages such as French and German. The troubadours sang of princely valor and true love of fair maidens—and everybody listened (including priests—secretly—behind closed doors).

(Note: For troubadour classroom background music, the four-CD set entitled *The Medieval Experience* [Archiv Production 449 082 2 by Deutsche Grammophon] is a good source.)

- **Song Writer:** Write a song for someone you love secretly in the style of the troubadours.
- **Costumer:** Create a troubadour costume.
- **Musician:** With a mandolin or guitar, pretend you are a troubadour singing the songs of what you have seen and heard during the Middle Ages.
- **T Chart:** Compare the troubadours of the Middle Ages to the musical groups of today. Use a T chart to compare how they are similar and different.
- **ADV Historical Research:** Using your library and the Internet, research how the Catholic Church's opposition to music and the

troubadours who composed thousands of joyful songs throughout the Middle Ages could exist side by side. When finished, report your findings to the class.

3.11.3   The Holy Calligraphy and Tessellations of Islam

The Koran makes no mention of images, but Muslims from the "Traditions of the Prophet" (*hadiths*) became strong iconoclastic believers. The word, rather than the image of God, became the center of Islam. Written Arabic was developed in order to express the words of the Koran. As a result, written Arabic, itself, became the major art form of Muslims (calligraphy), along with repeating patterns of nonrepresentational designs—tessellations.

In 1492, the Christian monarchs Ferdinand and Isabella were going through Spain destroying everything Muslim. But when they came to Granada, and its magnificent Alhambra palace on top of the hill, it was so beautiful, they could not destroy it.

(Note: The inscription here is taken from the magnificent Alhambra Palace in Granada, Spain [circa 1300 CE], where it is repeated over and over again on the palace walls.)

- **Personal Calligraphy:** Make a beautiful design out of your name and share it with your class.
- **Arabic Calligraphy:** In Arabic, the beautiful saying in the illustration says: "No one is a winner, but God!"

Illustration 3.11.3a.   *Arabic Calligraphy, circa 1300 CE, from Granada, Spain*

- **Practice Calligraphy:** Practice Arabic calligraphy yourself by repeating the example of Arabic art across a page—remember that Arabic is written from right to left.
- **Personal Tessellation:** Write the initials of your name into a beautiful triangle or circular design. Now repeat this design upside-down and right-side-up to fill up a page.
- **Arabic Tessellation:** Make a beautiful design on a page—it cannot be of a flower or any living thing—and then repeat this design upside-down and right-side-up to fill up the page.
- **Recreation of a Muslim Palace:** Display the calligraphy and tessellations developed by your class on the walls of your room as an example of what a Muslim palace during the Middle Ages might have looked like.
- **ADV Photo Research:** Go to the library or Internet to search for photographs of the Alhambra Palace in Granada, Spain (constructed 1248–1354). It is without question one of the most beautiful palaces in the world and the finest expression of Islamic calligraphy and tessellations in the world. Share what you find with your class. (See Abercrombie 1988 for a good source of pictures and a history of the Alhambra.)
- **ADV Comparative Research:** Compare the artwork of the Middle Ages in Europe—gothic churches, stained-glass windows,

Illustration 3.11.3b. *African Arabic Tessellations, circa 1200 CE*

and statues of Jesus—with the art of the Muslim world during the Middle Ages—calligraphy and tessellations.

3.11.4   The Gothic Cathedral—Suger's New Church (circa 1100)

All the early Christian churches of the Middle Ages were built with heavy walls and small windows, and were dark inside. Suger (1081?– 1151), the abbot of St. Denis near Paris, France, was no architect, but he disliked these early, dark, heavy Romanesque churches; he wanted to build a church that showed the light of God. His new church would have tall, slender, pointed arches and spires that pointed to God. The western major entrance to the church would have three large arched doors topped by a large rose window of stained glass. Because the massive walls of the early churches were too heavy to have large windows, Suger's new church would have flying buttresses to support thin, tall walls separated by large stained-glass windows. Each stained-glass window would tell a major story of Christianity. Suger's new church revolutionized church architecture and was copied in new forms all across Europe—and these churches represent some of the most magnificent buildings in the world.

- **Art Mart:** Based on an illustration of a Gothic cathedral, make a drawing of a Gothic cathedral to display on your classroom wall.
- **Field Work:** Find out if there is a church in your area that is patterned after one of the great Gothic cathedrals of Europe and visit it.
- **Model Making:** Make a model out of cardboard of a tall Gothic cathedral with flying buttresses.
- **Stained-glass Windows:** With colored pieces of paper, make a model of a stained-glass window that tells a story of someone you admire.
- **Stained-glass Demo:** Find out if someone in the art department of your school knows how to make stained glass and demonstrate the process to the class.
- **Imagine:** Imagine you are visiting Salisbury Cathedral in England, one of the greatest Gothic cathedrals. In a poem, describe your feelings as you enter this great cathedral constructed more than 800 years ago.
- **ADV Comparative Research #1:** Classic Greek temples always look very similar to each other, and yet Greece had no centralized state. Gothic cathedrals, on the other hand, always looked much

different from each other, even those constructed in the same state. Use your library and the Internet to see what you can find on this historical problem, and then report your findings to your class.

- **ADV Comparative Research #2:** Which do you think are greater—Greek temples, Roman temples, Gothic cathedrals, Islamic Mosques, or traditional Japanese temples? Defend your reasons. Why do you think they are so beautiful, and yet so different from each other?

3.11.5   *The Divine Comedy*—Seven Layers of Heaven and Hell

Dante Alighieri's (1265–1321) masterpiece, *The Divine Comedy*, is a transition point between the Middle Ages and the Renaissance. Really, it is a long triple-rhyming poem—the first written in a European language (Italian) that focuses on the dominant religious ideas of Europe during the Middle Ages. While guided through seven layers of heaven and seven layers of hell, Dante, in his masterpiece, realizes that humans freely decide the direction of their lives, which ultimately sends them toward heaven or hell. The Christian God of the Middle Ages still dominates the *Divine Comedy*, but human reason, from the Renaissance, gives humans the choice of deciding the direction of their fate. Dante is truly the bridge between the Middle Ages and the Renaissance (Boorstin 1992, 255–264).

(Note from the future: Dante's *Divine Comedy* is to this day considered to be a masterpiece of Italian poetry, even 800 years later. Dante's story of human choices does not fade and remains a great book to read in our own day.)

- **Quick Write:** In a short paragraph, quickly describe what you would like more than anything in the world and the worst possible thing that could happen to you—your personal heaven and your personal hell.
- **Poster Power:** Illustrate in a poster why Dante represents a major transition between the Middle Ages and the Renaissance.
- **You Were There:** As a roving reporter for Timeless TV Network, conduct an interview with Dante (a fellow student) and present it to your class.
- **ADV Reading Research:** Check out a copy of Dante's *The Divine Comedy* from your library and identify which parts of it reflect the Middle Ages and which reflect the Renaissance.

3.11.6   The Alhambra—The Crown of Muslim Spain

The Alhambra—The Red Fortress, completed in 1353, in Granada, Spain—is both the crown of Muslim Spain and the tragic reminder of the magnificence of the Muslim Renaissance in Spain while Christian Europe was still in its Dark Ages. After the destruction of Baghdad by the Mongols in 1258, the center of the Muslim Renaissance shifted to Muslim Spain—poets, artists, intellectuals, and translators from all over the Muslim world flowed into Spain. Lest we forget, many of these "Muslim" artisans, intellectuals, and translators during the Muslim Renaissance in Spain were Jews who wrote and spoke Arabic, Hebrew, and Latin. Many of the famous ancient Greek plays and books that we still have by such authors as Sophocles and Aristotle were translated from Arabic to Latin during the Spanish Muslim Renaissance. These translations certainly helped Christian Europe emerge from its Dark Ages into its own Renaissance.

The great tragedy of the Alhambra, however, is that it remains a symbol to the greatness of a Spanish Muslim Renaissance that is no more. For almost 400 years, the Christian Spaniards since El Cid (see TLP 3.2.4 above) sought to drive the Muslims out of Spain. The Alhambra became the last grand achievement of the Muslim Renaissance in Spain. Ferdinand and Isabella, in their military conquest to destroy all of Muslim Spain, captured the Alhambra in 1492, but could not destroy it be-

Illustration 3.11.6.   *The Alhambra, Crown of Islamic Spain*

cause it was so beautiful. Isabella met Columbus to support his voyages in one of the rooms of the newly conquered Alhambra in 1492. Over 300 years later, in 1832, the American author Washington Irving wrote a whole book describing the wonders of the Alhambra, and today, we can be thankful that it still exists for all to see its magnificence. If copying something is considered to be the best indicator of its beauty, then the Alhambra must be at the top of the list. Today, we can see buildings and university campuses all over the world that have copied the famous beautiful style of the Alhambra's red sandstone structures.

- **Quick Write:** Write a short essay describing a beautiful building you saw. When finished, share it with your class.
- **Drawing Board:** With a partner from your class, draw a picture that illustrates your image of what a beautiful building should look like. Be sure to share it when you finish.
- **Photo Shot:** As a newspaper reporter on a tight deadline, look through your library and the Internet to find as many photographs as you can of the Alhambra. When finished, write a short editorial on the magnificence of the Alhambra and how much fun it might be to travel and see it.
- **Time Traveler:** Travel back in time to when Columbus met Isabella in the Alhambra in 1492. Create a short dialogue between the two that describes the great beauty of the Alhambra and then present it to your class.
- **Our Loss:** Discuss with a partner in class how much great art we have lost in history and the ways in which we can work today to restore and keep safe great art—such as the Alhambra—for future generations.
- **ADV War or Peace?** With three members of your class, discuss why many countries and religions are intent on the military conquest of certain areas of the world. What are the alternatives to such military conquests? What are the advantages of avoiding such military conquests? Be sure to share your thoughts with the class.

3.12.0 SUCCESSES AND FAILURES OF THE MIDDLE AGES

3.12.1 Success or Failure?

- **Quiz Show:** This is the competitive quiz show that challenges teams to list as many reasons as possible why a person, place, or thing is the most important success or greatest failure of the Middle Ages.

1. Each student team of four draws the name of a medieval person, place, or thing from a hat.
2. Each team calls out its name, and the scorekeeper puts it on the board as the team's name.
3. Using any books or materials available, each student team has fifteen minutes to make as long a list as possible of reasons why the name is the most important of the medieval era.
4. The medieval names to be used can be as follows or developed from a larger list:

Justinian	Hagia Sophia	iconoclasts
Arab mathematics	Arab science	St. Augustine
the Crusades	the Black Death	St. Thomas Aquinas
gunpowder	the compass	the hourglass
Attila	Dante	Maimonides
Charlemagne	Ibn Batutta	Genghis Khan

Fall of Constantinople (29 May 1453)
The Alhambra
Europe's loss of Greek writing and thinking

5. A scorekeeper will keep track how many answers each team gives on the board.
6. The team with the most number of "valid" supporting reasons wins a free trip to the library.

3.13.0 MAJOR WORLD PROBLEMS FOR THE MIDDLE AGES

3.13.1 The Problem of Intolerance

Religious intolerance during the Middle Ages was brutal, inhumane, and long-lasting. At first, Christian iconoclasts destroyed only classical works of art and paintings. As the Church became more powerful, however, the intolerance turned toward other Christians who held even the smallest differences of religious opinion. As the Christian clergy were forbidden to shed blood, "burning at the stake" became the means of punishing other Christians (heretics) who shared different beliefs. In 1095, the Church turned to attacking the Muslims controlling the Holy Land (today's Israel/Palestine) with even bloodier results.

(Note from the future: Today, religious intolerance by all three monotheistic religions [Judaism, Christianity, and Islam] seems to be inescapable. Each believes that it has the one true God and will not accept the beliefs of other religions.)

- **An Inquisition (simulated):**
  1. The Inquisition has just met and concluded that all students wearing red in your class are to stand in a far corner of the room.
  2. The Inquisition (the rest of the class) must decide what punishment (simulated) the "Red Wearers" should receive for wearing the forbidden color.
  3. All "Red Wearers" must then stand in front of the class to receive their punishment (simulated).
  4. There is no defense for the "Red Wearers." The Inquisition has found them guilty, and they must receive their punishment (simulated).
  5. The Inquisition (simulated) is now over. All students may take their original seats.
- **The Inquisition Debriefed:**
  1. *Quick Write*: Both the members of the Inquisition and the "Red Wearers" should write down their impressions of their role in the simulation.
  2. *Pair Share*: Each two students should share their impressions of the simulation with each other and then with the class as a whole.
  3. *Class Debrief*: What was wrong with the Inquisition? What human rights did not exist with the Inquisition? What if the "Blue Wearers" were the next to be punished? How can we identify inquisitions before they start? How can an inquisition be stopped once it gets started?

(Note from the future: The Inquisition during the Middle Ages was a religious one. Throughout history, inquisitions tend to appear when certain people become intolerant of other people's beliefs. Sadly, we will see more inquisitions in the future whenever a few people believe in an ideology more than they believe in human rights.)

3.13.2   The Problem of Poverty

The poor did not have a chance during the Middle Ages. Society was strictly divided between the nobility (usually rich) and the peasants (almost always poor), with no chance of moving up the social ladder. The Church (rich) also preached to the commoners (poor) that it was good to be poor. How could the poor improve themselves? They couldn't! The Church considered education—reading and writing—to be sinful for everyone except the priests. Even earning money by charging interest (usury) was forbidden. The poor peasants were really stuck during the Middle Ages.

- **Quick Write:** Write down five ways that poor people in the United States today can pull themselves out of poverty.
- **Pair Share:** Share your Quick Write with a neighbor in the class and then with the whole class.
- **Newspaper Editorial:** As the ace reporter for the *Medieval Times* newspaper, visit a poor peasant family (students in class) during the Middle Ages and report on their living conditions and what plans they have for the future.
- **Group Project:** In groups of four (poor peasants), make a plan to escape from poverty during the Middle Ages and present your plan to the Peasant Assembly (the class). The group with the best plan gets to escape from poverty and join the Crusades.

3.14.0   MEDIEVAL ANTECEDENTS FOR THE FUTURE

3.14.1   The Economic Revolution of the Middle Ages

During the Middle Ages, Europe was transformed from vast forests and feudal estates into thriving economic towns where individual entrepreneurs began to thrive. Great fairs of cobblers, dressmakers, and tailors began on a small scale the free-enterprise capitalism that would come to dominate our own century.

- **Role Play:** Transform your classroom into a medieval faire with each student presenting a skill (dressmaking, candle making), a talent (musician, artist, jester), or merchandise (candy, popcorn) to sell for money in a small, early example of capitalism.
- **ADV Comparative Essay:** Compare the early capitalism of the medieval faire with the capitalism of the late 20th and early 21st centuries.

3.14.2   Results of the Inquisition

It is sad to report that the brutal Inquisitions in France, Spain, and Italy were successful. Beliefs about God other than those approved by the Roman Catholic Church were burned out (at the stake), and these countries remain overwhelmingly Catholic today. The Inquisition, however, was not as strong in the Germanic states to the north, and different ideas of a Christian God were not eliminated there.

(Note from the future: 300 years later, in these same Germanic states, the Protestant Reformation successfully rose up and became independent from the main church in Rome.)

- **You Were There:** As the anchorperson on the prime TV news program of the Middle Ages, Torquemada, the head of the Inquisition in Spain (a student in disguise) has granted you and your studio audience an interview. Each member of the studio audience should have three questions ready to ask His Excellency about the role of the Inquisition in the Catholic Church. Each of the members of the audience must be careful, however; if you rub him the wrong way, he might test your stamina on the rack.
- **ADV The Futurist:** Research your library and the Internet on information concerning the Catholic Church's current view of the Inquisition. Report your findings to the class.

3.14.3   End Point of the Middle Ages/Start of the Renaissance

The following are advanced research questions to answer about the end of the Middle Ages and the beginning of the Renaissance.

- **ADV Which Year?** Pick a year for the end of the Middle Ages and the beginning of the Renaissance and defend why you think that is the changeover date. (Note: Even historians cannot agree on a date for this change.)
- **ADV Dante:** Why is Dante considered the transition point between the Middle Ages and the Renaissance?
- **ADV Aquinas:** What would have happened if the Church had burned Thomas Aquinas for heresy rather than making him a saint? Since he is considered the father of the Renaissance, would the Renaissance have taken place without his leadership? Use

library and Internet resources to research this question and report your findings to the class.

3.14.4   Is Humankind Ready to Advance?

It is now time to judge whether or not humankind is ready to advance into the next era.

- **Viewpoints:** Five members from around Middleville (the class) will state their basic viewpoints of whether or not enough advances have been made during the Middle Ages to move forward. The five illustrious members are as follows:
  1. Letoc Betrink, the arch-conservative of Middleville, believes that humankind has gone far enough with enough progress. Betrink believes strongly that the good old days were the best and that humankind needs to hold strongly to past values and beliefs.
  2. Motar Derudzuk, one of the rising young voices in the town, is a more moderate conservative who believes that we need to be very cautious with any change and be very sure that no harm will come to Middleville if change takes place. Motar is willing to accept some change, but only in very small amounts and only when the time is right—and he wants to be the one to decide when that time will come.
  3. Pewik Wookbot, the wishy-washy middle-of-the-roader around town, is willing to accept change for a few minutes after one speaker, but may have a change of mind in an instant to oppose change after another speaker has finished.
  4. Yatdark Vatsmeer, the moderate progressive of the group, is willing to support change for the good of the people in Middleville. Vatsmeer is especially in favor of change when it will benefit Vatsmeer's own family directly.
  5. Queedril Varull, the radical progressive of the town, is very willing to support any change that will move humanity away from the drafty and damp old castle into something more modern and comfortable for humanity.
- **Take a Position:** Each member of Middleville (classroom) now must choose one of the five positions for humanity to take and support their position with evidence of what they have learned about the Middle Ages.

- **Vote:** A vote will then be taken of all peasants and nobles around town to determine whether or not humanity should move on to the next era. The consensus decision of the imaginary citizens of Middleville will determine their own future and the rest of humanity. (In reality, such decisions by people during the Middle Ages were key in deciding whether humans stayed the way they were or progressed to new levels of development.)

(For more great lessons on medieval world history, also see Ron Pahl's *Breaking Away from the Textbook: Creative Ways to Teach World History Volume III*, Unit 8.)

Renaissance, Reformation, and Explorations (1400 to 1600)

UNIT 4: TABLE OF CONTENTS

INTRODUCTION

There are, in history, ever-so-brief moments that explode with new ideas, new ways of expression, and triumphant masterpieces of art. The era of the Renaissance was just such an explosion of new ways of thinking, across Europe and the rest of the world. Rather than trusting in the mystical beliefs and superstitions of the Middle Ages, people of Middle East, Europe, and the world began to restore their trust in human reason. Such major historical changes do not start in isolation. The initial conditions must first be set—sometimes slowly for hundreds of years—before the right moment and the right person begin the change. This movement toward reason started during the Middle Ages. Major writings of ancient Greece and the Muslim Middle East in science, mathematics, and culture were translated from Arabic into Latin under enlightened 12th-century Christian governments in Spain and Sicily. These new ideas fed the minds of a few brave people who dared to think differently—St. Thomas Aquinas (13th century) and later Martin

Luther (16th century) in religion; Copernicus (15th century) and Galileo (16th century) in science; Giotto (14th century) and Leonardo da Vinci (16th century) in art; and Ibn Batutta (14th century) and Columbus (15th century) in exploration. The results of the changes brought by these thinkers were wondrous to behold. They set the model for other explorers of the mind to follow, down to our present era. But as with all periods of innovation and change, the Renaissance came to an end. The momentum of change brought by the era of the Renaissance was not strong enough and wide enough to continue with renewed energy. With complacency came decline and entropy in the Renaissance. Individuals, governments, and religions became resistant to change and wished to return to a more comfortable era when their minds were not challenged by new ideas. This ended the Renaissance.

THEMATIC LESSON PACS

4.1.0   HISTORICAL TIME LINE

4.1.1   A Renaissance History Time Line

- **Name Plates:** Photocopy six sets of the following fourteen names and items. Cut each name or item into a strip of paper. Place the strips of paper carefully into separate envelopes for each team and label the envelopes "4.1.1 The Renaissance History Time Line," for later use in class.
- **Team Power:** Break the class into six teams.
- **The Envelope:** Each team should be given an envelope containing the following random fourteen names and facts from the Renaissance era:
  1. Michelangelo started painting the Sistine Chapel — 1508
  2. Columbus discovered America — 1492
  3. Count Dracula lived in Transylvania — 1460
  4. Machiavelli wrote *The Prince* — 1512
  5. Mary, Queen of Scots, beheaded — 1586
  6. Martin Luther started the Reformation — 1517
  7. English defeated the Spanish Armada — 1588
  8. Mayan civilization disappeared — 1400
  9. Muslims and Jews expelled from Spain — 1492
  10. Beijing, China, the largest city in the world — 1500
  11. Incas had the best road system in world — 1500

12. Cheng Ho started to explore the West—1403
13. Vasco da Gama reached India—1497
14. Copernicus saw the sun as the center of the solar system—1473

- **Team Time Line:** The first job of each team is to correctly order the fourteen names and events according to time, with the oldest at the top and the most recent at the bottom. Each student should separately write the correct time line for the Renaissance names and events on a personal sheet of paper for later reference.
- **Team Look Up:** Once every member of the team has the Renaissance time line on a sheet of paper, each of the fourteen Renaissance names should be divided among members of the team to find out the meaning of each name from their textbook. Once found, the meanings of each Renaissance name can be shared with the members of the team to write on their own time lines.
- **Poster Power:** On a large piece of paper, each team should construct its own time line for the Renaissance using the fourteen names with descriptions and illustrations to demonstrate the meaning of each name. When finished, these can be presented to the class and displayed on the classroom wall.
- **Music Mart:** Each team should pick what they think is the most important name or event in the time line and then compose and present a short song or rap about the name or event. When finished, this can be presented to the class for their approval.
- **Journal Entry:** Have each team member write a short journal entry speculating about what they now know about the development of humans during the Renaissance—from the time line they developed—and possibly the most important things to happen during this era. When finished, students can first share their thoughts with their team and then with the class as a whole for general discussion about what they think are the most important things that happened during the era.

4.2.0   SEPARATING FACT FROM MYTH AND PROPAGANDA

4.2.1   Why Were Women Accused of Witchcraft?

Have you ever wondered why more women are not found in history books? Between 1450 and 1650 in central Europe, more than 100,000 women—including young girls—were burned at the stake as witches.

This mass killing of women did not take place in illiterate Russia or Scandinavia. It also did not take place in the Muslim Middle East. It took place in the center of Renaissance Europe—Italy, France, England, and Germany—where literacy and reason were flourishing. The printing press had just been invented (1454) and one of the first mass publications of a book by the Catholic Church was *Malleus Maleficarum* (*The Hammer of the Witches*) in 1487. It was a manual on how to catch female witches and kill them. Because of the manual, between 1510 and 1514, more than 450 females were burned at the stake for being witches in the small town of Brescia, Italy. Luther called for a reformation of the Church in 1517—but he did not call for an end to the mass killing of women throughout Europe. Any woman who spoke out, acted differently, or looked different was immediately suspected of being a witch. She could not defend herself, and there was no escape. Only in towns and states such as Venice, where accusations of witchcraft were banned, were women safe from the witch hunters. Why were there no great female artists, writers, and scientists during the Renaissance in Europe? The answer is clear. The horror of this Renaissance holocaust against women quickly silenced any creative or intellectual thoughts by the female half of Europe (Shlain 1999).

- **Quick Scare:** Describe what it would be like if someone accused you of being a witch. How would you feel? What would you do?
- **Bumper Sticker:** Create a bumper sticker that dramatically demonstrates the horror of the witchcraft holocaust against females in Europe during the Renaissance and Reformation.
- **Poster Power:** Create a poster that strongly protests the burning of females as witches during the Renaissance and Reformation in Europe.
- **Role Play:** With a partner, develop a short skit of a person accusing another of witchcraft and the person being accused of witchcraft. What would they say to each other? How would they react against each other?
- **ADV Witchcraft Inquiry #1:** Using your library and the Internet, research why people believe in witches. Accusations of witchcraft tend to be nothing more than people finding scapegoats for other problems. Research possible tensions in a society that might need scapegoats and might turn to accusations of witchcraft. When finished, report your findings to your class.

- **ADV Witchcraft Inquiry #2:** Many of the top scientists and re-ligious leaders of the Renaissance, and later Luther, Erasmus, and Newton, believed in witches. How could such learned men believe in witches?
- **ADV Witchcraft Inquiry #3:** Politicians today still regularly prac-tice "witchcraft" accusations, but under different names. People were accused of being "communists" during the 1950s—much as "witches" were accused during the Renaissance. Look to see if you can find more recent examples of political "witchcraft" accusations.

4.2.2   Was Count Dracula (circa 1460) Really a Vampire?

Yes, he really did live in a castle in Transylvania (Romania), he looked like the devil, and he loved blood. Bram Stoker—the author of *Dracula*—did not make that up. His real name was Vlad the Impaler (do not look up the word "impale" in the dictionary until after lunch!). What is forgotten in history is that Vlad—without any help from the rest of Europe—stopped the Muslim Turks from invading Romania and the rest of Europe. Today, he is considered one of the founding fathers of Romania. Poor blood-loving Vlad, however, was not a vam-pire (Shenkman 1993, 193–194).

- **Quick Blood:** In a short paragraph, describe your favorite vampire movie.
- **Map Attack:** Locate Transylvania and possibly Count Dracula's castle on a map, and calculate the distance from there to your hometown. Find out how much it would cost to fly to Transylvania (Romania) to visit Count Dracula's castle.
- **Vampire Art:** Draw or paint a picture—from your imagination—of Count Dracula.
- **Diary Entry:** As an imaginary vampire, write a description of your life, and the joys and sorrows of your life as a vampire.
- **ADV Vampire Analysis:** Research in your library and on the Internet how a "nice" guy like Vlad the Impaler can be made into one of the major creatures of modern horror mythology.

(For more great lessons on Vlad see "Will the Real Dracula Please Stand Up?" in Pahl, *Creative Ways to Teach the Mysteries of History Volume II.*)

4.2.3   Here There Be Dragons!

The early European maps of the known world during the 13th century had a strange statement: "Here there be dragons!" Were dragons at the edge of the known world? Of course not. But dragons to Europeans were feared mythological creatures that represented the scary unknown at the edge of the known world. Even the very earliest tale written in English, *Beowulf*, is about a dragon named Grendel who takes great pleasure in eating humans.

On the opposite side of the world, the Chinese revered dragons as good luck symbols. The five-clawed dragon was the special dragon that brought good luck to each emperor of China. Huge, colorful paper dragons would snake through each Chinese village and town as a symbol of good luck at the beginning of each new year.

Both the folk tales of European evil dragons and the folklore of happy Chinese dragons likely originated in the accidental discovery of dinosaur bones by ancient humans in different parts of the world. As it quite often happens in history, the facts of the sightings of these large prehistoric creatures' remains became exaggerated and soon developed into mythology and fiction.

- **Quick Dragon:** Close your eyes for a moment. Imagine a dragon. Now write a short description of the dragon you see. Share your description with the class.
- **Concept Web:** Draw a concept web of a dragon on the board and then see how many different types and names of dragons can be identified by students in the class.

Illustration 4.2.3.   *A Traditional Five-Toed Imperial Chinese Dragon*

- **Art Mart #1:** Create a drawing or a painting of a Chinese mythological dragon.
- **Art Mart #2:** Create a drawing or a painting of a European mythological dragon.
- **Art Mart #3:** Create a drawing or painting of the remains of a dinosaur, which was the likely origin of the mythological dragons of both China and Europe.
- **Quick Skit:** In a team of four, create a quick skit in which the conflicting mythologies of Chinese and European dragons come in contact with each other.
- **Folklore #1:** Find a story of an evil dragon from European folklore and read it.
- **Folklore #2:** Find a story of a good dragon from Asian folklore and read it.
- **Modern Dragons:** *Godzilla* and *Jurassic Park* films are modern mythological stories about dinosaurs. In a Pair Share, briefly discuss whether or not these stories are modern dragon stories, and then share your pair's ideas with the class.
- **ADV Inquiry:** Why are dragons so popular in mythology? They can be found in virtually every major culture. Research this topic in your library and on the Internet, and then share your findings with the class.
- **ADV Historical Dilemma:** European dragons represent the unknown and evil; Chinese dragons—on the other side of the world—represent good fortune and good luck. How come? Research this topic and then report your findings to the class.

4.3.0 LOCATION AND MOVEMENT

4.3.1 The Intellectual Shift of the World

The major source of new ideas during the Middle Ages (at least between the years 1000 to 1200 CE) was the Muslim Middle East—especially the enlightened Abbasid rulers of Baghdad. The Abbasid rulers gathered all the best thinking from ancient Greece, Persia, and India and translated it into Arabic. With the decline of the Abbasids after the Mongol sacking of Baghdad (1258 CE), enlightened and tolerant Christian rulers in Spain and Sicily during the 13th century accepted Muslim, Jewish, and Christian scholars into their courts to translate many of these major

Arabic intellectual works into Latin. With the new ideas from the Muslim world, Europe slowly began to pull itself out of the Middle Ages. This flowering of new ideas became especially noticeable in the city-states of Italy—Florence, Venice, and Milan—and began the intellectual, cultural, and artistic garden known as the Renaissance.

- **Map Think:** On a blank map of the world, trace the movement of the intellectual centers of the world between 1000 and 1500.
- **What If?** What would have happened if the Muslim intellectuals in Baghdad had not collected the major learning of the ancient Greeks? And what if these works had not been translated into Latin from Arabic? Would there ever have been a European Renaissance? Discuss these issues first in Pair Shares for one minute each and then share each pair's ideas with the class as a whole.
- **Poster Power:** Create a poster that illustrates the shift of intellectual thinking from the Muslim Middle East, through Spain and Sicily, into Europe.
- **Quick Skit:** In a team of four, create a short drama that illustrates the shift of new ideas from the Middle East to Europe during the Middle Ages.
- **The King's Scribe:** As the official scribe for King Alfonso X of Toledo in Spain, send out an advertisement for Muslim and Jewish scholars to work on translating important scientific works from Arabic into Latin.
- **ADV Research:** Using the resources in your library and on the Internet, research the impact that the Crusades and Christian attacks on the Muslims in the Middle East had on the transfer of important scientific works from Arabic into Latin during the Middle Ages.
- **ADV Question #1 from the Future:** Does the world have an intellectual capital today? If so, where would it be? If not, what are the major centers of learning today in the world? Discuss this issue first in a Pair Share and then in a general class discussion.
- **ADV Question #2 from the Future:** Are the inventions and technologies of today strong enough to protect the world from losing valuable learning? Interview teachers, parents, neighbors, and friends to learn their views on this issue, and report your findings to the class.

4.3.2   Timbuktu in 1492—114 Days by Camel!

Timbuktu (in modern Mali) in 1492 was the major commercial and intellectual center in West Africa. Camel caravans from Marrakech and Fez, Morocco, would bring blocks of salt and luxury goods south to trade for grain and gold. To travel by camel across the Sahara desert took 114 days. The gold from the Akan mines (in modern Ghana)—600 miles south of Timbuktu—supplied the gold to the countries of Europe and the Mediterranean during the Middle Ages and Renaissance. In exchange, blocks of salt and luxury goods were traded south. The strategic location of Timbuktu at the northernmost point of the Niger River and in the middle of West Africa made it a major trading center and the richest city in West Africa. It also became the major Muslim intellectual center for teaching the Koran and converting much of West Africa to Islam (see Ajayi and Espie 1965).

(Note from the future: The Portuguese explorations along the West African coast in the early 1400s circled around the old, slow camel caravans across the Sahara and made them obsolete. The merchants of Timbuktu and the Sahara middlemen were cut out of the gold trade, as the Portuguese could now make the trip shorter, cheaper, and safer by sea. After 1500 CE, Timbuktu faded as the major focus of history in West Africa.)

- **Map Attack:** On a blank map of Africa, trace the major trade route across the Sahara Desert from Marrakech and Fez, Morocco, to Timbuktu in modern Mali. How far is it between the two trade centers? If it took 114 days to travel one way between the two places, how many miles did they travel each day by camel? Also indicate how the Portuguese cut off this trade route between Europe and the gold fields in Ghana during the early 1400s.
- **You Were There:** Imagine pulling a camel for 114 days south across the Sahara Desert and then turning around and making the same trip again to the north. With three other camel drivers (from class), create a short skit describing the rigors of crossing the Sahara.
- **Plan a Camel Caravan:** Imagine the value of a camel caravan with 200 camels loaded with gold, water, and supplies traveling north across the Sahara. Plan a trip from Timbuktu to Marrakech for 50 merchants, 100 armed guards, 200 camels and their drivers, and all the food and water for 114 days.

- **Meet a Tuareg:** Riding camels, fierce veiled men called Tuaregs controlled much of the central Sahara Desert and demanded payment from any caravan passing through their territory. The favorite saying of the Tuareg was "Kiss the hand you cannot sever!" For one minute each, discuss with a partner in class what you will do when you meet a strong group of Tuaregs riding toward your caravan. When finished, share your ideas with the rest of the caravan (the class).
- **Art Mart:** Paint or draw a picture of a large camel caravan arriving in Timbuktu from the north after crossing the Sahara Desert.
- **Diary Entry:** Enter into your diary what it was like to be a member of a trading company crossing the Sahara Desert from Morocco to Timbuktu for 114 days on top of a camel.
- **ADV Historical Research:** Using your library and the Internet as sources, find out exactly what happened to the camel caravans and Timbuktu once the Portuguese began to bypass the arduous trans-Saharan trips. Be sure to tell your class what you found.

4.3.3 The World's Largest Cities in 1500 CE

The following are the important cities of the world in 1500 (Manley 1992, 33–34):

1. Rome in 1500 only had 100,000 people. (During the classic Roman Empire—300 CE—Rome held 1.5 million people.)
2. Istanbul (old Constantinople), the capital of the Muslim Ottoman Empire (in modern Turkey), had between 200,000 and 400,000 people.
3. Damascus (in modern Syria), one of the oldest cities in the world, had 57,000 people in 1500.
4. The most important city in ancient Greece—Athens—had only 12,500 people in 1500.
5. Cairo, Egypt, under Muslim Ottoman rule, had 400,000 people in 1500.
6. Viayanager (now Hampi), in India, had a population of 500,000 people, with a circumference of ninety kilometers (sixty miles) in 1500.
7. Tenochtitlan (Mexico City)—the capital of the Aztecs—had 150,000 people in the year 1500, before the arrival of the Spaniards.

8. Cuzco, Peru, the capital of the Incan Empire, had 45,000 people in 1500.
9. Beijing, China, had 672,000 people in 1500.
10. London, England, in 1500, had 60,000 people.
11. Madrid, Spain, was just a small village in 1500.

- **Rank Order:** Rank order the largest to the smallest city on the list for the year 1500.
- **Map It:** Locate all of the cities on a blank map of the world and list the size of each city next to its name.
- **Analysis:** Looking at a map of the major cities of the world on a map of 1500 (the one that you have just completed), what geographic factors can you identify with the largest cities of the world? What geographic features can you identify with some of the smallest cities?
- **Comparison:** In a short report, compare the size of your town today to the major towns in 1500.
- **ADV Historical Research:** Pick one of these above towns and determine its patterns of growth and decline. What factors led to these major demographic changes?

4.3.4 The Little Ice Age (1350–1850)

A little over 150 years ago, the world experienced the end of a 500-year-old cold snap. This cold snap was a far cry from the massive last Ice Age, which ended 12,000 years ago and lasted for thousands of years. The Little Ice Age did, however, cause major changes in how humans lived on planet Earth. The Black Plague struck Europe in 1347 and killed almost half of the population; it might have been related to the beginning of the Little Ice Age. At least five major volcanoes exploded each century, cooling Earth's atmosphere. Temperatures dropped. Glaciers advanced. Crops failed. The Vikings had to leave their Greenland settlements in 1492 because the weather became too cold. Thousands of people died in Iceland when their cattle froze to death and their crops failed. Farmers in northern Europe could no longer grow wheat because of the cold. Millions of people died from starvation. The cold snap and subsequent drought was also a contributing cause of the French Revolution in 1791. One saving grace was the discovery of America by Columbus: a discovery from the Andes Mountains of Peru brought a strange-looking food to Europe called the potato. It was very hearty and could grow well in very cold climates. Potatoes quickly became the major crop of northern Europe and saved the lives of many Europeans. The Cold Snap also did have a few good creative effects: it was during the cold summer of 1816 on Lake Geneva in Switzerland when, huddled around the fire, Mary Shelley's friends listened to her first reading of her new dark mystery novel *Frankenstein* (Fagan 1999).

- **Quick Write:** What is the longest you have gone without eating a meal? How hungry did you get? Write a short paragraph describing this unpleasant experience.
- **Cold Snap:** With a partner in class, imagine what it would be like if your town had to move to a warmer climate due to an advancing glacier. What plans would you have to make? What would you be sure to take, and what would you leave at home? Report your thoughts to your class.
- **Glacial Times:** As the four-person editorial staff of *The Glacial Times*, write a front-page first edition of the effect the global cold snap is having on your town. Be sure to include a catchy large banner headline and an interview with a victim of glacial expansion. When finished, place your front page copy on the bulletin board for all to read.
- **ADV Research:** Research your library and the Internet on the effects that the Little Ice Age had on the history of the world. Be sure to present your findings to the class.

4.4.0 POLITICS AND LEADERSHIP

4.4.1   The Most Powerful Nation on Earth—1500

Without question, the most powerful nation on planet Earth in 1500 was the Muslim Ottoman Empire in modern Turkey. In 1453, the Ottoman Turks captured ancient Constantinople (modern Istanbul) and formally ended the Christian Byzantine Empire—the last remnant of the Roman Empire. Within a few years, the Ottomans also conquered most of the Middle East, North Africa, the Balkans, and most of Greece. The Byzantine Christian point guard of Europe was no more. Christian Europe, for the first time in a thousand years, was open to attacks from the east. One of the great strengths of the Ottomans, however, was its toleration of the Christians and Jews who accepted Ottoman rule. Many Christians and Jews rose to prominence within this Muslim state. In 1492, when Christians were forcing Jewish and Muslims to flee Spain, the Ottoman Muslims openly invited the refugees—both Jewish and Muslim, many of them skilled craftsmen and scholars—to settle in the Ottoman Empire. These same Jewish and Muslim refugees from Christian intolerance in Spain revitalized the Ottoman Empire and, in turn, helped produce a Muslim Renaissance of culture and scholarship during the 16th century in Istanbul (Abercrombie 1988; Manley 1992).

- **Quick Map:** On a blank map of the Mediterranean, find and label Istanbul (old Constantinople), the capital of the Ottoman Empire. Shade in the different areas conquered by the Ottomans and the flight of the Jews and Muslims fleeing from Spain to Istanbul in 1492.
- **You Were There:** Interview the following (imaginary) people (from your class) who were present when Constantinople, the capital of the ancient Byzantine Empire, fell to the Ottoman Turks in 1453. Ask them what the final days were like and what their future plans were.
  1. Alexis, a high patriarch in the Greek Orthodox Church
  2. Fatima, the major wife of Mehmed, the new Ottoman sultan
  3. Constanis, a Greek Christian Byzantine who helped defend the large city wall around Constantinople
  4. Sophia, a Greek Christian noblewoman in Constantinople
  5. Ali, one of the first Muslim Turk soldiers in the Ottoman army who ran through the open door in the city wall of Constantinople
  6. Boris, the spy of the Ottomans who secretly opened the door and let the Ottoman troops into Constantinople in 1453
  7. Mehmed the Conquerer, the Ottoman sultan who captured Constantinople from the Byzantines in 1453
  8. Literus, the head librarian of the Byzantine library who just saw the last copies of the many major playwrights and scientists of ancient Greece go up in flames
- **Front Page:** With a team of student editors from your class, produce a front-page edition of the *Renaissance Times* newspaper that focuses on the Jewish refugees fleeing the Christians in Spain and becoming major artists and scholars in the Ottoman Empire.

Be sure to include interviews with Jewish refugees, and ask other Ottoman Muslims about the Jewish contributions to the Empire.
- **ADV Historical Research:** Using your library and the Internet, research the Ottoman Empire during the 16th century and its wide acceptance of other religions. When completed, report your findings to the class.

4.4.2   Was Lorenzo—Il Magnifico— a "Good" Dictator?

Can there be a good dictator? If so, then that dictator was Lorenzo de Medici (1449–1492). He was one of the richest men in Italy when he became ruler of Florence in 1469—at the young age of twenty. He never had any title except "citizen," and ruled Florence through a council of seventy advisors. His rule of the city for twenty-three years was legendary. Through his efforts, he kept the peace between the Italian city-states during his reign. He supported some of the greatest artists of the Renaissance, and he loved poetry, literature, and books. He supported some of the first major works to be written in Italian. His library of more than 1,000 hand-copied books was one of the largest during the Renaissance. He was also one of the first to reintroduce the study of ancient Greek and Roman writers. An ardent supporter of the first printing press (1471) in Florence, he quickly had major writers (such as Homer, Dante, and Euripides) published on that press. At the same time, he was also a dictator. He allowed no opposition to his rule, but his rule was so well-loved by the people of Florence that they gave him the political power of the city as long as he left them prosperous and happy. He was so generally well-liked that the Pope made Lorenzo's son Giovanni a cardinal in the Church at the age of fourteen (Giovanni later became Pope Leo X). Lorenzo was forty-three when he died in 1492 from gout and stomach problems. All of Italy mourned his passing (see Durant 1953, 110–142).

(Note from the future #1: Lorenzo de Medici's art collection today is the core of one of the greatest museums in the world today—the Uffizi Gallery in Florence. His library of a thousand hand-copied books was the major source upon which much of the rebirth of learning in Europe was based.)

(Note from the Future #2: One problem with great dictators and great kings: their sons are often very weak, if not terrible, rulers. Lorenzo's son Piero de Medici was such a son.)

- **Quick ID:** Write a short paragraph about the most impressive person you ever met and share it with your class.
- **Poet's Corner:** Write a short poem or rap about Lorenzo the Magnificent.
- **What If?** In a group of four students, discuss what would have happened if Lorenzo de Medici had not ruled Florence. Would Florence have been the center of the Renaissance without Lorenzo's benevolent rule? When finished, report your team's conclusions to the class.
- **Ace Reporters:** As the ace reporters of the *Renaissance Times* newspaper, your class has been granted an audience with Lorenzo de Medici (a member of your class dressed in costume). Each privileged ace reporter should have a minimum of three questions to ask Lorenzo. Be sure to be prompt. Lorenzo does not like people who are late.
- **ADV The Futurist:** Analyze whether or not a country, such as the United States, allows great leaders, such as Lorenzo de Medici, to rule without opposition. Or, should political checks and balances be kept in place ensure that even great rulers such as Lorenzo do not gain too much power?

4.4.3   Splendid Isolation—The Ming Emperor of China

The Ming emperors of China (1368–1644)—the sons of heaven—lived in splendid isolation behind the walls of their huge imperial palace in Beijing. To the north, the Great Wall of China shielded the Ming rulers and the Chinese from the Mongolians. To the south and east, the ocean shielded China from the outside world. To the west, the Himalayan Mountains provided another tall shield from the rest of the world. For a very brief time, China launched explorations into and across the Indian Ocean to the West under Cheng Ho, but no longer. China truly retreated into splendid isolation behind its many walls.

- **Quick Palace:** If you were an all-powerful Ming emperor of China during the Renaissance, with all of the wealth of China at your disposal, make a list of everything you would like to do. Cost is no object. Hand the list to your trusted eunuch (a fellow student) and have him or her read your list of wants to the members of your imperial palace (the classroom).

- **Home Boy:** What if you lived in isolation all of your life, in the same small town—without any TV, radio, or newspaper? Imagine a stranger suddenly entering your isolated little town. What would this strange person look like to you? How would you feel about this stranger? How would you treat this stranger? With four students, create a short skit that would illustrate what would happen when this stranger came to town.
- **Foreign Devils:** The Chinese called all foreigners "foreign devils." You are a foreigner visiting China during the Ming Dynasty. Everybody who speaks to you calls you "foreign devil" instead of your real name. Describe, in a short paragraph how you feel as the "foreign devil," and then share your thoughts with your class.
- **Analysis:** In a Pair Share, briefly describe—for one minute each—why you think the Chinese called all strangers "foreign devils." When finished, share your thoughts with the class.
- **ADV Historical Research:** Research in the library and on the Internet the impact of China's historical deep distrust of foreigners. What does it do for China's foreign policy? Be sure to report your findings to the class.
- **ADV Long-range Planning:** With a partner in class, devise a long-range plan for changing China's basic distrust of foreigners to trust.

4.5.0   SOCIAL AND ECONOMIC LIFE

4.5.1   Play Ball—In 1520 Mexico!

The Aztecs and all of Mesoamerica from Mexico to the Incas in Peru played a ball game called *tlachco*. At the invitation of Montezuma II, the Aztec king, Hernando Cortés, attended a game of *tlachco* in 1520. His description of the game was as follows:

> Their ball is made from gum from a tree which is kneaded together to make it round. The ball is black in color and bounces well. The *tlachco* ball court is long and narrow with high stone walls on either side and the ends. High at both ends of the court a protruding stone with a small horizontal hole in it serves as the goal. Players can strike the ball with any part of their body, but are penalized if they do not shoot the goal by bouncing the ball off their side or their bottom. If the ball hits the wall it

is considered out of bounds. The winners of a match receive mantels or the honor of being the winners. (Manley 1992, 160; Carey 1987, 86–88)

- **Quick Ball:** A foreigner who has never seen basketball asks you to describe the game to her. Write a short description of basketball so that she can understand the game.
- **Venn Diagram:** Using a Venn diagram, list the ways in which basketball and the Aztec *tlachco* ball game are similar to and different from each other.
- **Play *Tlachco*:** Set a box, a basket, or a hoop against a wall and see if you can hit a ball into the basket or hoop with your hip or bottom. Remember you can hit or kick the ball at any time, but your actual shot must be with your hip or bottom. Report to your class on your *tlachco* game.
- **Poster Power:** Make a poster advertising an important upcoming *tlachco* game between two rival Aztec teams in 1520. Illustrate your poster with a star player making a goal shot with his bottom.

(Note from the future: The Spanish conquerors of Mexico and Meso-america banned the game of *tlachco*, as well as everything else that was Aztec, because it was "the work of the devil." They tried to force the people of Mexico to speak only Spanish and play only Spanish games. Today, there are still over one million speakers of *Nahuatl* (the language of the Aztecs) (6% of Mexico) along with 60 other traditional American languages.)

4.5.2   Life as a Galley Slave (1703)

Life during the Renaissance was not all beautiful artwork and parties in the Vatican. For some, life was very harsh. The small city-states of the Renaissance along the Mediterranean were constantly at war with each other. Much of their naval warfare was done with large battle-ships, called *galleys*, in which hundreds of slaves pulled oars to move. Particularly harsh was the life of a galley slave: 300 slaves in a galley, five to an oar. The huge oars had to be kept in unison, and any sign of weakness was met with a whip across a sweaty, naked back. The heads of the slaves were shaved, and they slept chained to narrow planks of wood. During the day, the slaves were met with the cramped closeness of 300 sweating bodies and open wounds from the whips. At night, the

Illustration 4.5.2. *Drawing of a Venetian Slave Galley, circa 1500*

galley slaves were met with swarms of lice, cockroaches, and bugs that fed on their sweat and the blood of their wounds. Protestants, common criminals, and unlucky peasants all became galley slaves on these battleships of the Mediterranean Sea for such states of Venice and Genoa (Carey 1987, 193–198).

- **Quick Write:** Describe how you would feel if you were chained to a giant oar with 300 other slaves and were beaten with a whip if you did not pull in unison with the others.
- **Spin, Counter Spin:** With a partner from class, describe the beauty of a Renaissance galley being pulled across the water by hundreds of oars and then describe the horrors of the enslaved men underneath pulling the oars.
- **Bumper Sticker:** Create a Renaissance bumper sticker supporting the plight of the galley slaves.
- **Poster Power:** Draw a picture of what you think a galley might look like from the viewpoint of a slave.
- **Quick Skit:** With four classmates, create a small skit depicting what it was like being a galley slave.

- **ADV Historical Research:** Search your library and the Internet for more information on slave galleys of the Renaissance and report your findings to the class.

4.5.3   The Execution of Mary, Queen of Scots (1586)

The long rule of Elizabeth I, the Protestant queen of England, was not very peaceful. The Protestants and Catholics were constantly at war with each other. Mary Stuart, Queen of Scots, was Elizabeth's cousin, a Catholic, and queen of England—if Elizabeth died. Mary was tricked into supporting a plot to assassinate Elizabeth and was quickly executed for treason. We have a description of her last moments of life:

> Her prayers being ended, the executioners, kneeling, desired her Grace to forgive them her death. She answered: "I forgive you with all my heart." She never changed her countenance and continued to smile to all. With a Corpus Christi cloth pinned around her head to cover her face, the Queen knelt down upon the cushion and spoke aloud a Psalm in Latin as she laid her head upon the block. She quickly endured two strokes with the axe. The executioner then lifted her head to the view of all the assembly and stated in a loud voice: "God save the Queen" (Carey 1987, 136–138)

Eyewitness accounts say that there was absolute silence all over England and Scotland when Mary Queen of Scots was executed—even the people at the execution were silent. Everybody knew that she was innocent.

- **Quick Death:** Write a short paragraph describing why you support or oppose the death penalty.
- **Pair Share:** With a partner, make a list of all the possible reasons why people have been executed, and share this list with the class. As a class, make a larger list.
- **Free Verse:** Write a short poem describing the death of Mary, Queen of Scots.
- **Viewpoint #1:** As an English Catholic supporter of Mary, describe your feelings about her execution.
- **Viewpoint #2:** As an English Protestant supporter of Queen Elizabeth, describe your feelings about Mary's execution.
- **Viewpoint #3:** As James I, the next king of England, describe your feelings as your mother, Mary, is executed by your aunt, Queen Elizabeth I, for treason (under false pretenses).

- **Role Play:** As an important team of four lawyers (solicitors) during the reign of Elizabeth, write an opinion of Mary's trial for treason. She was arrested without any reason stated. She was given no lawyer. She was given no opportunity to defend herself. She was given no opportunity to appeal her death penalty. Your team must present a case either for or against her execution for treason.

4.5.4   Incan Medicine and Surgery

Before the invasion of the Americas by the Spaniards, the Incas could well have been among the best medical doctors in the world. They used a wide variety of plants and herbs for their medical practice—many of which are still used today in medicine, such as quinine. They also performed brain surgery, from which people survived and lived many years afterward. The Spanish, when they conquered Peru, viewed everything the traditional Inca did as evil, and they tried to stamp out traditional Incan medical practices. As a result, much of early Incan medicine was lost (Manley 1992, 47).

- **Quick List:** Make a list of all the plants you know that are used for medical purposes. Share this list with your class.
- **You Were There:** As the talk show host for the "You Were There" television show, interview the following guests on the subject of traditional Incan medicine. Be sure that each member of your studio audience has a minimum of three questions to ask our guests about traditional Incan medicine.
  Our Guests from Peru:
  1. De Las Vegas, a Spanish conqueror who thinks that only Europeans know anything about medicine
  2. Ignadio, a Spanish priest who thinks that the Incas are devil worshipers
  3. Qsquo, an Incan brain surgeon who has performed over 100 successful operations
  4. Atalqua, a traditional Incan herbal doctor whose vast knowledge of the use of medicinal plants has saved thousands of lives
- **Newspaper Editor:** As the editor of the *Renaissance Times* newspaper, write an editorial critical of the Spanish for rejecting Incan medical practices.

- **ADV Historical Analysis:** Using resources in your library and on the Internet, try to find out more on the loss of traditional Incan medicine after the Spanish conquest.

4.5.5   Pharmacy in 15th-century China

Li Shizhen (1518–1591) was perhaps the most famous medical doctor in China. During his lifetime, he compiled 11,000 prescriptions of different medical substances and the properties of each. His book is still used today by traditional doctors in China (Manley 1992, 43).

- **Quick Write:** Who is the most famous doctor you know? Write a short paragraph about this doctor and share it with your class.
- **List It:** With a partner in class, see how large a list of medicines you can make in a one-minute period. When finished, have each group of partners compare their lists for accuracy and see who has the most number of medicines.
- **ADV Historical Research:** Check your library or the Internet to see how much influence Chinese medicine has had on the development of Western medicine, and report your findings to the class.

4.5.6 Money, Money, Money

We all know and recognize paper money and gold, copper, and silver coins. What else can be used for money? One of the oldest currencies in the world is the cowry shell. Cowry shells come from the Maldive Islands in the Indian Ocean and the Philippine Islands, and have been used as units of currency throughout the world almost since the beginning of recorded history. Ancient Egyptian tombs contain cowry shells. Early Anglo-Saxon grave sites contained them. The earliest tombs in China, India, and the Middle East also contained cowry shells (Manley 1992, 88).

- **Quick List:** In one minute, make a list of all the different things that might be used for money, and share it with your class.
- **What If?** What if you did not have any money? What would you do? With a partner, discuss for one minute each of the different techniques you would use to acquire things you wanted without money. When finished, share your ideas with your class.

- **Create Money:** Money is defined as something with a trusted constant unit of value—something that people can trade, but know that it is always worth the same amount all the time. With a team of four, create a new type of money and then propose it to the class.
- **Map Attack:** On a blank map of the world and using an atlas, illustrate where cowry shells came from and how they must have traveled to reach ancient Egypt and ancient England thousands of years ago.
- **Why Cowries?** In groups of four, discuss the features of cowry shells that made them ideal international currency in ancient times—as well as in the Renaissance—in many places of the world.
- **ADV Other Money?** Research your library and the Internet to discover what other items have been used as money across the world and throughout history. When finished, report your findings to the class.
- **ADV The Futurist:** In a brief essay, speculate on what kind of money we can expect to see in the future.

4.5.7.   Elizabeth of York—The Queen of Hearts

Talk about a centerpiece of English history! You might not have heard about Elizabeth of York (1466–1503), but you will not forget her when you find out that she was the original Queen of Hearts in your handy deck of playing cards. The new game of card playing was sweeping across England and Europe in the late 15th century—everybody wanted to play cards, and Elizabeth of York was no exception. In honor of Elizabeth of York, her husband Henry VII standardized the deck of playing cards and proclaimed that she was the Queen of Hearts. Obviously, Henry VII loved his wife—together they had seven children, including a little red-haired guy who would later become King Henry VIII. Their marriage had also been the final seal that ended the War of the Roses between the Yorks—Elizabeth's family, and the Tudors—Henry's family. The next time you play a game of cards, look carefully at the Queen of Hearts, and you will see that she is holding a rose in her hands—a symbol of the end of the War of the Roses. Take a second look at the Queen of Hearts, and you will see that Elizabeth of York was also the fashion queen of her day with her gabled head dress and her fancy jeweled dress (Leon 1999).

Illustration 4.5.7. *Elizabeth of York, Queen of Hearts*

- **Quick Write:** As the Queen of Hearts, Elizabeth of York, write a quick thank-you note to your hubby, King Henry VII of England, thanking him for making you the Queen of Hearts.
- **Soap Opera:** With four other students, create a short one-page 15th-century English soap opera that tells the story of the end of the War of Roses, Elizabeth and Henry, and the Queen of Hearts. When finished, present your soap opera to the class.

- **Banner:** Create a banner for your class that either is in favor of or against Elizabeth of York becoming the Queen of Hearts. Be sure to be able to explain your reasons for your banner.
- **Rumper Sticker:** Write a snappy rumper sticker to go on the back of King Henry VII's horse to describe his Queen of Hearts.
- **ADV Henry VIII's Childhood:** As an Internet project, research the childhood of King Henry VIII, son of Henry VII and Elizabeth of York, and show how they influenced his growth into one of the most powerful kings in English history.

4.6.0 RELIGIOUS THOUGHT

4.6.1   The Renaissance Popes—Alexander VI and Leo X

Never was there such magnificent church art as that made during the Renaissance—and never was there more corruption, fraud, and worldliness in the Church as during the Renaissance. Rodrigo Borgia (1431–1501) and Giovanni de Medici (1475–1521) became true Renaissance popes. In 1492, Rodrigo became Pope Alexander VI and used the papacy as a position of power rather than religious leadership. He openly sold Church positions for money and bribed political and religious leaders for the political advantage of the Church. He openly recognized his mistresses and his two children—Caesar and Lucrezia. Popes were not supposed to have mistresses, wives, or children, but that did not seem to bother Alexander VI.

Giovanni became Pope Leo X in 1513. He was the son of Lorenzo de Medici; through his father's wealth and power, he became a church cardinal at the age of fourteen and a pope at the unheard of age of thirty-seven. Leo, like his father, loved art, music, and laughter. Under Leo, musicians played and jesters performed at Church functions. The Pope even played cards with the cardinals of the Church. But Leo was also an intellectual and supported the revival of ancient (non-Christians) Greek thought, such as that of Plato and Aristotle. The Vatican was obviously the best place to be to have a good time, but was this any way for the leader of the Christian Church to act (see Durant 1953, 404–440)?

- **Quick Write:** In a short paragraph describe how you think a major religious leader should act.

- **Quick Drama:** With a group of four students, create a short skit that dramatizes what the Church in Rome was like under Popes Alexander VI and Leo X.
- **You Were There:** As the host of the popular television program "You Were There," interview the following guests (students) on the topic of the Renaissance popes:
  1. Pietro, a pious Italian pilgrim who has come to the Vatican in Rome to be blessed by the pope
  2. Nicholi, a Catholic Renaissance priest who thinks that it is important for Christians to have a good time and enjoy the fruits that God has given us on Earth
  3. Johann, a German priest who thinks that it is sinful for Christians to have fun with earthly things such as art, music, and dance
  4. Lucrezia, daughter of Pope Alexander VI and firm believer that the Church should support art and the joy of living
- **ADV Research Question:** From a historical perspective, was it more important to have the Renaissance popes be major supporters of the great art works of Michelangelo and others in literature and music, or to continue the pious iconoclastic Christianity of the Middle Ages?

4.6.2   Revolt of the German Churches—1517

A minor German monk by the name of Martin Luther (1483–1546) made a pilgrimage to Rome to visit the Holy City of Pope Leo X—the Vatican (see 4.6.1 above). Rather than feeling holy, he was shocked by what he saw. The offerings he had been collecting from his poor worshipers in Germany were being used to build the largest church in the world, with expensive marble, solid gold statues, jewels, and magnificent paintings and frescos by Renaissance masters such as Michelangelo. He returned to Germany angry at what he saw. In his anger, in 1517, he nailed "Ninety-five Theses" on the door of his church at Wittenberg in Germany. These were ninety-five reforms he believed the Church in Rome should make in order to return to the simple Christianity he saw being practiced in the Bible. If left alone, Luther would certainly have been burned at the stake for heresy, but several princes from northern German states were tired of Roman rule and willingly hid and protected him.

- **Quick List:** With a partner in class, make a list of things that irritate you about your school and tape this list to your classroom door.
- **Historical Analysis:** From the reading above, list the major things that Luther did not like about the practices of the popes in Rome.
- **Rumper Sticker:** Create a Renaissance rumper sticker for horses supporting either the Renaissance popes or Martin Luther.
- **Poster Power:** Draw a picture of Martin Luther nailing his Ninety-five Theses on the church door in 1517.
- **ADV Historical Analysis:** Why are the Ninety-five Theses of Martin Luther one of the important turning points in world history? Research your library and the Internet for answers to this question. When finished, report your findings to the class.
- **ADV Venn Diagram:** Compare the Christianity of the early Middle Ages and the Christianity practiced by the Renaissance popes, noting the similarities and differences.
- **ADV Research Problem:** What were the major historical influences from the Middle Ages and earlier that influenced the Protestant rebellion of Luther and the northern German churches? Research your library and the Internet to find the answer to this question.

4.6.3   The Preliminary Conditions of the Reformation

Major revolutions do not happen in isolation. The field of any revolution is plowed before the seeds of revolution are planted. This is certainly true with the Reformation. Italy during the Middle Ages controlled the religion and much of the wealth of Europe. By 1517, this was rapidly changing (Durant 1957, 332–333).

1. People, not just the priests, were learning to read.
2. People started reading the Bible on their own.
3. People started to think on their own, and stopped listening to the priests.
4. People started reading the ancient non-Christian Greeks—Homer, Aristotle, and Plato—once again.
5. New ideas of science and mathematics from the Muslim intellectuals were being read.
6. New scientific ideas by Copernicus and others questioned the thinking of the Church.

7. Erasmus (1466–1536) and the other humanist thinkers were quietly and intellectually pushing the Church to reform.
8. The new printing press rapidly spread revolutionary ideas.
9. The rulers and priests in Germany were angry at seeing money earned in their states being sent to Rome to build rich palaces and churches.
10. The Muslims now controlled the eastern Mediterranean after the Crusades, cutting off Italy from the spices and silks of India and China.
11. The Portuguese now sailed directly to India around Africa, bypassing the Italian middlemen and thereby offering cheaper prices for spices and silks.
12. The northern German merchants now traded with the Portuguese, not the Italians.

- **Concept Web:** Using "Preconditions for the Reformation" as the center, map a concept web of the factors leading to the Reformation.
- **Mural Power:** Divide each of the preliminary conditions leading to the Reformation among the members of the class and have them illustrate and label their specific preliminary condition and present it to the class. These preliminary conditions can then be displayed along the classroom wall.
- **Map Attack:** On a blank map of the world, trace the changes in trade routes in 1517 that benefited the Portuguese and Germans but not the Italians.
- **ADV Essay:** Pull the major preconditions for the Reformation together and describe each precondition as a piece of wood feeding a fire—the fire of revolution.
- **ADV Research:** Compare the preconditions of the Reformation to other revolutions in history. How are they similar? How are they different? Use your library and the Internet to discover sources of information on this question.

4.6.4   The Success of the Protestant Revolt

Luther's key pronouncement (1520) was that every person had the right to interpret God and the Bible according to his own judgment. This concept of "free will" was a major change from the medieval

Catholic Church. Suddenly, everyone could read the Bible and make up his or her own mind about God. Luther translated the Bible into the language of the people—German. Other reformers did the same in other languages. Intellectuals such as Erasmus, and churchmen, even in Italy, read and watched Luther with great interest. The new invention of the printing press rapidly spread every pamphlet of Luther's across Europe. The princes of northern Europe and Germany quickly lined up behind Luther against the pope in Rome. As his success grew, Luther became more dogmatic and personal rather than just pushing for religious reform. He forgot his early pronouncement of "free will" and began to see his own views as superior to everyone else's—except for those of angels. His attacks against his opponents (Catholics and Jews) became even more vicious toward the end of his life. Although the political leaders of northern Europe stayed with Luther politically, many of his early supporters left him and stayed within the Catholic Church (Durant 1957, 420–437).

- **Quick Write:** Imagine you are a candidate for the United States Congress. How would you ensure that the people going to the polls would vote for you and continue to support you? Make a list of things you would do to guarantee your reelection, and share it with the class.
- **Pair Share:** With a partner, discuss the basic issue of the Reformation: Does an individual have the "free will" to have personal views about God, or does a religious leader such as the pope have the right to say how we should think about God? Share your pair's views with the class.
- **Political Analysis:** In teams of four, discuss how a political candidate can win an election: by stating radical views and stating what you think or by taking a more moderate position to gain more supporters? Share your team's views with the class.
- **ADV Research #1:** Could Luther have been more successful as a moderate in working to reform the whole Catholic Church (such as Erasmus tried), or did he reach his maximum success as the radical leader of the breakaway Protestant churches? Use sources in your library and on the Internet to find this information.
- **ADV Research #2:** Compare the results of other radicals and other moderates in history to see which ones have been more successful at bringing about needed change.

4.6.5   Erasmus (1466–1536) — The Middle Position

Erasmus — the rationalist of the Reformation — had openly called for Church reform in his book *In Praise of Folly* long before Luther. Luther read the works of Erasmus and used many of his thoughts in his Ninety-five Theses. Erasmus, in turn, strongly supported Luther's initial criticism of Church practices in 1517, but Erasmus was openly critical of Luther when he later changed to openly attack the Pope himself and the whole Church.

In a letter to Luther in 1519, Erasmus wrote:

> I confine myself to literature as far as I can, and keep aloof from other quarrels, but generally I think courtesy to opponents is more effective than violence. It might be wiser of you to denounce those who misuse the Pope's authority than to censure the Pope himself. So also with kings and princes. Old institutions cannot be rooted up in an instant. Quiet argument may do more than wholesale condemnation. Avoid all appearance of sedition. Keep cool. Do not hate anybody. Do not be excited over the noise you have made. (Durant 1957)

Luther rejected Erasmus as a weak Catholic and continued to directly attack the Pope. The Catholics, in turn, distrusted Erasmus and accused him of being a secret Lutheran. Erasmus wanted reason, not emotion, to rule. Afraid for his life — from both sides — Erasmus fled to Basel, Switzerland, where he could continue his intellectual life of the Renaissance. In Switzerland, he was safe from the bloodshed of the coming Thirty Years War fought between the Catholics and the Protestants (Durant 1957, 427–437).

- **Quick Write:** Describe in a short paragraph a time in your life when two friends were arguing, and you refused to take either side. In return, they were both angry with you.
- **Quick Draw:** Draw a picture of Erasmus struggling to maintain a reasonable neutral position in the fight between the Protestants and Catholics, and share it with your class.
- **Pair Share:** With a partner in class, discuss why you think Erasmus risked his life to steadily maintain a neutral position in the Reformation? When finished, share your ideas with the class.
- **ADV Historical Analysis:** Look through history to identify other individuals who worked hard to maintain neutral positions during major struggles or issues. What was the result of their struggles?

- **ADV Take a Stand:** Pick a major hot issue of today. Define both the pro and con positions of each side, and then describe a neutral position between both sides. Now decide which position you will take and describe why you have picked this position.
- **ADV Position Analysis:** Is it often harder to take a neutral position on some issues than to go along with the crowd and either support or attack something? Write a short position statement on this topic and share it with your class.

4.6.6   The Failed Compromise of Ratisbon in 1541

Pope Leo X and many of the popes after him did not understand Luther's Protestant Reformation. They thought it was just a religious quarrel between German monks, and they were more interested in the joyful delights of the Renaissance. The reality of the Reformation came home to the Church leaders when a large irregular army of German Protestants attacked and sacked Rome in 1527. Cardinals and leaders alike began to reform the excesses of the Renaissance popes and looked for ways to compromise with the Lutherans. Leading Protestants and Catholics met in 1541, in the town of Ratisbon in the Alps, to work out a compromise. They agreed to compromise on everything, except on the power of the Pope to change wine into the blood of Christ during communion—and the compromise failed. On this seemingly small point of theology, the Protestant and the Catholic churches permanently split and went their separate ways (Durant 1957, 921–933).

(Note from the future: The real struggle that Luther started in 1517 was not between the Renaissance and the Reformation. It was Luther's desire to return to the deep religious faith of the Middle Ages and his opposition to the still-developing Enlightenment, which focused on individual freedom, political rights, religious freedom, and scientific thought, and which would fully emerge after 1600.)

- **Quick Write:** Describe an instance in your life when you and a friend or family member failed to reach an agreement in an argument. What was the precise thing on which you disagreed? On reflection, could you now reach a compromise on this issue? Share your reflections with the class.
- **You Were There:** As the host of this popular TV talk show, conduct an imaginary interview of the Protestant and Catholic

theologians (students) who attended the Ratisbon Conference in 1541. Quiz them on why they failed to reach a compromise, which resulted in a divided Europe. Could these (student) theologians reach a compromise now?

- **ADV Research #1:** Examine the records of history for other conferences that failed to reach compromises and resulted in major fighting. Use the resources in your library and the Internet to research this topic.
- **ADV Research #2:** Using your library and the Internet, compare the clashes throughout history between the faithful of one religious belief and those who wish to have the freedom to reason and believe in their own ways.

4.7.0   CONQUEST AND WARFARE

4.7.1   Joan of Arc—The Strange Teenage General of France

Warfare during the Renaissance was rather strange, with bands of hired thugs (*condottieri*) fighting for whoever paid the most. Perhaps the strangest war during this period was the Hundred Years War (1337–1453), which, of course, did not last 100 years. Subtract the dates and you will come up with 116 years.

Even stranger was a young teenager during the Hundred Years War named Joan of Arc. Her actions during this strange war stirred the patriotic spirit in Frenchmen, and she (much later in history) became the symbol of France, with her own statue in Paris. Joan was a teenage girl who dressed in boys' clothes and heard voices from God. In most other instances, she would have been quickly locked up. She was, however, given the task of leading the French army during several battles during the Hundred Years War. She amazingly won a couple of battles, but then was captured and burned at the stake by the English for being a witch (Shenkman 1993, 49–50, 143–145).

- **Quick Write:** Make up your own story of a symbol or hero of your own imaginary country and share it with the class.
- **Historical Question:** With a partner in class, discuss why someone would call a war the Hundred Years War when it really lasted 116 years. When finished, share your ideas with the whole class. Are there other such misnamed wars and events in history?

- **Newspaper Reporter #1:** As the top reporter of the *Renaissance Times* newspaper, write up your recent (imaginary) interview with Joan of Arc for a front-page feature article and format it on a word processor.
- **Newspaper Reporter #2:** As the military analyst for the *Renaissance Times* newspaper, report on your (imaginary) interview with the French military general who picked Joan of Arc to lead his army.
- **Question from the Future:** What would happen today to a general who picked a young teenage girl to lead his army?

4.7.2   Agincourt (25 October 1415)— One of the Great Battles of All Time

Jehan de Wavrin, a French knight, gave his eyewitness account to one of the major battles of the Hundred Years War—Agincourt. Ten thousand English archers and knights under Henry V met 50,000 French knights in full armor. It rained all night in the narrow, boggy field of Agincourt. Two forward battle lines of English archers—armed with powerful long bows—rained arrows down on the tightly packed French knights mounted on horseback in full armor and banners. The fully armored French knights were so heavy that their horses quickly became mired in the mud and could not move. The English arrows continued to rain down on the French, wounding horses and knights alike, but they could not move forward into the English arrows or backward into the field of thousands of knights behind them. Out of arrows, the English forces advanced with axe and broadsword to kill or capture all the knights wounded or stuck in the mud. The rest of the French army fled the battlefield (Carey 1987, 68–76).

(Note from the future: The battle was one of the greatest in English history and became a battle cry for the English during wartime. Shakespeare's play *Henry V* and Sir Lawrence Olivier's World War II film *Henry V* focused on the Battle of Agincourt.)

- **Quick Write:** Describe a game your school has played in which everybody imagined that you would lose, but you really finally won. How do you feel?
- **Quick Skit:** In teams of four students each, write and dramatize a short skit of the Battle of Agincourt. Divide up the class and have

half of the teams create skits from the English point of view and the other half of the teams from the French point of view.

- **Art Mart:** Draw a picture of the Battle of Agincourt depicting the English long bowmen against the fully armored French knights on horseback.
- **Spectator:** As a spectator watching the epic Battle of Agincourt from a hidden spot in the woods, describe what you saw in a short article for the *Renaissance Times* newspaper.
- **ADV Historical Research:** Why do humans so often take such great pride in battles they have won and the great numbers of people they have killed?

4.7.3   The 130 Ships of the Spanish Armada (1588)

Philip II of Spain was fuming mad with Elizabeth I of England. He was Catholic and she was Protestant. She refused his proposal of marriage. Elizabeth's father, Henry VIII, never paid back the immense dowry when he divorced Philip's sister, Catherine of Aragon. Elizabeth had also just beheaded Mary, Queen of Scots—her cousin, a Catholic, and next in line to be queen of England. Philip's answer was to invade England. He gathered 130 ships from Portugal, Venice, and the Vatican to attack. Elizabeth had spies everywhere and knew long in advance of the Spanish plans. She gathered 197 ships under Sir Francis Drake and waited. The tall Portuguese galleons were slow, heavy, and did not sail well when going upwind. The prevailing winds blew south from England to Spain, making it very hard for the Portuguese galleons to reach England. After a few small clashes, Drake sent a flaming ship into the tightly packed Spanish fleet, scattering them. A large storm came up, pushing the Spanish fleet north to Scotland. Sailing around Scotland, many of these Mediterranean galleys—veterans of the Battle of Lepanto against the Turks—did not sail well in the rough seas of the open Atlantic and sank. Others crashed into Ireland, because the Spanish maps did not have the location of Ireland marked correctly on their maps. Most of the large, old Portuguese galleons, however, got home safely, and England proclaimed a great victory over the Spanish (Shenkman 1993, 119–122).

- **Quick Cheer:** As the leader of an English cheering squad, develop and present to your class a cheer for the English before the battle with the Spanish Armada.

- **Counter Cheer:** As the leader of a Spanish cheering squad, develop and present to your class a cheer for the Spanish after the battle of the English fleet (even though you did not do so well in the battle).
- **Map Attack:** On a blank map of Europe, mark the major movements of the Spanish Armada during its attempted invasion of England. Label your map to explain why the Spanish invasion was not successful.
- **History or Myth?** With a partner in class, discuss whether or not the English were correct to proclaim victory over the Spanish Armada—or did Mother Nature deserve the credit for stopping the invasion force? Explain your answer to the class when finished.
- **Eyewitness:** As an imaginary eyewitness to the battle with the Spanish Armada of 1588, write a description of the battle from your viewpoint and then share it with the class.
- **ADV Research:** Using your library and the Internet, find how many "great" battles in history were really won by one army getting lost, a giant storm interrupting the fighting, or a major accident taking place. Report your findings to the class.

4.8.0   TRAGEDY AND DISASTER

4.8.1   The Expulsion of the Jews and Muslims from Spain in 1492

The new Christian rulers expelled the Jews as well as the Muslims from Spain in 1492. An estimated 300,000 Jews were forced to leave Spain that year, although many remained as nominal Christians. Waves of Jewish expulsions swept Europe during the Middle Ages and the Renaissance; England in 1290 and France in 1394 are specific examples. Often, however, they were quickly invited back. Christians during the Middle Ages and Renaissance believed in the sin of usury, which was making money by charging interest. Jewish merchants and bankers had no such sin as usury. As a result, kings, nobles, and rich Christian merchants needed the Jewish bankers to handle their monetary transactions so that the Church would not punish them. Jewish bankers paid for Columbus's voyages to the New World in 1492, not the jewels of Ferdinand and Isabella. Many former Spanish Jews and Muslims were also quickly accepted by Muslim rulers in Morocco, Turkey, and Egypt, which led to a second Muslim-Jewish Renaissance in the Middle East (Manley 1992, 32).

- **Quick Write:** Imagine you were a Jew or a Muslim in 1492 being forced to leave your home and your country in Spain by Christian armies. Describe how you would feel. What would you do?
- **Ace Reporter:** As the hot-shot reporter for the *Renaissance Times* newspaper, write on-the-spot interviews of Muslims and Jews being forced out of Spain, and make them feature articles for the next edition of your paper.
- **Newspaper Editor:** As the editor of the *Renaissance Times* newspaper, write a critical editorial concerning the expulsion.
- **Quick Money:** *Usury*—making money by charging interest—was a sin for early Christians. With a partner in class, discuss what would happen to the banking system in the United States today if this were still a "sin" for Christians. Share your thoughts with the class when finished.
- **ADV Right On #1:** What human rights are violated when one set of people expels people from another ethnic group or religion from a country? What actions, if any, should be used to prevent such actions in the future?
- **ADV Right On #2:** What human rights are violated when one set of people stops people from another ethnic group or religion from entering a country? What actions, if any, should be used to prevent such actions in the future?

4.8.2   Why Did the Mayan Civilization Collapse So Quickly?

The estimated population of the classical Maya Civilization in 800 CE was a staggering eight to ten million. Without a question, it was one of the most advanced and largest ancient civilizations in the world, but something happened in 700 CE to change all that. A massive 200-year drought covered most of southern Mexico and Central America. The lush tropical rain forests of the region could support all the people if there was enough rain. Without moisture, however, the poor soil of the rain forests simply collapsed and could grow very little food. The many Mayan city states such as Copan, Palenque, and Tikal fought viciously to control the diminishing food supplies. Millions of Mayans died not only from warfare but from simple starvation. The magnificent stone temples, pyramids, and cities of the Maya simply were abandoned and were taken over by the rain forests. Post-classical Mayan cities (1000–1600 CE), after the drought, created many beautiful symbols of Mayan civilization, as Chichen Itza and Uxmal, but they did not have the full splendor of the early Maya cities. Thank goodness, the Mayan people are still with us in southern Mexico, but their powerful city-states with major temples, pyramids, and governments are only something to be remembered in history. Why did such a people with very advanced thinking in mathematics and astronomy disappear? Mayan archaeologists today do not fully know why. The Mayan city-states were constantly at war with each other near the end—that is one clue. Another clue is that the tropical rain forest soils, as in all of Central America, are not very fertile. The success of the Mayan civilization could have been the cause of its decline. An educated guess might be that too many people trying to farm poor soil led to fighting between cities over new land, overcrowding, and the eventual decline of the Mayans (Fagan 1999).

- **Quick Write:** Describe what happens to a herd of animals when there is too little food and too many animals. Describe several actions that could be used to prevent this situation.
- **Poster Power:** Make a poster depicting the struggle of the last years of the Mayan civilization. Label the different images in your poster and share it with your class.
- **Bumper Sticker:** Create a Mayan bumper sticker promoting efforts to save the Mayan civilization.
- **Map Attack:** Research in the library and on the Internet the location of the major ancient Mayan city-states in Central America; using a map of the area, present your findings to the class.
- **ADV Future Research:** What problems will the world face if the food supply decreases and the population increases? What actions can be taken to delay or prevent such a tragedy?

4.8.3   Genocide of the Native Populations of the Americas

The eyewitness descriptions of the Spanish atrocities against the native Americans in the Caribbean Sea by the Dominican missionary Bartolomé de las Casas curdle the blood:

The Spaniards with their horses, spears, and lances began to commit murders and strange cruelties as they entered into the towns and villages, sparing neither children nor old men nor women with child. They taught their fierce dogs to tear them to pieces at first view. In my presence without cause I saw three thousand souls—men, women and children—put to the edge of the sword without cause what so ever. I saw there such great cruelties, that never any man living either have or shall see the like. (Carey 1987, 82–84)

The Spaniards also carried the deadly disease of smallpox to the Americas and effectively wiped out most of the native population of the Caribbean islands and the Americas. A major factor in the success of the Spanish conquests of the Aztecs in Mexico and Incas in Peru was smallpox. The Spanish attacked both peoples during raging epidemics of smallpox, which left these American empires powerless to stop the small Spanish armies. The combined Spanish atrocities and epidemics of European diseases rapidly wiped out most of the native peoples of the Caribbean and the Americas. The estimated population of Mexico in 1500 was 25 million; by 1600, the native population of Mexico was one million people (McNeil 1977, 183–190).

- **Quick Write:** Describe what happens when someone in your family gets a bad cold or the flu. Imagine in a short paragraph what would happen if this were a major unknown disease that was killing people across the nation.
- **You Were There:** As the host of this popular TV show, interview the following eyewitnesses (students in costume) to the Spanish conquest of the Americas:
    1. Atahulpa, the Inca Emperor who died of small pox during the Spanish conquest
    2. Montezuma II, the Aztec emperor who was stabbed to death by the Spanish during the Spanish attack
    3. Pizzaro, the leader of the Spanish attack against the Incas
    4. Cortez, the leader of the Spanish conquest of Mexico
    5. Malenche, the young native woman who aided Cortez by serving as his translator and spy against the Aztecs
- **ADV Today #1:** For class discussion, if a group, like the Spanish in 1519, attempted to kill such a large number of people today, what actions could be taken by the rest of the world to stop such inhumanity?
- **ADV Today #2:** For class discussion, should the United States and other countries in the world have the right to develop and use specially designed weapons, such as deadly diseases, to kill people? What can be done to prevent this from happening?

4.8.4   The Dreaded Spanish Inquisition

In 1622, William Lithgow, an Englishman, was brought before the Inquisition in Spain and charged with heresy against the Church. In order to force a confession from him, he was placed on the dreaded rack and tortured. Amazingly, he survived the ordeal and later wrote a description of his experience.

> I was brought to the rack, then mounted on the top of it. My legs were drawn through the two sides of the three-planked rack. A chord was tied about my ankles. As the levers bent forward, the main force of my knees against the two planks burst asunder the sinews of my hams, and the lids of my knees were crushed. My eyes began to startle, my mouth to foam and froth, and my teeth to chatter like the doubling of a drummer's sticks. My lips were shivering, my groans were vehement, and blood sprang from my arms, broken sinews, hands and knees. Being loosened from these pinnacles of pain, I was hand-fast set on the floor, with this incessant importation: "Confess! Confess!" (Bronowski 1973)

- **Quick Write:** Why do some people in power—now and throughout history—think they have the authority to torture people? Write a short paragraph on your views of this question.
- **Poster Power:** Create a poster that illustrates your views on the use by governments of human torture both in the Inquisition and today.
- **Pro and Con:** In teams of four, discuss the problem of a historical organization such as the Church that wants to make sure its members follow an established set of beliefs. Is it better for such an organization to force members to follow a set range of beliefs, or is it better for the organization to convince members by reasonable argument to follow a set of beliefs? Each team should then present its views to the class for full discussion.
- **ADV Action Research:** Student teams of four members each should contact Amnesty International for information concerning governments and organizations that are still torturing people today, and then report to the class on what they find.
- **ADV Historical Research:** Using the library and the Internet, research the history of the Inquisition of the Catholic Church, and find out the opinion of the Church today regarding this dark page in its history. Be sure to report your findings to the class.

4.9.0 EXPLORATION AND DISCOVERY

4.9.1 Why Not the Vikings?

Why did the Vikings not get credit for discovering America? In 986 CE, a Norwegian, Bijarni Herjolfsson, mistakenly sailed past Greenland and landed in modern-day Labrador, in Canada. In 1000 CE, Leif Eriksson took Herjolfsson's boat farther south to Newfoundland, where the Vikings later founded a settlement at L'Anse-aux-Meadows in what the Vikings called Vineland because of all the grapes growing there. The site was excavated by Icelandic archaeologists between 1960 and 1964, and their findings are available for viewing today. These discoveries of America were a full 500 years before Columbus. Why did the Vikings not get credit for these discoveries?

The answer is simple: communication. The Vikings of 1000 did not know how to read or write, and were not on very friendly terms with the rest of Europe. Viking ships were constantly attacking the communities of Europe along the coast. Western Europe had no strong governments. The only strong states at the time were the Byzantine Empire in modern Turkey and the Islamic Empire in Baghdad, and these two powerful states were more interested in the Silk Road to the east and certainly had no interest in lands to the west of Greenland (Manley 1992, 62).

- **Quick Discovery:** If you were the first to discover something new in science or in space, how would you advertise it to the world?
- **Poster Power:** Make a poster illustrating the Viking discovery of North America.
- **Bumper Sticker:** Make a bumper sticker celebrating the Viking discovery of America.
- **Madison Avenue:** As the top four salespeople (students) of the Viking Advertising Company, develop a hot ad campaign to promote the Viking discovery and downplay Columbus with jingles, thirty-second prime-time TV ads, and a junk mail blitz. When finished, present your ad campaign to your class for their approval.
- **ADV Historical Analysis:** Compare the reasons why the world knew little, if anything, about the Viking discoveries, yet knew within a year the discoveries of Columbus in 1492.

4.9.2   Zeng He (Cheng Ho)—The Great Chinese Explorer (1405–1433)

Between 1405 and 1433, the Chinese emperor's grand eunuch Cheng Ho (Zeng He) conducted major explorations by sea to the east across the Indian Ocean. His great fleet of ships contained giant five-masted sailboats over 426 feet (130 meters) in length, with as many as five decks. (All three of Columbus's little caravels could have fit on the deck of one of Cheng Ho's junks.) The purpose of Cheng Ho's explorations was to demonstrate China's greatness to the world. Wherever Cheng Ho visited, if the local ruler proclaimed China was the greatest nation in the world, Cheng Ho would then shower the ruler with gifts. The great fleets of Cheng Ho sailed to India and then later down the eastern coast of Africa to modern Mozambique. In 1433, the isolationists came to power in China and retreated behind the great Chinese wall. They strongly opposed Chinese ships going out to contact strange foreigners. Following a seemingly regular theme in Chinese history, this giant nation retreated once again into isolation. They kept Cheng Ho at home and destroyed his great ships (Boorstin 1983).

- **Quick Map:** On a blank map of the world, trace the route Cheng Ho's Chinese junks traveled in 1433 to "discover" India and East Africa, and then trace the route of Columbus's trip to the "New World" in 1492.
- **Map Attack:** Measure the length of Cheng Ho's voyage of discovery versus Columbus's voyage of discovery. Which is greater in length?
- **Pair Share:** Discuss with your partner why Columbus is mentioned in every world history textbook and Cheng Ho mentioned in very few textbooks. Share your pair's views with the class.
- **Historical Importance:** In terms of historical change, which voyage was the more important, that of Columbus or that of Cheng Ho? Support your conclusion in a short essay and present it to your class for comments.
- **How Come?** In a Pair Share, and then in a full class discussion, examine why the European explorers began their expeditions in search of gold and the Chinese began their expedition in search of new countries to whom they could give gifts of gold and silks.
- **ADV What if?** In 1433, the fleets of Cheng Ho had already been down the east coast of Africa and might have rounded the Cape

of Good Hope at the tip of South Africa and sailed into the Atlantic Ocean. Perhaps they even sailed to America in 1428. What if the Chinese had continued to sail up the west coast of Africa and "discovered" Europe? Hypothesize how that would have changed history.

- **ADV Research into the Future:** Chinese history is full of cautious contacts with the rest of the world and then rapid reversals to full isolation from the world. The Great Wall, the burning of Cheng Ho's ships, and other such isolationist cycles are a major theme in Chinese history. Use resources in your library and on the Internet to explore this major theme in Chinese history and report your findings to your class (Boorstin 1983).

4.9.3   Why Was Prince Henry of Portugal So Important?

The Portuguese were different from the Spanish. While Spain looked to Italy and the Renaissance, Portugal looked to the Atlantic Ocean with England to the north, and Africa to the south. While Spain supported Columbus on a lucky whim, Portugal carefully planned its explorations, step by step, for more than 100 years. Portugal also had the ideal man for explorations—Prince Henry the Navigator. He liked the intellectual excitement of exploration, and opened his own school of exploration at Sagres, on the southernmost tip of Portugal, shortly after 1415. Mapmakers, navigators, and shipbuilders all came to Sagres to study with Prince Henry. He designed a special ship for exploration—the caravel. It was small, fast, and able to sail tight to the wind with lateen sails. Prince Henry and the Portuguese also did not have the ethnic prejudices of the Spanish. Prince Henry's father was Portuguese and his mother was English. He borrowed much of his caravel's design and sails from the Arabs. His main navigators were Arab and his main mapmakers were Jewish.

His main interest was the coast of Africa. When his ships started to explore down the coast, he did not know that it would become the route to India. The Atlantic coastline of Africa was unknown past Cape Bojador and looked exciting. He sent ships to explore it, and suddenly the world became a larger place (Boorstin 1983, 156–164).

- **Quick Write:** If you want a new fresh idea, whom do you turn to among your friends? Why do you turn to this friend for new ideas?

- **T Chart:** Compare the differences between the Portuguese and the Spanish. How did these differences affect the explorations of these two countries?
- **Map Attack:** On a large map of Africa, find Cape Bojador (off the Western Sahara and south of the Canary Islands), which was the limit of Europe's knowledge of Africa in 1415. On a blank map of Africa, write "unknown" on Africa south of Bojador. On your map, draw in mythological dragons to depict the "unknown" south of Bojador, much as mapmakers did before Prince Henry. Now imagine what may lie beyond the Cape and share your ideas with your class.
- **Letter Writer:** As an imaginary visitor to Prince Henry's school of navigation, write a letter to a friend describing the excitement of the place.
- **ADV Historical Research:** New discoveries and explorations do not happen by accident; someone has the initial ideas to look for something new. Look back in history in your library and on the Internet to find other such people who had new ideas and led the way for further explorations.

4.9.4   Columbus—Who Was He?

We all know the story of the poor weaver's son from Italy who got the support of the queen of Spain to discover America. It makes a great "poor boy makes good" story—almost mythological—but is it true? Let's look at some recent questions about Columbus to see if the story holds up.

1. We know that Columbus easily and regularly had access to the royal courts of Portugal and Spain, but 15th-century Europe had a very tight class society. Royalty and commoners (especially weavers) did not mix. Was Columbus really a poor commoner, or was he secretly a member of the nobility?
2. Columbus spoke fluently in Spanish and Portuguese, and wrote in an interesting mixture of Portuguese and Spanish, but never in Italian. Was he really Italian?
3. The best navigators of the era attended Prince Henry's navigation school at Sagres in Portugal. Columbus was obviously very good at navigation. Did he secretly attend the school? Only Portuguese navigators attended.

4. Columbus told King Ferdinand and Queen Isabella of Spain that his request for support had been turned down by King John II of Portugal. If so, why did he sail directly to Lisbon and report to the king of Portugal after his first voyage—before he sailed back to Spain?

Columbus remains a mystery. Was he really who he says he was? Barreto (1992) thinks that Columbus was a secret agent of the Portuguese, who was used to send the Spanish off in another direction—west—and away from Portugal's recently discovered (1486–1487) route to India around Africa. No one realized, however, that there were two unknown continents out west, and Columbus accidentally tripped over them on his way to China. What is the real story about Columbus? We do not know. The truth is out there for us to discover.

(Be sure also to see Pahl, *Creative Ways to Teach the Mysteries of History, Volume I,* for more great lessons on the mysterious explorer we call Columbus.)

- **Quick Write:** In a short paragraph, describe the story you heard about Columbus in grade school.
- **T Chart:** Compare the story of Columbus described in a textbook with the story described above. Which sounds more realistic to you? Why?
- **Write a Letter:** Imagine you lived in 1492 and are really excited by Columbus's recent discovery. Write a letter to him. What would you say? What would you ask him?
- **ADV Research:** Read three different articles about Columbus from the Internet or library and report to the class about your findings.

4.9.5 Why Did Columbus Become So Famous?

What did Columbus do that made him so famous? Answer: His discovery of America was one of the major change points in world history. He had a crazy idea that he could sail west directly to China and India. People laughed at him and called him crazy, but he stuck to his idea. He finally got support from Spain to try it out in three little ships, but he really failed in what he wanted to do. He thought he was in China or India, and did not realize he was in the Americas. But wow, for an accident, it was a real discovery! Gold, lots of new foods, lots of new animals, and lots of different people. It opened peoples' eyes and made them realize the world was very different from what they had been taught. It was also the world's first media event. The printing press had just been invented, and some of the first news printed was that of Columbus's discoveries. News of Columbus was quickly printed in almost every major European language. For the first time in history, people were excited about something in print, and they could not wait for more to come. He had the P.R. (public relations) machine that the Vikings never had.

- **Quick Write:** Do you think that people who have a different but very interesting idea should stick with it, or listen to people around them who make fun of it?
- **Diary Entry:** Imagine you are one of the first people in the world to read that Columbus just discovered that you can sail west to reach India and China. How do you feel? What does it mean to you? Write in your diary what his trip meant to you.
- **Stern Sticker:** Make a stern sticker to stick on the backside of the *Nina*—the flagship of Columbus—to show what you think about Columbus.
- **Hot Off the Press:** Make an imaginary mock-up of the first printed sheet announcing Columbus's new discoveries and share it with your class.
- **What If?** What if Columbus never made it to America? Do you think someone else would have found it? Discuss this issue in a Pair Share and then in a full class plenary session.
- **ADV Research:** How much luck and how much skill enabled Columbus to accidentally discover the Americas? Use your library and the Internet to research this question, and report your findings to the class.

4.9.6   How Did Vasco da Gama Change the World in 1497?

A young twenty-eight-year-old sailor from Portugal by the name of Vasco da Gama (1469?–1524) made an extraordinary voyage in 1497. Da Gama's trip, however, was not an accidental discovery, such as that by Columbus. For most of the 15th century, the Portuguese had slowly and carefully been exploring down the west coast of Africa. The key discovery that enabled da Gama to sail to India was the rounding of the

Cape of Good Hope (the southern end of Africa) by Bartholomew Diaz in 1486–1487. The Portuguese were quite excited by the discovery by Diaz. They now knew that they could sail around Africa by ship to reach the rich spices of India and avoid the Arab middlemen. Da Gama's trip was also successful because his was the first voyage of exploration to really understand that the world was round and to take advantage of the circular ocean currents. To do so, he was the first to fully use the counterclockwise ocean currents of the south Atlantic. From Portugal, he traveled southwest across the Atlantic and the equator along the coast of Brazil, and then followed the currents back to the east across the south Atlantic to the Cape of Good Hope. Sailing up the east coast of Africa to Malindi (in modern Kenya), he hired a Muslim geographer to take him to Calicut (modern Kozhikose) in India. Again following the currents, da Gama returned to Portugal a rich man with a boatload of pepper and spices from India. In one trip to India, the Portuguese had learned the basic round shape of the world, the shape of its major continents, and the direction of the world's major ocean currents. This one trip by a young Portuguese sailor ended the domination of the Italian city-states, such as Venice, over the trade between Europe and Asia. The monetary advantage enjoyed by Italy—that had paid for much of the glories of the Renaissance—was now gone (Boorstin 1983, 172–177).

- **Quick Write:** Think of one small thing you did that really changed your life, and describe it to the class.
- **Map Attack #1:** On a blank map of the world, trace the route of da Gama from Portugal to India and back. Be sure to remember the counterclockwise ocean currents that da Gama followed in the south Atlantic.
- **Map Attack #2:** After plotting da Gama's route from Portugal to India and back, calculate the length of the trip in miles and kilometers, and then estimate how long the voyage took if his ship traveled approximately 150 miles a day.
- **Poster Power:** Make a poster to illustrate the immense impact da Gama's voyage had on Europe and the rest of the world in 1498.
- **Music Mart:** With a partner, write a short song, poem, or rap about da Gama's voyage to India and perform it for your class.
- **Diary Entry:** As a sailor for da Gama on his voyage to India, make a diary entry describing what it was like to be the first to sail from Europe to India and back.

- **ADV Historical Comparison:** Use information on the Internet or your library to compare the voyage of da Gama with the voyage of Columbus. Which was longer? Which had more immediate economic impact? Which had a longer-range impact?

4.9.7   Was Magellan the First Around the World?

The Portuguese navigator Magellan (1480–1541) started his around-the-world expedition from Spain in 1519, with five ships and 270 men. They sailed down the east coast of South America, through the Straits of Magellan, and into the Pacific. They crossed the Pacific. In Malaysia, Magellan died in a small, silly battle in 1521. Juan del Cano (d. 1526), who chronicled the voyage, continued to sail west across the Indian Ocean, then around Africa, and somehow made it back to Spain in 1522, with one battered ship and twenty starving men. This was certainly one of the most amazing trips human beings have ever taken, but the question remains: Who was the first to go around the world? Del Cano—because he completed the trip back to Spain? Or, Magellan because he had already been in Malaysia on another trip? And do not forget Enrique, Magellan's Malaysian slave who had gone around the world with Magellan and stayed in Malaysia when Magellan died (Manley 1992, 64).

- **Quick Write:** Imagine traveling on a voyage with your friends, and you were one of the only who returned alive. Describe your feelings in a short paragraph.
- **Map Attack:** On a blank map of the world, trace the amazing voyage of Magellan.
- **Ace Reporter:** As the ace reporter of the *Renaissance Times* newspaper, you are on the scene when Del Cano brings his ship into port after returning from around the world. Describe the scene and Del Cano's first impressions of the trip. With your editorial team, make a bold front-page edition of this late-breaking event.
- **Chart It:** On a chart, compare the expeditions of Columbus, da Gama, and Magellan. Based on your comparison, which was the most important?
- **ADV Research:** Find out from the Internet or your library how sailors managed to survive on early sailing explorations such as Magellan's. What did they eat when their regular food gave out or became rotten?

4.10.0 INVENTION AND REVOLUTION

4.10.1 Why Was Copernicus (1473–1543) Not Burned at the Stake?

The medieval Christian Church believed that the Earth was the center of the universe because humans (God's creations) lived on Earth. To say that it was not true was heresy and a sin, punishable by being burned at the stake. Copernicus, a Polish churchman, discovered that the sun, not the Earth, was the center of our solar system—contrary to the teachings of the Church. For fear of being burned at the stake, Copernicus did not publish his findings until 1473—the year of his death. True to his fears, both the Catholic and Protestant churches condemned his findings as heresy. Even Martin Luther was bitterly opposed to these new radical ideas of Copernicus. "Such crazy ideas will turn the world upside down," said Luther. In a way, Luther was right; the discoveries of Copernicus completely changed how humans viewed planet Earth. The Church, however, was not ready for such new ideas. Copernicus was declared a heretic, and his books were burned; luckily for Copernicus, he died before his book was published (Boorstin 1983).

- **Quick Think:** Watch the sun, the moon, and the stars as they move across the sky. Make an argument from your direct observations that the Earth, not the sun, is the center of the universe.
- **What If?** In a Pair Share, discuss this topic with a partner: If you made such a gigantic discovery, such as Copernicus had, that was so much against the teachings of the Church, would you hide what you learned, or would you tell everybody of your new discovery and be willing to die for what you found?
- **Art Mart:** Make a drawing or a painting that illustrates the great conceptual change of planet Earth that Copernicus made for human beings.
- **Quick Skit:** With a team of four students, create a short drama that illustrates the conflict Copernicus faced with the Catholic and Protestant churches of his day.
- **ADV Research:** Using your library and the Internet, examine why both Protestants and Catholics—bitter enemies during the Reformation—declared that Copernicus's findings were heresy and had his books burned. Also find out who—if anybody—had the courage to support Copernicus during this period.

- **ADV The Futurist:** Using resources in your library and on the Internet, research how the Church finally came to accept the discoveries of Copernicus.

4.10.2   Was the Printing Press the World's Greatest Invention?

Was the invention of the printing press one of the greatest inventions of any age? The art of paper-making came into Europe during the Middle Ages from the Muslims in Spain. The art of printing with blocks was invented in China, but the written Chinese language (with more than 50,000 separate characters) was impractical for an early printing press. The invention of carving separate letters and words of a language on moveable blocks, covering them with ink, and then printing them on paper was an invention by Laurens Janszoon Coster (circa 1370–1450) in the Netherlands in 1440. About 1455, after Coster's death, Johann Gutenberg (circa 1397–1468) printed the first Bible and made Coster's invention famous. Suddenly, the written language was easy to read, cheap, and easy to duplicate. It created one of the major revolutions in the history of the world (Manley 1992, 103).

(Note from the future: The Vikings did not have a printing press—in fact, they did not even know how to read or write. As a result, the rest of the world did not notice the Viking discovery of America circa 1000 CE. In 1492, after Columbus rediscovered America, the printing press was ready and waiting for him. Within two years after his return, Columbus's description of the New World had been printed in almost every major European language by more than 100 different presses. Due to the printing press, everyone in Europe knew very quickly about Columbus. No one ever heard of Leif Eriksson. The same is true of the Reformation in 1519. Luther's proclamations against the Church in Rome were very quickly printed and spread across modern Germany. Without the printing press, Luther's Reformation of the Church likely would not have succeeded. It is also an irony that great Muslim scholars of the Middle East were not able to convert the beautiful structure of written Arabic into a typeface for printing for several hundred years later [Boorstin 1983, 510–516].)

- **Quick Print:** Cut thirteen potatoes in half and, in the open halves, carve the letters of the alphabet. Cover each of these potato letters with tempera paint and then press them onto a piece of paper, forming a letter to a friend.

- **Medieval Copyist:** One of the major jobs of monks during the Middle Ages was copying Bibles, the Koran, and other religious books by hand. A time warp suddenly crosses your classroom and everyone in the class is in a monastery during the Middle Ages. There are no printing presses. Everything we want to have must be copied by hand. Every student monk is to be assigned one paragraph (not too long) to be copied in neat printed letters so the people of the next generation can read it. When finished, now imagine copying an entire Bible by candlelight. What did the invention of the printing press do to the written word?
- **Poster Power:** Create a poster that illustrates the importance of the printing press to world history.
- **ADV Imagine:** What if the printing press had never been invented? What would our life be like today? What inventions based on the printing press would never have taken place? What would education be like today without the printing press?

4.10.3   Airplanes in the Renaissance

Airplanes are not 20th-century inventions. Leonardo da Vinci was flying cardboard models of airplanes and helicopters in 1500. Endlessly watching the graceful ravens taking off and landing near his castle window, Leonardo carefully designed and flew cardboard gliders that copied the graceful aerodynamic shapes of ravens' wings. With wind-up screw motors, he also designed and flew the first cardboard helicopters. What he did not design, however, was a means of designing a human-powered airplane. He worked endlessly on plans for a human to fly by flapping his airplane's wings, but it never worked. The Renaissance in which Leonardo lived was still dominated by a very powerful Church that did not like new ideas. As a result, Leonardo wrote all his plans for airplanes and helicopters backward, in mirror writing, so that no one would accuse him of witchcraft (Manley 1992, 103).

- **Paper Airplane:** Make a paper airplane and then measure how far it flies.
- **Design Comparison:** How many different paper airplane designs are known by members of your class?

- **Test Pilot:** Test out different paper airplane designs to see which one flies the farthest. Which one can stay in the air the longest? Which one can fly in circles? Which one can fly in loops?
- **Aerodynamic Design:** Discuss in teams of four and then the whole class the aerodynamics of each paper airplane. What makes each fly and do different tricks? Why does one paper airplane fly farther than the others? Why is one paper airplane design better than the other?
- **Bird Watching:** Watch the graceful flight of a large bird like a crow, a hawk, or seagull near your home and school, like Leonardo did. What do you notice about the bird's flight that makes it take off and land so easily?
- **Bird Landing:** Make a drawing of a bird's wings and tail when it is landing, and describe why you think the bird does this.
- **Role Play:** Imagine you are Leonardo da Vinci (500 years ago) watching ravens in the sky and making the world's first paper airplanes. Describe your discoveries in an essay and then read it to the class.
- **ADV Research:** Using the resources in your library and on the Internet, examine the basic principles of aerodynamics for modern airplanes and compare them to the fundamental discoveries of Leonardo in 1500.

4.11.0   ART AND CREATIVE THOUGHT

4.11.1   Why Was Petrarch the Father of the Renaissance?

Francesco ("Petrarch") Petracco (1304–1375) is acknowledged as one of the fathers of the Renaissance. Writing in exile from Avignon, the native Florentine became the rage of all Italy with his expressions of pure love and the love of Nature in the Italian language. He wrote imaginary letters to the great Greek and Roman writers—Homer, Cicero, and Livy. In so doing, he alone revived an interest in the classical world. Rather than extol the virtue of faith in the Church, he cherished the simple personal pleasures of love, watching Nature, and even climbing mountains—just for the joy of doing pleasurable things. With Petrarch, suddenly, an individual's feelings, emotions, and pleasures were important. With his concern for individual pleasures and not religious doctrine of faith, Petrarch certainly became one of the major fathers of the Renaissance (Durant 1953).

- **Quick Write:** Describe a scene from Nature you enjoy and why you enjoy it.
- **Quick Poem:** Describe this simple natural pleasure of yours in a short poem à la Petrarch.
- **Ace Reporter:** As the ace reporter for the *Renaissance Times* newspaper, develop a list of questions to ask Petrarch in an interview. With a partner, develop a set of answers you think Petrarch might say to your questions, and then present your interview to the class.
- **ADV Literary Research:** Research the Internet or your library for something by Petrarch, read it, and then share your impressions of it in class.

4.11.2   Want a Good Laugh from the Middle Ages? Read Chaucer's *Canterbury Tales*!

Geoffrey Chaucer (1340?–1400) wrote a very funny set of poetic stories in English, called *The Canterbury Tales*, between 1386 and 1399. The Middle Ages were really not a very fun time. There was one exception: religious pilgrimages. These pilgrimages were not really meant to be fun, but people traveling together toward holy sites sang, told funny stories, met interesting people, and basically had a good time. In reality, religious pilgrimages became the tourist industry of the Middle Ages. As did Boccaccio, Chaucer wrote one of the first human comedies since the classical period of ancient Greece and Rome. Chaucer's thirty pilgrims were all sorts of people—such as a knight, a nun, a clerk, a man of law, and a miller's wife. Each told funny tales, each had a moral, and all were quite entertaining. *The Canterbury Tales* was one of England's first steps toward the Renaissance.

- **Quick Write:** Write down a funny story you recently heard, and share it with your class.
- **Ad Campaign:** Put together an ad campaign to sell *The Canterbury Tales* on the open market with an ad poster and a thirty-second TV spot.
- **ADV Quick Publish:** Compare the stories that members of your class have told. If your collected stories are good enough, print

them together and sell them to other students as a class project to earn money for a class party.

4.11.3   Black Plague and Human Comedy — 1348

Giovanni Boccaccio (1313–1375) thankfully survived the Black Plague that struck Florence and killed half of its population in 1348. His famous comedy *Decameron* is based on this attack of the Black Plague, and with it, Boccaccio became the first writer of the Renaissance. There are no morals or religious teachings in Boccaccio's *Decameron*. These are only 100 tales told by seven young ladies and three young men who have come together to escape the plague. The stories are of love, courage, cowardice, humor, wisdom, deceit, and foolishness. Boccaccio's tales are the first book in the world of modern short stories. One story is of Ghismunda, who falls in love with her father's valet. The father disapproves of someone so lowly for his daughter and kills his valet. To console his daughter, the father gives her a solid gold goblet containing the valet's heart. In the final scene, she puts poison in the goblet and tells her father: "Will you say I consorted with a man of low condition? Poverty does not diminish anyone's ability, it only diminishes his wealth! Many kings and great rulers were once poor, and many of those who plow the land and watch the sheep were once very rich, and they still are." She then drinks the poison to be reunited with her lover's heart (Boorstin 1992, 266–275).

- **Quick Disaster:** Imagine you are caught in a major disaster in which thousands of people die. You and your friends seriously think the world is about to come to an end. To take your minds off the disaster, write down several things you would talk about to other surviving friends. Would it be something sad, funny, or serious?
- **Ace Reporter:** As the ace reporter of the *Renaissance Times* newspaper, give an eyewitness account of the Black Plague as it hits Florence in 1348. With your editorial team (groups of four students), develop a front-page edition focusing on the plague and people's reactions to it (McNeill 1977).
- **Writer's Corner:** In Boccaccio's style, write a short story with a twist or two in its plot about love, anger, fear, joy, or lying. Share your short Boccaccio-style story with your class.

- **Music Mart:** Make up a funny song with a partner about the Black Plague—something Boccaccio would like—and share it with your class.
- **ADV Literary Research:** Using the Internet and your library, determine how many great pieces of literature were written in times of crisis? Why does this happen?

4.11.4   Brunelleschi's Dome

Filippo Brunelleschi (1377–1446) and his buddy, the sculptor Donatello (1389?–1466), were fanatics about ancient Rome. They drew and measured almost every ruin they could find in ancient Rome. The result was a Florentine architect who understood and who could, once again, create buildings that paralleled the grandeur of the Pantheon in ancient Rome. Florence had begun its cathedral in 1296, and it was to be the grandest in Europe, with a dome 138.5 feet across. The difficulty was that no one since the ancient Romans knew how to build such a large dome. In 1425, Brunelleschi got the final contract to complete the dome, using an ingenious trick that is still used by architects today. He used a tall outer dome to give the cathedral height and then a false inner dome, which would look more full to the viewers inside the cathedral. The two domes together strengthened each other and the whole structure. To make the outer dome stronger, he made it into an octagon similar to a Gothic church from the Middle Ages, but it was a true dome and the largest built since ancient Rome, more than 1,200 years before. Brunelleschi's dome in Florence represented the full expression of the Renaissance in Italy—a rebirth of the grandeur of ancient Greece and Rome (see Symcox 1991).

(Note from the future: This same double dome was used in building other giant domes, such as that of St. Paul's Cathedral in London and the dome of the Capitol Building in Washington, D.C. Both used Brunelleschi's design as a model [Boorstin 1992, 384–391].)

- **Quick Write:** Describe the most impressive building you have ever seen. What made it impressive to you?
- **Cheer Leader:** Create a Renaissance cheer to encourage Brunelleschi to finish his famous dome.
- **Quick Calc:** With rulers or a measuring tape, measure 138.5 feet across an area in your school yard. This is the diameter of

Brunelleschi's dome in Florence. Have all the students in class stand in a circle of this diameter to represent the size of Brunelleschi's dome. Impressive, isn't it?

- **Model Mart:** Create a cardboard model of the cathedral at Florence and especially Brunelleschi's dome. Describe how you constructed this dome out of cardboard.
- **What If?** Imagine being the construction foreman in charge of all the materials (the rock, cement, and brick) used to create Brunelleschi's dome. Describe in a short paragraph or two what your average workday would be like.
- **ADV Architectural Comparison:** Using your library and the Internet, compare the size and shape of some of the great domed buildings in the world—the Parthenon, the Blue Masjid in Istanbul, St. Peter's in Rome, St. Paul's in London, and the Capitol Building in Washington, D.C. How are they similar and different from each other?

4.11.5   Da Vinci's Revolution in Oil Painting

During the Middle Ages and earlier, pictures were painted on walls and wood, usually with a mixture of colored pigment and egg yolk. That all changed radically with the Renaissance. Starting with Jan van Eyck (d. 1441) in the Netherlands, painters started to paint with slow-drying, oil-based paints. These oil-based paints enabled the artist to slowly layer subtle different shades of hue and color to make very realistic skin tones. The oil-based paints were also superior at refracting light, resulting in very bright colors. Two well-known Italian painters quickly became champions of this new way of painting—Leonardo da Vinci and Raphael. One of the first oil paintings by Leonardo is also perhaps the most famous in the world, *La Gioconda* (otherwise known as the *Mona Lisa*). Within 100 years (by 1550), every major painter of the Renaissance was painting in oils (Manley 1992, 128).

(Note from the future: Until the invention of acrylics in the late 20th century, virtually every major artist in the world in the past 400 years after the Renaissance used oil as a major way of painting.)

- **Art Mart:** Paint a picture of a person using watercolors.
- **Close-up and Personal:** With a set of paintings from the Renaissance in your library or on the Internet, use a magnifying glass to look closely at an oil painting from the Renaissance. Can you see

the careful layering of different hues and colors that soften the painting and make it look so personal and lifelike? Describe, in a short paragraph, what you see.
- **Gallery Walk:** Pick out four or five great oil paintings from the Renaissance by Leonardo, Raphael, and others.
  1. Which one is the most impressive? Why?
  2. Which one is the most realistic? Why?
  3. Which one is the most colorful? Why?
  4. Which one do you like the best? Why?
- **ADV Art Critic:** Compare your work of art with a great Renaissance painting, such as the *Mona Lisa*. Describe the differences between the colors and textures of your watercolor and the Renaissance oil painting.
- **ADV Art Research:** Using resources in your library and on the Internet, describe in an essay what oil painting did for the Renaissance over 400 years ago, and what it did for the whole history of painting.

4.11.6   Painting the Ceiling—Ugh!—In 1512

Michelangelo Buonarroti (1475–1564) at age thirty-three did not want to paint the Sistine Chapel ceiling. He was perhaps the greatest sculptor the world had ever seen. He told Pope Julius repeatedly that he did not want to do it. The Pope bullied him, yelled at him, hit him with his cane—and Michelangelo finally agreed to do it. He started painting the 132 × 44-foot ceiling in 1508 and finished it in 1512. He did not enjoy the exhausting experience, and described what it felt like: "I live here in great toil and great weariness of body, and have no friends of any kind and don't want any, and haven't the time to eat what I need."

We can pity poor Michelangelo toiling alone and cold, endlessly perched atop a 100-foot scaffolding with the pope continually screaming at him. But the end product is perhaps the greatest painting the world has ever seen—and remains so almost 500 years later (Jeffery 1989, 688–713; Boorstin 1992, 407–419).

- **Quick Write:** Imagine working alone as a painter for three years on a ceiling 100 feet in the air. Describe your feelings in a short paragraph.
- **Poster Power:** Create a poster for Pope Julius to hang outside the Vatican to advertise for a painter of the Sistine Chapel in 1508.

- **Scaffold Sticker:** Create a scaffold sticker for Michelangelo to use to express how he felt as he painted the Sistine Chapel.
- **Art Mart:** Create a design for painting the ceiling of your classroom and present it to your class.
- **Pro or Con:** In a Pair Share, stage a mock argument over whether or not Pope Julius was ultimately correct in forcing Michelangelo to work hard on the Sistine Chapel.
- **ADV Sistine Tour:** Find a large art book illustrating the different sections of the ceiling of the Sistine Chapel. Write down a brief description of each section of the painting and then describe your favorite section to your class.
- **ADV Art Research:** Using resources in your library and on the Internet, compare Michelangelo's Sistine Chapel with any other major work of art in the world. How do they compare? Report your findings to the class.

4.11.7   Revolt Against the Renaissance

Not everyone loved Renaissance art. The old medieval Christian iconoclastic idea that painting pictures of humans was evil still existed in Germany and elsewhere. At several times during the Reformation, Church art was destroyed by iconoclastic Protestant mobs. Most of the destruction of Renaissance art, however, took place in England under the rule of Henry VIII. He joined the Protestant revolt in 1538 against the authority of the pope in Rome, officially to annul his marriage to Catherine of Aragon. Unofficially, however, he wanted to take control of all the Church's wealth in England. By creating his own "Protestant" Church, Henry also took control of all Church property. All gold and silver items were immediately taken by the crown and melted down. Major paintings were smashed, books were burned, altars were destroyed, and stained-glass windows broken. Virtually all Church art in England before 1538 was destroyed by mobs under the direction of Henry VIII (Manley 1992, 128).

- **Quick Write:** What is your immediate reaction when you see a work of art that has been disfigured or destroyed, such as Michelangelo's *Pieta*?
- **Pair Share:** In a Pair Share, discuss for one minute each whether or not people with religious values that oppose certain kinds of art have the right to destroy art they do not like.

- **Class Discussion:**
  1. Do artists have the right to make any kind of art they want?
  2. Should certain rules be placed on artists to make only certain kinds of art?
  3. What penalties should be placed on people who deface or destroy art?
- **Poster Power:** Make a poster either supporting or opposing the right of artists to create anything they want.
- **Make a Right:** In groups of four, make a list of the fundamental rights all artists should have, and present this list to the class.
- **ADV The Futurist:** Explore your library and the Internet for information on groups today that oppose certain types of artwork. What arguments do these groups have against artistic freedom, and what position do you take today on this issue? Present your views on the subject to the class.

4.12.0   SUCCESSES AND FAILURES OF THE RENAISSANCE

4.12.1   Success or Failure?

This is the competitive quiz show that challenges teams to list as many reasons as possible why a person, place, or thing is the most important success or failure of the Renaissance, Reformation, and Age of Exploration.

1. Each student team of four draws the name of a Renaissance, Reformation, or Age of Exploration person, place, or thing from a hat.
2. Each team calls out its name, and the scorekeeper puts it on the board as the team's name.
3. Using any books or materials available, each student team has fifteen minutes to make as long a list as possible of reasons why that name is the most important of the era.
4. The Renaissance, Reformation, and Age of Exploration names to be used can be as follows or developed from a larger list:

Mona Lisa	the Sistine Chapel	Inquisition
Martin Luther	Giotto	Leonardo da Vinci
Michelangelo	Cheng Ho	Columbus
Magellan	Vasco da Gama	Brunelleschi's dome

Petrarch	Chaucer	Boccaccio
Henry VIII	Pope Leo X	Lorenzo de Medici
Black Plague	Copernicus	Prince Henry of Portugal

5. A scorekeeper will keep track of how many answers each team gives on the board.
6. The team with the most number of "valid" supporting reasons wins a free trip to the library.

4.13.0   MAJOR WORLD PROBLEMS FOR THE RENAISSANCE

4.13.1   How Does a Renaissance in History Start?

The Renaissance was a glorious period in human history—magnificent art was created, important inventions were made, major scientific discoveries were made, and new worlds were discovered. But the question remains, how does such a period get started? What necessary elements come together to produce a chain reaction of creative thinking in art, religion, politics, and discovery? The world today would be a very dreary place if the Renaissance had not taken place.

- **Inquiry #1:** Ask some friends if they would like to go play baseball or something else fun. Why does a question to start something work some of the time and not work at other times?
- **Inquiry #2:** Why do friends sometimes start joining in to help with something, but other times you are left to do something all alone?
- **ADV Inquiry #3:** In teams of four, examine from library readings and interviews the influence of the following factors in making an activity, product, company, or even a country successful.
  1. Key individuals who influence others into new ways of thinking
  2. An environment accepting enough of new ways of thinking
  3. The availability of financial support to new ways of thinking
  4. Sustained and renewed popular and financial support to continually search for new ideas and thinking
- **Plenary Session:** When finished, present your team's findings to the class in the form of a skit, a poster, or a panel discussion.

4.13.2   What Causes a Renaissance in History to End?

Good or bad, every era in history sooner or later comes to an end. The factors that cause a decline vary. Initial conditions that enabled the era, such as economic prosperity, can disappear. The initial energy of the individuals who started an era such as the Renaissance can fade and not be revitalized with new ideas. The era may also be replaced by a more energetic era with newer ideas. All of these factors contributed to the decline of the Renaissance.

Specifically, three major events spelled the end of the Renaissance. The first was political. Although the Italian city-states were unrivaled during the Renaissance for art, their politics remained strictly medieval, with small city-states constantly fighting petty little wars. Machiavelli sought to unify the city-states against their much larger national neighbors—Spain and France—but his calls went unheeded. In 1527, a German Protestant army invaded Catholic Italy and sacked Rome. Three years later, in 1530, Spain formally took control of the Italian city-states (until 1796). The second cause was religious. By 1535, the Protestant Reformation was in full swing in northern Europe and no longer dependent on Rome. The third cause was economic, from multiple fronts. The Protestant Reformation now deprived the Catholic Church in Rome of the rich donations from the new Protestant Churches in Germany. In 1488, the Portuguese had rounded the Cape of Good Hope in Southern Africa on their way to India. By 1502, the Portuguese could sell pepper in Europe at half the price that the merchants in Italy did, due to their cheaper sea route. Suddenly, Italy was no longer the political, religious, and economic power it once was. The Church, the political power, and the money were no longer there to support the great artists. The Renaissance was over (Durant 1953, 686–723).

- **Quick Write:** Name a sports team or musical group that used to be your favorite. What happened to them? Why did they decline? What would they have to do to become a favorite of yours again?
- **Chart It:** Chart the factors on a time line that led to the decline of the Renaissance in Italy.
- **Map Attack:** On a blank map of the world, illustrate how the Portuguese, after 1488, were able to obtain cheaper pepper from India than the Italians, who had to obtain it from traders traveling along the Silk Road.

- **You Were There:** Imagine that you were a great artist, Domingo de Siena, in Florence, and you were supported with the highest salary, the finest apartment, and many rich patrons. Suddenly, it is over. No one has the money to hire you. You are out of work, with no apartment and no friends. Describe your feelings in a letter to a friend.
- **Poster Power:** Make a poster illustrating the three major things that caused the rapid decline of the Renaissance in Italy.
- **Historical Analysis:** In groups of four, discuss possible ways that the Italian city-states could have prevented the decline of the Renaissance. When finished, share your ideas with the class.
- **ADV Historical Research:** Using resources in the library and on the Internet, examine the decline of several different eras in history and compare their similarities and differences. When finished, report your findings to the class.
- **ADV The Futurist:** Research the decline of the Renaissance with the decline of a nation or company during the 20th century. When finished, share your conclusions with the class.

4.14.0 ERA ANTECEDENTS FOR THE FUTURE

4.14.1 Is Humankind Ready to Advance?

It is now time to judge whether or not humankind is ready to advance into the next era. Five members from around the Renaissance Village (the class) will state their basic viewpoints of whether or not enough advances have been made during the Renaissance, and whether humankind should move forward. The five illustrious members are as follows:

1. Letuck de Betrink, the arch-conservative of Renaissance Village, who believes that humankind has gone far enough with enough progress. Betrink believes strongly that the good old days were the best and that humankind needs to hold strongly to past values and beliefs.
2. Monardo Derudzuk, one of the rising young voices in the town, is a more moderate conservative who believes that we need to be very cautious with any change and be very sure that no harm will come to Renaissance Village if change takes place. Monardo is willing to accept some change, but only in very small amounts

and only when the time is right—and he wants to decide when that time will come.

3. Peeangelo Wookbot, the wishy-washy middle-of-the-roader around the village, is willing to accept change for a few minutes after one speaker, but might have a change of mind in an instant to oppose change after another speaker has finished.

4. Yakurnicus Vatsmeer, the moderate progressive of the group, is willing to support change for the good of the people in Renaissance Village. Vatsmeer is especially in favor of change that will benefit Vatsmeer's own family directly.

5. Quether Varull, the radical progressive of the village, is very willing to support any change that will move humanity away from the drafty and damp old castle into something more modern and comfortable for humanity.

- **Pick a Position:** Each member of Renaissance Village (classroom) now must choose one of the five positions for humanity to take and support their position with evidence of what they have learned about the Renaissance.
- **Class Vote:** A vote will then be taken of all peasants and nobles around town to determine whether or not humanity should move on to the next era. The consensus decision of the imaginary citizens of Renaissance Village will determine their own future and the rest of humanity. (In reality, such decisions by people during the Renaissance were key in deciding whether humans stayed the way they were or progressed to new levels of development.)

Full Thematic Table of Contents

Traditional World History: Chronological and Regional Table of Contents

UNIT 1 PREHISTORY

Global Thematic Learning Pacs

Early and Middle Stone Ages (1 Million BCE to 10,000 BCE)

Late Stone Age or Neolithic (10,000 BCE to 3000 BCE)

UNIT 2 ANCIENT HISTORY

Ancient Global Thematic Lesson Pacs (3000 BCE–450 CE)

Ancient Egyptian Thematic Learning Pacs (3000 BCE–450 CE)

Ancient Rome Thematic Learning Pacs (3000 BCE–450 CE)

UNIT 3 THE MIDDLE AGES

Middle Ages Global Thematic Learning Pacs (400 CE–1400 CE)

Early Middle Ages European Thematic Lesson Pacs (450 CE–1095 CE)

UNIT 4 RENAISSANCE, REFORMATION, AND EXPLORATIONS

Global Renaissance Thematic Learning Pacs (1400–1600)

Southern Europe Thematic Lesson Pacs (1400–1600)

Renaissance Art and Literature Thematic Learning Pacs (1350–1600)

Northern Europe and Reformation Thematic Learning Pacs (1400–1600)

Africa, America, and Asia Thematic Lesson Pacs (1400–1600)

Exploration and Discovery Thematic Lesson Pacs (1400–1600)

Basic Map Resources

Absolutely the best source of maps for any world history class is the CD-ROM by Broderbund entitled "Maps N Facts." Any map of any country or continent can be instantly analyzed or printed out for duplication, along with a massive wealth of CIA data on any area of the world. Available from Broderbund, P.O. Box 6125, Novato, CA 94948.

An excellent map source on the Internet or CD is Bruce Jones Designers' World of Maps (see https://www.bjdesign.com), from which you can download excellent sets of maps for both the IBM PC and Mac computers for a low initial price.

The Internet also contains a wealth of other map sources for a wide variety of needs. For example, the library at the University of Texas, Austin, has a large collection of Asian maps available on the Web at http://www.lib.utexas.edu/PCL/Map_collection/asia.html. A West End London bookstore, Altea Maps & Books, sells antique maps online at http://www.antique-maps.co.uk. For a comprehensive site of world maps on the Web, The Map Guide! at http://wwww.algonet.se/~cristar/index.htm lists almost every map available on the Web by continents, countries, and region. Check them out!

Recommended Classroom Background Music by Time Period

UNIT 1—PREHISTORIC CLASSROOM BACKGROUND MUSIC

Ancient humans sang music and played instruments such as the drum (hollow log), whistle (hollow reed), and harp (stretched animal intestines), but we do not know what ancient music really sounded like. Members of your class, however, are free to experiment and produce sounds that might have sounded like that of ancient humans.

Perhaps the best example of what early harp music sounded like is *The Art of Harp* from the International Harp Festival, Volume One (Earth Beat CD R272496) available from Earth Beat, P.O. Box 1460, Redway, CA 95560. This CD is an awesome collection of harp music from such distant locations as Ireland, Germany, and Uganda.

UNIT 2—ANCIENT CLASSROOM BACKGROUND MUSIC

Written music does not appear until Unit 3 (the Middle Ages), but we do have some idea of what kind of instruments were played from written descriptions and from wall paintings of the ancient Egyptians, Greeks, and Romans. Following these models and ancient instruments still used in the Middle East, Ali Jihad Racy has produced an interesting CD entitled *Ancient Egypt* [LYRCD 7347] produced by Lyrichord Discs, 141 Perry St., New York, NY 10014. We really do not know how ancient Egyptian music sounded, but Racy's CD is likely to be as close as we can get to the way it might have sounded.

For ancient Greece, a CD from France is entitled *Musique de la Grece Antique* by the Atrium Musicae de Madrid under the leadership of

Gregorio Paniagua [Harmonia Mundi HMA1901015]. The CD gives us a fascinating glimpse of the music of ancient Greece based on the rare fragments of papyrus and marble containing music hymns or comments concerning music. Examples include the "Premier Hymn to Apollo" found on a marble slab at Delphi in 1893 and a "Hymn to the Sun" based on a Byzantine papyrus preserved by Galileo in Venice in 1581.

UNIT 3—MEDIEVAL CLASSROOM BACKGROUND MUSIC

The last few years have also seen a renaissance of recordings of music from the Middle Ages. Most impressive is the four-CD set entitled *The Medieval Experience* [Archiv Production 449 082 2 by Deutsche Grammophon] containing Gregorian chants, songs of troubadours, motets, and masses from the Middle Ages, played and sung by such distinguished groups as the Early Music Consort of London and the choir of the monks of the abbey of Notre Dame de Fontgombault. Also impressive are recent CDs celebrating the Jewish, Christian, and Muslim multicultural contributions to the medieval music of Spain. *Iberian Garden* [Dorian Discovery DIS 80151] by the Altramar Medieval Music Ensemble contains fascinating medieval selections from all three religious groups. More specific is *Musique Arabo-Andalouse* [Harmonia Mundi CD 90389] by the Atrium Muisicae de Madrid. The sheer elegance and beauty of Muslim culture in Andalucia [Al Andalus] is captured musically in this recreation of the music of Muslim Spain during the Middle Ages, based on the musical traditions of the descendants of Muslim Andalusians still living in Morocco.

UNIT 4—RENAISSANCE CLASSROOM BACKGROUND MUSIC

A wide variety of CDs exist that reconstruct the music of the era of the Renaissance and Explorations. *Canzoni e Danze* [Deutsche Grammophon Archiv Production D111360] by Piffaro: the Renaissance Band creates a delightful wind ensemble of canzoni and dances played on such archaic instruments as bagpipes, shawns, sagbuts, recorders, crumhorns, and harps. *A Song of David: the Music of the Sephardim and Renaissance Spain* [Dorian Discovery DIS 80130] played by La Rondinella reconstructs Jewish Ladino Sephardic music of Spain before their expulsion in 1492 and still preserved by the Jewish Ladino communities in the Balkans. *1492—Music from the Age of Discovery* [EMI Classics D115591] by the Waverly Consort presents a fascinating selection of songs such as a praise to Fernando [King Ferdinand] for conquering the Moors; a sad love song of three Moorish girls; an Arabic Andalusian instrumental piece; and selections from the palace song book of the Duke of Alba.

Recommended CD-ROMs and Websites by Time Period

UNIT 1—PREHISTORIC CD-ROMS AND WEBSITES

One of the best classroom CD-ROMs available on early humans and prehumans is *Investigating Olduvai—Archaeology of Human Origins* by Jeanne Sept and produced by the Indiana University Press at www .indiana.edu/iupress or 800-842-6796. Through interactive detective work, students learn archaeological field principles, early human pre-history, and early African archaeology. Updates on the Olduvai CD-ROM can also be obtained from the same website.

UNIT 2—ANCIENT CD-ROMS AND WEBSITES

Thousands of websites focus on ancient history. A few of the better ones are:

- Ancient Egypt Resources at www.historylink101.com/ancient _egypt.htm contains a wide list of links to almost any topic on classical Egypt from mummies and Nefertiti to ancient Egyptian medicines and writing your name in hieroglyphics.
- Ancient Civilizations on the Internet at http://www.ancient civilizations.co.uk/home_set.html from the British Museum is a great global site on ancient civilizations such as Egypt, Indus River Valley, Inca in South America, and many more.
- Exploring Ancient World Cultures at http://eawc.evansville.edu/ provides a discussion of all the major classical civilizations of the world—China, India, the Middle East, as well as Egypt, Greece, and Rome, with hyperlinks to other sites.

UNIT 3—MEDIEVAL CD-ROMS AND WEBSITES

Argos–Limited Area Search of the Ancient and Medieval Internet at http://aros.evansville.edu/index.htm is an excellent starting ground for any study of the Middle Ages with hyperlink jumps to sites on the Byzantine Empire, The Labyrinth (a World Wide Web server for medieval studies), and women and gender issues during the Middle Ages. Voted as one of the best sites on Islam by many sources, http://www.mosque.com is a rich multimedia source on the religion of Muhammad.

UNIT 4—RENAISSANCE CD-ROMS AND WEBSITES

Three notable CD-ROMs exist on the Renaissance era: *Leonardo the Inventor* (CD-ROM 37 0072 00); *Explorers of the New World* (CD-ROM 0069 0150 00 by Future Vision Multimedia of Great Neck, New York. Telephone: 516-773-0990); and *Uffizi—A Virtual Tour* (Lifestyle Software Group. Telephone: 904-794-7070), an absolutely beautifully designed CD-ROM guiding the viewer carefully through the world's oldest art gallery.

Several outstanding websites on the Internet also exist on the era: The Renaissance website http://renaissance.dm.net/compendium/home.html offers a delightful Compendium of Common Knowledge of the Elizabethan era in England 1558–1603 for writers, actors, and reenactors of such items as games, money, food, language, nobility, and dueling. Welcome to the Renaissance Faire at http://renfaire.com is a how-to-do-it manual for Renaissance Faires, from costumes and language to historical perspectives, and links to California Renaissance Faire sites for specific advice. On the Reformation, the best place to start is http://infoseek.com/topic/education/history/reformation, which leads to a variety of educational sites on the era, including a usefulness ranking and a teachers' chat room on the Reformation. For advanced research on the Reformation, The Protestant Reformation at http://history.hanover.edu/early/prot.htm provides links to approximately forty of the major authors and texts on the Reformation. The Columbus Navigation Homepage at http://www1.minn.net/~keithp/index.htm also provides an interesting site focused on the history, navigation, and specific voyages of Columbus.

Annotated Bibliography

Abercrombie, Thomas J. 1988. When the Moors Ruled Spain. *National Geographic 174* (July): 86–119.
A beautiful illustrated depiction of the Muslim history of Spain.
———. 1991. Ibn Batutta—Prince of Travelers. *National Geographic 180* (December): 2–49.
A beautifully told and photographed record of Ibn Batutta's fourteenth-century travels.

Ajayi, J. F. Ade, and Ian Espie. 1965. *A Thousand Years of West African History.* Ibadan (Nigeria): Ibadan University Press.
A classic and masterful source for information on West African history.

Assmann, Ian. 1997. *Moses the Egyptian.* Cambridge, Mass.: Harvard University Press.
A powerful reexamination of the role of Moses in the development of monotheism.

Astarita, Tommaso. 2005. *Between Salt Water and Holy Water—A History of Southern Italy.* New York: W. W. Norton & Company.
Totally ignored in our history books is Roger II of Sicily. Who says that Muslim, Christian, and Jew must be at continual war with each other? During the Crusades, Roger II ruled Sicily peacefully, integrating all three groups into his kingdom.

Barreto, Mascarenhas. 1992. *The Portuguese Columbus—Secret Agent of King John II*, translated by Reginald A. Brown. New York: St. Martin's Press.
If you think history is boring, try reading Barreto. This work by Professor Barreto is a report on a lifelong focus on the validity of the evidence about the man we call Columbus. It turns the conventional wisdom about Columbus upside down.

Boorstin, Daniel J. 1983. *The Discoverers.* New York: Random House.
Without question, the best book on the discoveries of humankind—social, political, scientific, and just sheer adventure—is this volume by Boorstin. It should be required reading for every student of history.

————. 1992. *The Creators: A History of the Heroes of Imagination*. New York: Random House.

————. 1994. *Cleopatra's Nose—Essays on the Unexpected*. New York: Random House.

Bromer, Jeff. 1988. Joan of Arc Rides to the Rescue of New Orleans. *Old News* (November): 1–5.

Old News is a great and inexpensive resource for history teachers and can be obtained at 400 Stackstown Road, Marietta, PA 17647 or by phoning 717-426-2212.

Bronowski, J. 1973. *The Ascent of Man*. Boston: Little, Brown.

A beautiful and brilliant history of the human intellect.

Bryant, Vaughn M. July/August 2007. Artifact: This Microscopic Maize Pollen Grain. *Archaeology 60*: 4, p. 72.

A summary of recent research that pushes the use of maize back to 10,000 years ago in the Americas.

Campbell, Joseph. 1968. *The Hero with a Thousand Faces*. Princeton, NJ: Princeton University Press.

Canby, Cortland. 1961. *Epic of Man*. New York: Time, Inc.

A magnificently illustrated coffee table book on the rise of human history.

Capra, Fritjof. 1996. *The Web of Life*. New York: Anchor Books.

A brilliant synthesis of recent thinking tying together the ideas of complexity, Gaia, and chaos theory with explanations of living organisms, ecosystems, and social systems.

Carey, John, ed. 1987. *Eyewitness to History*. New York: Avon.

Perhaps one of the most extensive collections of firsthand historical accounts of major events in world history.

Chadwick, John. 1958. *The Decipherment of Linear B*. Cambridge: Cambridge University Press.

A fascinating and detailed account of how the ancient Linear B writing of ancient Greece was decoded.

Chambers, E. K. 1930. *William Shakespeare*. Oxford: Oxford University Press.

A classic source on information about the Elizabethan bard.

Chandler, Graham. November/December 2007. Desertification and Civilization. *Saudi Aramco World*. 58:6, 36–43.

Collingwood, R. G. 1956. *The Idea of History*. New York: Galaxy.

A classic source on the philosophy of history.

Confucius. 1971. *Confucian Analects: The Great Learning and the Doctrine of the Mean*. New York: Dover.

This small book captures the essence of Confucian thought.

Dubos, Rene. 1974. *Beast or Angel? Choices That Make Us Human*. New York: Scribner.

A fundamental book for the beginning of human history, focusing on a discussion that should take place at the start of every class in history.

Durant, Will. 1939. *The Life of Greece*. New York: Simon & Schuster.

———. 1944. *Caesar and Christ*. New York: Simon & Schuster.

———. 1950. *The Age of Faith*. New York: Simon & Schuster.

———. 1953. *The Renaissance*. New York: Simon & Schuster.

———. 1954. *Our Oriental Heritage*. New York: Simon & Schuster.

The first part of Durant's monumental eight-volume history of the world. Readable, insightful, and always one of the best general references for world history up to the 19th century.

———. (1957). *The Reformation*. New York: Simon & Schuster.

Ebrey, Patricia E. 1991. *Chinese Civilization and Society*. New York: Free Press.

A book of social and political historical sources on Chinese history.

Edwards, Mike. 1996. Lord of the Mongols: Genghis Khan. *National Geographic 190* (December): 2–37.

An excellent short history of the Mongols and their infamous leader Genghis Khan, with the usual magnificent photographs, illustrations, and maps of the National Geographic Society.

Eisenman, Robert. 1997. *James—The Brother of Jesus*. New York: Penguin.

A powerful academic inquiry into the early history of Christianity focusing on the leadership of James in Jerusalem between 30 CE and 69 CE and using such sources as the Dead Sea Scrolls.

Ellwood, Robert S., Jr. 1980. *An Invitation to Japanese Civilization*. Belmont, Calif.: Wadsworth.

A short and lively introduction to the social and intellectual history of Japan.

Fagan, Brian. 1999. *Floods, Famines and Emperors*. New York: Basic Books.

We went through a mini Ice Age between 1400 and 1850, and do you think it is mentioned in our history books? Fagan does a masterful telling of the impact of this long cold spell on world history.

Fletcher, Sir Banister. 1896. *A History of Architecture on the Comparative Method*. London: B. T. Batsford.

A beautiful old book full of architectural drawings of some of the great buildings of the world.

Gabrieli, Francisco. 1957. *Arab Historians of the Crusades*. New York: Dorset Press.

Perhaps the only readily available Muslim source of firsthand accounts of the Crusades.

Grant, Michael. 1964. *The Birth of Western Civilization—Greece and Rome*. New York: McGraw-Hill.

One of the best of the many magnificently illustrated books on ancient Greece and Rome.

Guedj, Denis. 1996. *Numbers: The Universal Language.* New York: Abrahms.
A beautiful and very readable history of numbers and mathematics.

Gumus, Dogan. 1994. *Ancient Ephesus.* Istanbul: DO-GU Yayinlari.
A beautifully illustrated guidebook to ruins of the ancient Greek and Roman city of Ephesus in southwestern Turkey.

Hall, Stephen S. July, 2007. The Last Hours of the Ice Man. *National Geographic 212*: 1, 68–81.
Who would have imagined that a fully intact frozen human from more than 5,000 years ago would be found in an Alpine glacier?

Healey, John F. 1990. *Reading the Past: The Early Alphabet.* Berkeley: University of California Press.
A short, very easily read book on the early forms of modern writing.

Hesse, Hermann. 1951. *Siddhartha.* New York: New Directions Paperbacks.
Perhaps the best short and easy-to-read introduction to the life of the Buddha (Siddhartha).

Jacobus, Lee A., ed. 1994. *The World of Ideas.* Boston: St. Martin's.

Jean, Georges. 1992. *Writing: The Story of Alphabets and Scripts.* New York: Abrahms.
A fun and beautifully edited book, good enough to just look at the pictures and all the different scripts of the world—if you're not in the mood to read.

Jeffery, David. 1989. A Renaissance for Michelangelo. *National Geographic 176* (December): 688–713.
A visual treat of the restoration of Michelangelo's ceiling of the Sistine Chapel in the Vatican.

Josephus, Flavius. 1988. *Josephus: The Essential Writings,* translated by Paul L. Maier. Grand Rapids, Mich.: Kregel Publications.
The primary source document for the history of the Jewish people during the early years of the current era and likely a major source of information for early Christian writers, such as Luke.

Kennedy, Paul. 1987. *The Rise and Fall of the Great Powers.* New York: Random House.
A powerful study of the cycles of political states.

Koning, Hans. 1991. *Columbus: His Enterprise—Exploding the Myth.* New York: Monthly Review Press.
A critical but very readable investigation into the myths about Columbus and the brutality of the Spaniards against the people of the Caribbean. Not a very pretty picture of our "hero" Columbus.

Kuiseko, Ryokushu. 1988. *Brush Writing—Calligraphy for Beginners.* Tokyo (Japan): Kodansha International.
An excellent step-by-step guide to Japanese calligraphy.

Kunzig, Robert. 1997. The Face of an Ancestral Child. *Discover 18* (December): 88–101.

A valuable update on the latest excavations of early human archaeological sites from the past one million years.

Leon, Vicki. 1995. *Uppity Women of Ancient Times.* Berkeley: Conari Press. 160–161.

A delightful romp through ancient history focusing on those many women who did not make it into our history books.

———. 1999. *Uppity Women of the Renaissance.* Berkeley, Calif.: Conari Press.

Leon does it again with women in the Renaissance. A very enjoyable book to read and use in lesson planning.

Manley, Deborah. 1992. *The Guinness Book of Records—1492.* New York: Facts on File.

Simply one of the most interesting books in print. Each page is full of economic, social, political, and geographic information about the year 1492.

McNeil, William H. 1977. *Plagues and People.* New York: Anchor Doubleday.

The classic source for information on the black plague and other epidemics.

Mee, Charles L., Jr. 1993. *Playing God—Seven Fateful Moments When Great Men Met to Change the World.* New York: Simon & Schuster.

An excellent source on the meeting between Attila and Pope Leo I, Cortez and Montezuma, and the meetings at Versailles and Yalta following World Wars I and II.

Meskill, John. 1965. *The Pattern of Chinese History.* Boston: D. C. Heath.

An excellent short source for the major problems confronting Chinese history (for example, cycles, development, or stagnation). One of Heath's series of Problems in Asian Civilizations.

Michael, Franz. 1986. *China through the Ages.* Boulder, Colo.: Westview Press.

An interesting high-level history of the major trends in Chinese history.

Miller, Peter. July, 2007. Swarm Theory. *National Geographic 212*: 1, 126–147

A fascinating article on the phenomena of "swarming" not just for bees and grasshoppers, but also humans.

O'Neal, Dennis. 2007. Modern Human Variation: An Introduction to Modern Human Diversity. *Available at http://anthro.palomar.edu/vary/Default.htm.*

Pahl, Ron H. 1997. Maybe Shakespeare Was Right about "Race." *Multicultural Education* (spring): 12–17.

An important article on the historical evolution of the word "race" in the English language.

Pearson, Carol S. 1989. *The Hero Within: Archetypes We Live By.* San Francisco: Harper and Row.

A masterpiece of understanding the role that myths and archetypes play in shaping the lives of individual humans and nations.

Pellegrino, Charles. 1993. *Unearthing Atlantis—An Archaeological Odyssey.* New York: Vintage.

A must-read for anyone interested in the early history of the Mediterranean. Focused on the gigantic volcanic eruption on the Greek Island of Thera (1628 BCE), Pellegrino's look weaves the implications of this eruption into the history of the whole area. Fascinating.

Powell, Eric A. July/August, 2008. The Shah's Great Wall. *Archaeology* 36–41.

Sardar, Zuauddin, and Zafar Abbas Malik. 1994. *Introducing Muhammad.* New York: Totem Books.

A delightful, beginning introduction to Muhammad and Islam written in a well-illustrated, semi-cartoon format.

Severin, Tim. 1978. *The Brendan Voyage.* New York: Avon Books.

Severy, Merle. 1983. The Byzantine Empire—Rome of the East. *National Geographic 164* (December): 709–736, 746–766.

A beautiful journey with the Byzantines in the best National Geographic tradition.

Shenkman, Richard. 1993. *Legends, Lies and Cherished Myths of World History.* New York: HarperCollins.

A delightful romp through history, exposing many cherished beliefs as frauds or at least rather rich embellishments.

Shlain, Leonard. 1999. *The Alphabet Versus the Goddess—The Conflict between Word and Image.* New York: Penguin.

A brilliant study of the mental differences between male and female, and the negative impact illiteracy has had on females throughout history.

Shreeve, James. March, 2006. The Greatest Journey. *National Geographic 209*: 3, 60.

Spielman, Andrew and Michael D'Antonio. 2001. *Mosquito: A Natural History of Our Most Persistent and Deadly Foe.* New York: Hyperion.

Sussman, Robert W. 1997. Exploring Our Basic Human Nature: Are Humans Inherently Violent? *Anthro Notes 19* (fall): 1–6, 17–19.

A great starting point for any thoughtful class on the history of humanity.

Symcox, Linda. 1991. *Crowning the Cathedral of Florence: Brunelleschi Builds His Dome.* Los Angeles, Calif.: UCLA National Center for History in the Schools.

An excellent short monograph on the rediscovery of dome construction during the Renaissance.

Tschanz, David W. July/August, 2007. History's Hinge—'Ain Jalut. *Saudi Aramco World.* 58:4, 24–33.

Another major battle that changed the course of history and preserved Islamic civilization, but is totally ignored in our history books.

Tschanz, Edmund. 1997. The Arab Roots of European Medicine. *Aramco World 48* (May/June): 20–31.

Tsu, Lao. 1972. *Tao Te Ching*. Translated by Gia-Fu Feng and Jane English. New York: Vintage.

This edition of the Tao Te Ching cannot be any more beautiful. A dual Chinese–English edition with photography and layout that captures the essence of the Tao.

Ulrich, Robert. 1971. *Progress or Disaster? From the Bourgeois to the World Civilization*. New York: New York University Press.

Watson, Francis. 1974. *A Concise History of India*. London: Hames and Hudson.

A well-written and illustrated history of India from the Aryan invasions to rule of Indira Gandhi.

Williams, A. R. March 2006. Licorice Power. *National Geographic 209*: 3.

Who would have imagined that licorice has such great medical properties, with its roots going back to ancient Rome, India, and China?

Wilson, Cleveland. 1975. *The Living Socrates*. Owings Mills, Md.: Stemmer House.

A clear and simple application of Socrates to modern living.

Wood, Francis. 1996. *Did Marco Polo Go to China?* Boulder, Colo.: Westview Press.

A scholarly study of the story of Marco Polo that questions whether or not it is true.

About the Author

Ron Pahl is a longtime world history buff who does not like history teachers who bore their students with endless lectures. He has climbed the pyramids of Giza in Egypt several times, sat with his feet in the reflecting pool of the Taj Mahal in India, and meditated with monks at Ankhor Wat, Cambodia. Why can't students actively simulate such exciting historical experiences in the classroom? His belief is that students learn more in active, rigorous, and enjoyable classrooms, and he has applied this belief to his high school classrooms for more than twenty years. He currently teaches and coordinates the social studies teacher education program at California State University, Fullerton.

Breinigsville, PA USA
15 December 2010
251520BV00001B/4/P